UNPEOPLE

Mark Curtis is a former Research Fellow at the Royal Institute of International Affairs (Chatham House) and has written extensively on British and US foreign policies. His books include *The Ambiguities of Power: British Foreign Policy since 1945* (Zed, London, 1995); *The Great Deception: Anglo-American Power and World Order* (Pluto, London, 1998); *Trade for Life: Making Trade Work for Poor People* (Christian Aid, London, 2001); and *Web of Deceit: Britain's Real Role in the World* (Vintage, London, 2003). He has worked in the field of international development for the past eleven years and is currently Director of The World Development Movement. His website is: www.markcurtis.info.

ALSO BY MARK CURTIS

Web of Deceit: Britain's Real Role in the World

Mark Curtis

UNPEOPLE

BRITAIN'S SECRET HUMAN RIGHTS ABUSES

VINTAGE

Published by Vintage 2004

6 8 10 9 7 5

First published in Great Britain by
Vintage, 2004

Vintage
Random House, 20 Vauxhall Bridge Road,
London SW1V 2SA

www.rbooks.co.uk

Addresses for companies within
The Random House Group Limited can be found at:
www.randomhouse.co.uk/offices.htm

The Random House Group Limited Reg. No. 954009

A CIP catalogue record for this book
is available from the British Library

ISBN 9780099469728

The Random House Group Limited supports The Forest Stewardship
Council (FSC), the leading international forest certification organisation.
All our titles that are printed on Greenpeace approved FSC certified paper
carry the FSC logo. Our paper procurement policy can be found at:
www.rbooks.co.uk/environment

MIX
Paper from
responsible sources
FSC® C013604

Set in Scala by SX Composing DTP, Rayleigh, Essex
Printed and bound in Great Britain by
CPI Antony Rowe, Chippenham, Wiltshire

CONTENTS

INTRODUCTION

This book is an attempt to uncover the reality of British foreign policy since the invasion of Iraq in 2003. It also analyses several major episodes in Britain's past foreign policy, exploring in detail formerly secret government files which have been ignored by mainstream commentators. They expose the truth behind British governments' supposed commitment to grand principles such as human rights, democracy, peace and overseas development.

Britain is bogged down in an unpopular occupation in the Middle East, the state has become widely distrusted by the public, accusations of spying on the UN have further undermined its international role, while Britain has effectively been marginalised in the EU. Seen from within the establishment, Tony Blair has become the greatest public liability since Anthony Eden, whose mistake was not his invasion of a foreign country (normal British practice) but his defeat, in the Suez crisis of 1956.

Massive public opposition to the invasion of Iraq has troubled the government and may prove to have deterred it from other ventures. Yet the course of New Labour's foreign policy since the invasion has been disastrous in terms of human rights, and is continuing to occur outside any meaningful democratic scrutiny.

British foreign policy is guided by a tiny elite – not just the handful of ministers in successive governments, but the civil servants, ambassadors, advisers and other unaccountable Whitehall mandarins around them, who set the country's agenda and priorities, and define its role within the world. Since March 2003, these decision-makers have been implementing a series of remarkable steps: first, Britain is deepening its support for state terrorism in a number of countries; second, unprecedented plans are being developed to increase Britain's ability to intervene militarily around the world; third, the government is increasing its state propaganda operations, directed towards the British public; and fourth, Whitehall planners have in effect announced they are no longer bound by international law.

The principal victims of British policies are Unpeople – those whose lives are deemed worthless, expendable in the pursuit of power and commercial gain. They are the modern equivalent of the 'savages' of colonial days, who could be mown down by British guns in virtual secrecy, or else in circumstances where the perpetrators were hailed as the upholders of civilisation.

The concept of Unpeople is central to each of the past and current British policies considered in this book. Through its own intervention, and its support of key allies such as the United States and various repressive regimes, Britain has been, and continues to be, a systematic and serious abuser of human rights. I have calculated that Britain bears significant responsibility for around 10 million deaths since 1945 (see table), including Nigerians, Indonesians, Arabians, Ugandans, Chileans, Vietnamese and many others. Often, the policies responsible are unknown to the public and remain unresearched by journalists and academics.

In this book, I aim to document for the first time the secret record of certain episodes in government planning. The declassified files to which I refer are instructive not only for the light they throw on the past. They are also directly relevant to current British foreign policy surrounding Iraq, military intervention and the 'war against terror'. British interests and priorities have changed very little over time; essentially, the only variation has been in the tactics used to achieve them.

Of the basic principles that guided the decisions taken in these files, there are three which seem particularly apposite when considering current events.

The first is that British ministers' lying to the public is systematic and normal. Many people were shocked at the extent to which Tony Blair lied over Iraq; some might still be unable to believe that he did. But in every case I have ever researched on past British foreign policy, the files show that ministers and officials have systematically misled the public. The culture of lying to and misleading the electorate is deeply embedded in British policy-making.

A second, related principle is that policy-makers are usually frank about their real goals in the secret record. This makes declassified files a good basis on which to understand their actual objectives. This gap between private goals and public claims is not usually the result, in my view, of a conscious conspiracy. Certainly, planned state propaganda has been a key element in British foreign policy; yet the underlying strategy of misleading the public springs from a less conscious, endemic contempt for the general population. The foreign-policy decision-making system is so secretive, elitist and unaccountable that policy-makers know they can get away with almost anything, and they will deploy whatever arguments are needed to do this.

The third basic principle is that humanitarian concerns do not figure at all in the rationale behind British foreign policy. In the thousands of government files I have looked through for this and other books, I have barely seen any reference to human rights at all. Where such concerns are invoked, they are only for public-relations purposes.

Currently, many mainstream commentators would have us believe that there is a 'Blair doctrine', based on military intervention for humanitarian purposes. This is an act of faith on the part of those commentators, a good example of how the public proclamations of leaders are used unquestioningly to set the framework of analysis within the liberal political culture. If there is a Blair doctrine, it does indeed involve an unprecedented degree of military intervention – but to achieve some very traditional goals. The actual impact of foreign policies on foreign people is as irrelevant now as it ever has been.

PART I

IRAQ

I

OCCUPYING IRAQ: THE ATTACK ON DEMOCRACY

Current British policy towards Iraq is in many ways nothing new. Many aspects of the invasion and occupation are normal, permanent features of British foreign policy, in particular: the violation of international law, the government's abuse of the UN, its deception of the public and its support for US aggression.

Yet what the Iraq episode has revealed to large numbers of people is the nature of British foreign policy-making: a cabal of unelected advisers around its chief, the Prime Minister, taking decisions in an unaccountable and increasingly centralised way and contemptuous of restrictions on its authority from public opinion and international law.

Indeed, the British and Iraqi public have something in common: they are both seen as a threat to policy-makers, to be overcome with violence in the case of Iraq and propaganda in the case of Britain. There is a symmetry between the attack on democracy in Britain (evident in the invasion, opposed by the majority of the public) and the attack on democracy in Iraq (evident in the occupation, which is attempting to impose Anglo-American priorities on an increasingly popular resistance movement).

British democracy in action

The three key actors at the centre of the Iraq episode – Downing Street, parliament and the media – illustrate the current nature of 'democracy' in Britain.

Blair's cabal – consisting of his closest foreign policy advisers in Downing Street – has been heading an unprecedented propaganda campaign to deceive the public, and has appropriated the power of the state to an unprecedented degree, even to the point of capturing its legal functions. Britain's 'democratic' political system has been revealed as more a kind of personalised autocracy. There are, moreover, no formal mechanisms within the British political system to restrain it. The Hutton and Butler inquiries were set up by the Prime Minister and predictably cleared the government of acting in bad faith or for 'sexing up' intelligence on Iraq, in defiance of all the evidence. They suggest a stage-managed lack of accountability which would be hard to match outside the former Soviet bloc.

Consider also the failure of the various all-party parliamentary committees to hold the government to account. For example, the Foreign Affairs Committee's report on the decision to go to war found that 'ministers did not mislead parliament' and agreed with the government that Iraq was 'a real and present danger'. It also concluded that the claims made in the government's September 2002 dossier, alleging all manner of threats from Iraq which have since been shown to be nonsense, were 'well-founded on the basis of the intelligence then available'.[1] These select committees are the primary means by which policy-making is scrutinised on behalf of the public.

On the eve of the invasion the majority of the British public, 58 per cent, were shown to be opposed to the war. Air Marshal Brian Burridge, Commander of British forces in the invasion, later noted that 'we went into this campaign with 33 per cent public support'.[2] Yet parliament still backed war; indeed, more

MPs voted to oppose the government over the proposed ban on fox-hunting than did over the invasion of Iraq – perhaps evidence that to those who supposedly represent the British people, animals are more important than (un)people. Following the parliamentary debate on the Butler report in July 2004, only 41 MPs voted against the government. At the same time, an opinion poll showed that 55 per cent of the public believed that Tony Blair lied over the war. The 'democratic deficit' in British political culture is now gaping.

The invasion of Iraq highlights the need for a transformation in the way Britain is governed – something which now seems obvious even to some supporters of the war. Keeping discussion of this largely off the mainstream media agenda must count as one of the great elite propaganda successes, another sign of the extreme lack of democracy in mainstream British culture. While many in the media praise themselves for not letting Blair 'draw a line' under the Iraq affair, they have indeed done so on its most important aspect.

In this light, the media's increasing criticism of Blair personally is a sideshow: it is the system, not the individuals that preside over it, which is the problem. Protecting the system is a basic function of the mainstream media – we can expect that once Blair falls and different faces are in power (no doubt promoting essentially the same policies), the real issue will become even more deeply buried. Indeed, many in the media are now openly calling for Blair to resign precisely because he has become a liability to the system: ever larger numbers of the public no longer trust it, and know that 'democracy' is a facade, thus posing a threat to the wider elite. Yet the problem for that elite is that it is hard even for them to remove the Blair cabal since the beast they have created is indeed so centralised.

It is true that, since the occupation began, there has been considerable criticism of government policy in the mainstream media, and some thorough reporting of the revelations from the Hutton inquiry in the *Guardian* and *Independent*. This stance is partly explicable by the media's need to defend itself

9

against Alastair Campbell, Blair's former Director of 'Communications', and from the Hutton report's attack on the BBC. It is also worth remembering that the parameters of acceptable debate have been widened from within the establishment, much of which was opposed to invading Iraq, for self-interested reasons: the April 2004 letter, speaking out against British policy in Iraq and Israel and signed by 52 former senior diplomats, shows how Blair's cabal has succeeded in alienating even members of its own elite.

Yet the government was able to invade and occupy Iraq because of much of the media's failure to expose obvious propaganda and to be regularly willing simply to parrot it. By the time the September 2002 dossier was published, it was clear that Blair's cabal was bent on invading Iraq and would find any justification for doing so. Yet the mainstream media failed systematically to ridicule the document as obvious state propaganda. Much of it has been taken at face value, not only by the tabloid press, with only mild criticisms and analysis. From then until the invasion period, the litany of British and US government claims of Iraq's possession of weapons of mass destruction (WMD) and links to al Qaeda was consistently reported uncritically.

Just as unquestioning has been the portrayal of the 'intelligence' agencies and the 'security services' as independent, neutral actors providing objective material for a government to act upon. Yet much of the 'intelligence' agencies' work is to promote disinformation, a role discussed in chapter 3.

Also absurd has been the media's compliance in a portrayal of Britain as a force bent on reducing WMD. Not only is Britain a leading nuclear power with no intention of abolishing its own arsenal (in defiance of its international obligations), it is also developing a new generation of such weapons. While the debate over Iraqi WMD was taking place, the British delegation at the UN was opposing several General Assembly resolutions calling on the nuclear states to reduce and abolish their arsenals. In the 57th session of the UN General Assembly, which began in September 2002, Britain voted against three such resolutions and abstained on two others. In all of these votes, more than a hundred states voted in favour, while Britain could count less than five allies (one of which was invariably the US).[3] None of this has been reported in the mainstream media, which preferred to take seriously New Labour's moral commitment to abolishing WMD.

The ideological role of the mainstream media over Iraq has been well-documented in various academic studies and also by the organisation Medialens, which currently provides the most incisive analysis of media reporting. It has noted, for example:

> The important lies – that past experience proved war was necessary to enforce Iraq's disarmament, that its alleged weapons of mass destruction represented a serious threat, that there was a 'moral case for war', and that the US/UK governments were making 'desperate efforts to find a diplomatic alternative' to war – went almost completely unchallenged by the BBC and the media generally.[4]

The portrayal of the BBC as either neutral or even opposed to the war is another staggering public relations achievement. In reality, the institution's 'news' output has been shown by independent analysis to consistently support the priorities of the state.[5] Blair's 'moral' commitments in Iraq are rarely questioned; the done thing is to question only the tactics for achieving his assumed 'humanitarian' objectives. It is almost never mentioned that hundreds of thousands of Iraqis lie dead thanks partly to sanctions previously maintained by Britain and the US. The mainstream media also continues to broadcast the British and American assertion that they are seeking 'democracy' in Iraq while the insurgents are never described as the resistance movement which they represent.

In May 2004, a huge amount of media attention was paid to abuses of Iraqis in custody by US soldiers. But these gruesome acts were a sideshow to the hundreds of Iraqis being massacred in Falluja and elsewhere at the same time. The Abu Ghraib diversion ensured that these uprisings barely made the news, and their suppression was rarely described as the slaughter it was.

Invasion, occupation

The Blair government ordered British forces into a brutal invasion and occupation not in response to a threat from Iraq but to promote traditional foreign policy goals and to demonstrate the special relationship with the US. This is at a time when the US has clearly announced its intention to rule the world by force, outside of international law and free from restrictions imposed by many multilateral institutions or agreements. Blair has acted as the world's major apologist for US foreign policy under the Bush administration. 'There has never been a time when the power of America was so necessary, or so misunderstood', he told the US Congress in July 2003.[6]

Washington's decision to invade Iraq appears to date to two days after September 11th 2001, when Defence Secretary Donald Rumsfeld and his deputy Paul Wolfowitz argued to strike Baghdad but decided on Afghanistan first. One week later, at a private dinner in Washington, George Bush asked Tony Blair for his backing in removing Saddam, according to Christopher Meyer, the former British ambassador to the US. Bush agreed with Blair on the need to strike Afghanistan first but said that 'we must come back to Iraq', to which, according to Meyer, Blair 'said nothing to demur'. Within weeks of September 11th Sir Richard Dearlove, head of MI6, reportedly flew to Washington for policy discussions with US National Security Adviser Condoleeza Rice on regime change in Iraq and on al Qaeda.[7]

Tony Blair's decision to join the US in invading Iraq appears to have been taken in September 2002 at the latest and possibly as early as April 2002 – at meetings with President Bush.[8] The

Butler report is interesting in this respect, and refers to British 'changes in policy towards Iraq in early 2002'. In March, the government considered two options 'for achieving the goal of Iraqi disarmament' – 'a toughening of the existing containment policy; and regime change by military means'. The Butler report states that:

> The government's conclusion in the spring of 2002 that stronger action (although not necessarily military action) needed to be taken to enforce Iraqi disarmament was not based on any new development in the current intelligence picture on Iraq. In his evidence to us, the Prime Minister endorsed the view expressed at the time that what had changed was not the pace of Iraq's prohibited weapons programmes, which had not been dramatically stepped up, but tolerance of them following the attacks of 11 September 2001.

Butler also notes that at this time 'there was no recent intelligence that would itself have given rise to a conclusion that Iraq was of more immediate concern than the activities of some other countries'.[9]

Britain apparently joined US military planning for an invasion of Iraq in June 2002, at which point, according to British military chiefs, a target date of 'spring of 2003 or autumn of 2003' was considered. More specific military planning, including 'media operations', began in September 2002.[10]

This date coincides with Blair's ordering the production of a dossier, intended to make the case for war, while claiming that it was simply outlining the intelligence that Britain had on the threat posed by Iraq. For months, and possibly up to a year, the pretence was maintained to the public that the decision to go to war had not been taken.

By early 2003, the real threat posed to Whitehall by Iraq was not possession of WMD but the fact that Iraq was beginning to cooperate with the weapons inspectors. On 7 March, two weeks before the invasion, chief UN weapons inspector Hans Blix told the Security Council that Iraq, although by no means fully cooperating, was taking 'numerous initiatives . . . with a view to resolving longstanding open disarmament issues' and that 'this can be seen as "active", or even "proactive" cooperation'. After the invasion, Blix reported to the Security Council that his weapons inspections commission, UNMOVIC, 'has not at any time during the inspections in Iraq found evidence of the continuation or resumption of programmes of weapons of mass destruction or significant quantities of proscribed items – whether from pre-1991 or later'.[11]

The invaders' actual aims were essentially to ensure that Iraq has a pro-Western government, that it provides the US with the military bases necessary for a redesign of the Middle East, and that oil flows in accordance with US and UK interests; attainment of the latter two objectives will provide an alternative to US reliance on Saudi Arabia. The British interest in securing new foreign energy supplies is outlined in chapter 4.

That the Iraqi WMD threat was largely a pretext for securing fundamental US interests was conceded by Deputy Defence Secretary Paul Wolfowitz, who told *Vanity Fair* magazine that the issue of WMD was chosen for political expediency: 'The truth is that for reasons that have a lot to do with the US government bureaucracy, we settled on the one issue that everyone could agree on – which was weapons of mass destruction – as the core reason'. A 'huge' outcome of the war, he noted, was the opportunity for the US to pull troops out of Saudi Arabia.[12]

Jay Garner, the retired US General who initially ran the occupation authority in Iraq, recently noted that:

> One of the most important things we can do right now is start getting basing rights . . . Look back on the Philippines around the turn of the 20th century: they were a coaling station for the navy, and that allowed us to keep a great presence in the Pacific. That's what Iraq

is for the next few decades: our coaling station that gives us great presence in the Middle East.[13]

Indeed, by early 2004 the US press was reporting that 'US military engineers are overseeing the building of an enhanced system of American bases designed to last for years'. Fourteen 'enduring bases' were being constructed with plans to operate from former Iraqi bases in Baghdad, Mosul, Taji, Balad, Kirkuk and in areas near Nasiriyah, near Tikrit, near Falluja and between Irbil and Kirkuk. The number of US troops currently in Iraq – around 110,000 – was expected to remain the same through to 2006.[14]

There was a further reason given for war, by Blair, repeated on many occasions in speeches and press conferences. This goal was the same as that given for the bombing of Yugoslavia in 1999 and Afghanistan in 2001, which again went largely unreported. Blair said a month before the invasion that if 'we fail to act' then 'when we turn to deal with other threats, where will our authority be? And when we make a demand next time, what will our credibility be?' In a press conference at Camp David in February he similarly said that if 'we back down' and if 'the world walks away' then 'think of the signal that would have sent right across the world to every brutal dictator'.[15]

What Blair is saying is that the rulers of the world must show the underlings who's boss, otherwise their 'credibility' may be challenged. The demonstration of brute power has value. After the invasion Blair said:

> You can see in relation to countries like Syria and Iran, where we have still got big issues we need to discuss with them and we need to resolve with them, and yet we can do that now in a completely different atmosphere than was possible a few months ago.[16]

Translated: now that we've whacked Iraq, our other enemies are more easily brought into line. Such is the viciousness that lies behind the facade of British foreign policy.

The invasion was extremely brutal. Figures vary from 10,000 civilian deaths alone, with at least 20,000 injured, to another estimate of 22,000–55,000, a figure which includes military and civilian deaths from diseases caused by the war's destruction of health infrastructure.[17]

US and British officials are not counting the number of civilian deaths, during either the war or the occupation. 'We have no viable means of ascertaining the numbers of Iraqis killed or injured during the conflict', the government has stated on several occasions. It has also refused calls in parliament to make a survey of the number of deaths during the invasion period.[18]

British and US forces used around 13,000 cluster bombs containing 2 million bomblets, which killed or wounded more than 1,000 civilians. Around 90,000 bomblets remain unexploded, according to US-based organisation Human Rights Watch, littering the country with what are effectively landmines.

Britain used 2,170 cluster bombs containing 113,190 submunitions. The government, however, had the audacity to claim in June 2003 that 'we are aware of no proven civilian casualties caused by UK cluster weapons'.[19] By contrast, Human Rights Watch reports:

> UK forces caused dozens of civilian casualties when they used ground-launched cluster munitions in and around Basra. A trio of neighbourhoods in the southern part of the city was particularly hard hit. At noon on 23 March, a cluster strike hit Hay al-Muhandissin al-Kubra (the engineers district) while Abbas Kadhim, thirteen, was throwing out the garbage. He had acute injuries to his bowel and liver, and a fragment that could not be removed lodged near his heart . . . Three hours later, submunitions blanketed the neighbourhood of al-Mishraq al-Jadid about two and a half kilometers northeast. Iyad Jassim Ibrhaim, a twenty-six-year-old carpenter, was sleeping in the front room of his home

when shrapnel injuries caused him to lose consciou
ness. He later died in surgery. Ten relatives who were
sleeping elsewhere in the house suffered shrapnel
injuries. Across the street, the cluster strikes injured
three children.

The US and Britain also conducted air strikes against media,
electrical and civilian power distribution facilities. 'Some of the
attacks on electrical power distribution facilities in Iraq are
likely to have a serious and long-term detrimental impact on the
civilian population', due to the effects on water and sewage
treatment plants and medical care, Human Rights Watch
comments. The US destruction of three separate Iraqi media
facilities 'was of questionable legality' since there was no
evidence that the media was used to support Iraq's military
effort, it notes further.[20]

Between 1,000 and 2,000 tonnes of depleted uranium were
also used. According to the Uranium Medical Research
Council, the main cities of Iraq are poisoned with radiation
from these shells and missiles.[21]

Immediately after the fall of the Saddam regime, the
occupation took a predictably violent course. From the outset,
US troops opened fire on unarmed civilians, killed peaceful
demonstrators and even shot at ambulances, killing or
wounding their occupants. Hundreds of people were killed in
the first year of the occupation, mainly by US forces, who often
resorted to brutish methods of population control. Homes were
being demolished as a form of collective punishment, which are
illegal acts. The press also reported the existence of a secret
police force operating with British approval in southern Iraq
that had been accused of kidnapping suspects who were
subsequently mistreated in detention and, in some cases, 'disappeared'. Israeli advisers were also reported to be training US
special forces in 'aggressive counter-insurgency operations',
including the use of assassination squads.[22]

asing opposition to the occupation, as well as
against US and Iraqi targets, the US stepped
vember 2003. It was then that new 'offensive
gan, directed at Iraq's 'growing guerrilla
d which involved heavy equipment such as
the use of aircraft for the first time since Bush
declared the war over. A further, even more dangerously violent
phase began in April 2004, when, in response to the killing of
four US private security guards, the US decided to clamp down
on Shia cleric Moqtada al-Sadr. It launched horrific attacks on
Falluja and other cities that killed hundreds of people, half of
whom were civilians and children. British forces killed up to 40
people in a massacre near the town of Amara in May 2004.[23]

The attack on Falluja started with eliminating the power
supply and involved days of intense bombardment, including
pounding the city with 500lb bombs. Reports suggested that
US troops shot randomly at people and targeted ambulances,
while US marines closed the main hospital for the city's
300,000 people for more than two weeks in order to use it as a
military position, a violation of the Geneva convention.
According to aid workers, many wounded died as a result. After
the attack, aid workers described the city as a ghost town after
inhabitants poured out in their tens of thousands.[24]

As a result of these operations, one member of the US-
appointed Iraqi Governing Council suspended his membership and another called them 'mass punishment for the people
of Falluja', which was 'unacceptable and illegal'. The attack on
Falluja was, however, completely backed by Tony Blair, who
told MPs that 'it is perfectly right and proper that they take
action against those insurgents', adding that 'I deeply regret
any civilian death in Falluja, but it's necessary that order is
restored'. Blair justified the attack under the general pretext of
fighting 'former regime elements' and 'outside terrorists'. Yet,
as the *Guardian* reported, 'those from Falluja could not
understand the claim. The insurgents were not terrorists but
Iraqis, they did not support the old regime and were merely

fighting a patriotic war against American occupation'. The Falluja massacre was quickly passed over in the media, whereas the terrorist killing of 200 people in Madrid received intense coverage for over two weeks.[25]

By May 2004, it had become clear that the US and Britain were confronting an increasingly popular resistance movement. The occupation resembled previous colonial attempts at subjugating nationalist uprisings, and a war of national liberation, uniting various groups, was emerging. Contrary to the public proclamations of British ministers, a leaked Foreign Office memo of May 2004 noted that the insurgency had 'a reservoir of popular support, at least among the Sunnis'.[26]

The response was plain. 'We are going to fight them and impose our will on them and we will capture or, if necessary, kill them until we have imposed law and order upon this country', the US administrator, Paul Bremer, sounding tellingly like a viceroy, said before he left the country after the fictional 'transfer of power' in mid-2004.[27]

A report by the US-based Centre for Economic and Social Rights in June 2004 noted that 'the Bush administration is committing war crimes and other serious violations of international law in Iraq as a matter of routine policy'. It documented ten categories of violations. These included: 'unlawful attacks' involving 'widespread and unnecessary civilian casualties'; 'unlawful detention and torture' involving indiscriminate arrests with around 90 per cent of those detained being innocent bystanders swept up in illegal mass arrests; and 'collective punishment', involving 'taking a cue from Israeli tactics in the occupied territories' by demolishing civilian homes, sealing off entire towns and villages and 'using indiscriminate, overwhelming force in crowded urban areas'.[28]

US and British occupation forces have consistently acted with impunity. Human Rights Watch reported in October 2003 that there were 94 civilian deaths in Baghdad alone 'involving questionable legal circumstances that warrant investigation'. But the US military was 'failing to conduct proper investigations into civilian deaths resulting from the excessive and indiscriminate use of force'. One year into the occupation not a single US soldier had been prosecuted for illegally killing an Iraqi civilian.[29]

As of mid 2004, the deaths of 75 Iraqi civilians at the hands of British forces were being investigated by the British military. 'British troops, and those who command them, can kill with impunity because there is no effective mechanism for accountability within domestic or international law', commented Phil Shiner, a lawyer acting for those killed by British forces. The British military maintains a discreet unit within US-run Camp Bucca prison near the port city of Umm Qasr, in which US soldiers have been known to abuse Iraqis.[30]

A Red Cross report of May 2004 noted 'a number of serious violations of international humanitarian law' by US forces, including 'brutality' in custody, 'physical or psychological coercion during interrogation', prolonged solitary confinement in cells without daylight and 'excessive and disproportionate use of force, resulting in death or injury'. Methods used included hooding, handcuffing, 'pressing the face into the ground with boots', threats, being stripped naked for several days, acts of humiliation and exposure to loud noise. These methods, which involve war crimes, have become standard US practice, employed both at Guantanamo Bay and in Afghanistan, and perhaps also at other US detention centres in Pakistan, Jordan and Diego Garcia. Indeed, they have been taught to US and British military intelligence soldiers at bases in Britain and elsewhere and are known as 'resistance to interrogation' techniques. They also perhaps best signal the Bush administration's view of international law, exemplified in Bush's own response to September 11th: 'I don't care what the international lawyers say, we are going to kick some ass'.[31]

The war against democracy

It seems to be inconceivable in the mainstream that Britain could be opposed to democracy in Iraq or elsewhere. Rather, it is axiomatic that Britain is a supporter of democracy; the only apparent concession is that some 'mistakes' might be made along the way or else leaders may have too high 'ideals'. As a result, Blair's and Bush's statements about wishing to bring democracy to Iraq are rarely countered, even despite the evidence that the opposite is the case.

In the period of occupation alone, Britain has given its backing for blatantly flawed elections in Russia, Chechnya and Nigeria. In truth, Britain and the US have a general aversion to genuine democracy, particularly in the Middle East, where the most popular political movements tend to have weird ideas about using resources for national development purposes, rather than for the benefit of Western corporations.

In Iraq, military force has been quickly followed by economic occupation. The country is currently being subjected to the usual dose of market fundamentalism common to the Western vassal states of the Third World – a process described as 'reconstruction' in the mainstream media. The US occupation forces – in the guise of the Coalition Provisional Authority (CPA) – have proceeded to enact a series of economic 'reforms' in Iraq decreeing widespread privatisation, full foreign ownership of Iraqi banks and factories and the ability for investors to repatriate 100 per cent of profits. CPA order number 12 on 'trade liberalisation policy' decreed the abolition of all trade tariffs and Iraq's 'development of a free market economy'.

'Reconstruction' is being managed and implemented almost solely by foreign expertise. The strategy, which involves handing out multimillion dollar contracts to firms close to the Bush administration, has provoked lobbying by the British government to make sure that 'British companies secure a large slice of the new contracts', in the words of Foreign Office minister Mike O'Brien. By the end of 2003 there were five staff from Britain's Department of Trade and Industry working in Iraq as secondees to the CPA 'to support British firms in Iraq', Trade Secretary Patricia Hewitt noted. 'We expect UK companies to play a significant role in the redevelopment of Iraq', she stated, while her department was ensuring that British businesses 'access opportunities' there. This contradicted her earlier assertion to parliament that the government 'is not in this for business opportunities'.[32]

According to former World Bank chief economist Joseph Stiglitz, the US 'is pushing Iraq towards an even more radical form of shock therapy than was pursued in the former Soviet world'. Today, Stiglitz notes, there is a consensus that economic shock therapy 'failed' and countries 'saw their incomes plunge and poverty soar'. Rapid privatisation is likely to have even more serious consequences in Iraq and 'the international community should direct its money to humanitarian causes such as hospitals and schools, rather than backing American designs'.[33]

The economic 'reforms' imposed on Iraq are almost certainly illegal under international law. The terms of the Geneva Conventions of 1949 and the Hague Regulations of 1907 require existing laws in an occupied country to be respected. Since the passing of UN Security Council resolution 1483 in May 2003, the British government has been arguing that this 'provides a sound legal basis' for the privatisation and other reforms enacted by Paul Bremer's occupation authority. Yet resolution 1483 still requires full compliance with 'obligations under international law', which include the Geneva and Hague provisions.[34]

The Iraqi oil industry appeared to have escaped privatisation and is instead slated to be state-run, partly due to fears of inflaming nationalist anger. Tony Blair told the House of Commons on the eve of war that 'the oil revenues, which people falsely claim that we want to seize, should be put in a trust fund for the Iraq people, administered through the UN'. Later, Britain co-sponsored the May 2003 UN resolution which in effect gave the US and UK control over Iraq's oil revenues, with no UN-administered trust fund.[35]

One key business opportunity is exporting arms. Britain has already secured a special exemption from the UN arms embargo and has been providing arms to Iraq since October 2003. This is in the form of 'sub-machine guns and pistols which are to be used by private security firms contracted to provide close protection for employees' of the CPA. In a parliamentary answer in March 2003, Mike O'Brien said that Britain would support the lifting of the UN arms embargo 'as and when circumstances warrant'.[36]

A further lucrative business is that of the 'private security guards' (ie, mercenaries) operating in the country. With contracts estimated to be worth around $1 billion, British companies are believed to have the biggest share. Around 1,500 former British soldiers and police officers, including former SAS officers, marines and paratroopers are working in Iraq, much of which is being paid for by British taxpayers. The Foreign Office and Department for International Development are reported to have spent nearly £25 million on hiring bodyguards and security advisers to protect their civil servants. The US recruitment of thousands of mercenaries has included veterans from the Pinochet regime in Chile and apartheid regimes in South Africa. Private contractors were also reported to be supervising interrogations in prisons.[37]

The electoral systems in Iraq have been manipulated in much the same way as its economic resources. The country's leading Shia cleric, Grand Ayatollah al-Sistani, led the campaign to insist on early elections. He was opposed by Washington and London, presumably out of fear that their own favoured candidates would not win. 'The Bush administration wanted an orderly process it could control', the *Washington Post* commented.[38]

The media generally reported faithfully what was billed as a 'transfer of power' to Iraq at the end of June 2003 – even though it had become clear several months earlier that precisely the opposite was intended by the Anglo-US occupation forces. An 'occupation order' issued in March 2004, for example, signalled the US' intention to retain control of the Iraqi military after this 'transfer of power'. It also called for the US to appoint several key officers – an army chief of staff, national security adviser and inspector-general – for terms lasting several years. In practice, any Iraqi government was unlikely to replace the appointees before national elections in 2006.

The Associated Press also reported – under the headline 'US will retain power in Iraq after transfer of sovereignty' – that 'most power will reside within the world's largest US embassy [being built in Baghdad], backed by 110,000 troops'. The *Wall Street Journal* reported that 'Bremer and other officials are quietly building institutions that will give the US powerful levers for influencing nearly every important decision the interim government will make'. In a series of edicts issued in the spring, Bremer 'created new commissions that effectively take away virtually all of the powers once held by several ministries'. He also announced that US and international 'advisers' would remain in virtually all remaining ministries after the 'handover'. By mid-2004, Foreign Office minister Mike O'Brien stated that 'almost 200' British officials had been seconded to the occupation authority and Iraqi ministries in recent months.[39]

The US under-secretary of State, Marc Grossman, admitted that what was being transferred was 'limited authority'. The former top State Department official for the Middle East, Edward Walker, noted that Iraq's budget would effectively continue to be run by the US since it would control the doling out of billions of dollars in US aid. He said that 'it's definitely not really a transfer of sovereignty when you don't control the security of your country and you don't really have an income'.[40]

Tony Blair managed to tell the House of Commons: 'There should be full sovereignty transferred to the Iraqi people and the multinational force should remain under American command'. His official spokesperson explained the need for Iraq 'to have full indivisible sovereignty – which means the Iraq government must give its consent to the role of the multinational forces after 1 July'.[41]

The 30 June 'handover' was a consolidation of US power, and

in effect a constitutional coup. It even appointed into power Iyad Allawi, a CIA and MI6 asset and also the source of the British government's claim that Iraq could deploy WMD within 45 minutes. It was as openly undertaken a coup as can be imagined, further exemplifying the attitude of the occupiers towards democracy.

Another anti-democratic Anglo-American strategy in determining Iraq's future is to ensure that the Kurds in the north are kept as far from independence as possible. During the invasion of Iraq, Britain and the US specifically assured Turkey that the 'territorial integrity' of Iraq would be preserved. US leaders have reportedly assured the Turkish government of the need for 'a federation system' for Iraq giving Kurds limited autonomy. In contrast, some Kurdish leaders claim that Washington promised them more widespread autonomy in a federal system just before invading Iraq; which has been denied by the US. In early 2004 the agreed interim Iraqi constitution provided the Kurds with powers to veto any future permanent constitution, and contained guarantees of self-rule in the Kurdish region. However, these powers were not retained in the UN Security Council resolution that was passed in June 2004. US officials rejected strong Kurdish lobbying due to concerns about offending Iraq's Shia leaders who were opposed to granting the Kurds such powers.[42]

One of the British government documents revealed in the Hutton inquiry is a question-and-answer sheet on the September 2002 dossier, in one part of which is stated: 'We wish to see autonomy (not independence) for the Iraqi Kurds'. This basic position has not changed over time. The view in 1963 was that 'our interests are best served by a strong and united Iraq', according to then Foreign Office official Percy Cradock, who was later to become a chairman of the Joint Intelligence Committee.[43]

Washington and London's perennial policy towards the Kurds is evident in the declassified documents, and is worth briefly reviewing to understand the likely course of events in contemporary Iraq.

Consider a secret Foreign Office paper from August 1963, which notes that 'there is no prospect of an independent Kurdistan since this would mean dismembering several other states besides Iraq'. The British interest is described as 'the existence of a strong, friendly Iraqi government able to ensure order throughout the country' either by agreement with the Kurds or by 'military control'. A strong and united Iraq acted as a counter to Nasser's Egypt in the Arab world and helped 'to ensure that the various oil-producing territories remain under divided political control'. The paper also notes that it is in British interests to see a negotiated settlement to the Kurdish problem 'though preferably not such a settlement as would seriously weaken the authority of the central government by its concessions to the Kurds'.

Britain should seek to cultivate good relations both with Iraq and the Kurds but:

> The first are much more important . . . if we favour the Kurds against the Iraqis we would alarm neighbouring countries with Kurdish minorities . . . When faced with the need to make a choice we should therefore recognise the overriding importance of good relations with the Iraqis and that it is in our interest [sic] that their authority should prevail throughout the country.[44]

The Kurds are regarded as a tool for applying pressure on regimes in Baghdad when necessary. In the early 1960s, for example, the British began to encourage a new Kurdish insurrection in Iraq in order to destabilise the nationalist regime of Abdul Qasim. The files show that the British ambassador in Baghdad was quite willing to 'keep an open mind' about the possibilities of the Kurdish revolt 'bringing about his [Qasim's] downfall'. He suggested in September 1962 that Britain should not therefore encourage a settlement between Baghdad and the Kurds but rather remain on the sidelines. Britain should not give direct assistance to the Kurds, he said, 'but perhaps we need not worry too much if others do'.[45]

However, once Qasim had fallen in 1963 and a favoured regime assumed power in Baghdad, British policy changed to all-out support to the government (see Chapter 5). The US pursued the same policy, providing arms to the Kurds from 1961–1963 to undermine Qasim; two days after his fall, the US began to arm the new military regime to fight the same Kurds it had previously armed.[46]

The sequence was essentially repeated for Saddam Hussein. When Saddam was a favoured ally in the 1980s, his massacre of the Kurds was tacitly accepted. After he became an official enemy upon his invasion of Kuwait in 1990, the Kurds were once again favoured and covertly supported. Now that the US controls things in Baghdad, the Kurds are regarded largely as a threat to be kept in their box.

The balance sheet

These then are some of the major considerations to be taken into account. There have of couse been positive developments in Iraq: the terrible Saddam regime has fallen, making for some improvements in freedom of expression and association, and the establishment of new media and civil society organisations. But these real gains seem dwarfed by the reality of the increasingly violent occupation. There is a range of harsh consequences, not only for Iraqis but for Unpeople everywhere.

The first is the scale of violence and killings in Iraq, which have been more brutal than in Saddam's last years, while provisions for basic needs such as health have remained static or worsened for many. Second is a rise of terrorism both in Iraq itself and elsewhere, apparently spawned by US and British strategy. Third are the long-term consequences for ordinary Iraqis of the economic occupation, from which the population is likely to benefit little.

Fourth are the consequences for human rights elsewhere. Following the brazen violation of international law committed in invading Iraq, other states – China, Russia, Indonesia, Nepal etc. – have used the cover of a 'war against terrorism' to launch attacks on their populations. Indeed, the global human-rights conventions and international law, to which states should be held to account, are coming under unprecedented attack in favour of the law of the jungle.

Human Rights Watch has provided a devastating critique of the US and British claim to be acting in defence of human rights in Iraq. Its Director Kenneth Roth has written:

> The invasion of Iraq failed to meet the test for a humanitarian intervention. Most important, the killing in Iraq at the time was not of the exceptional nature that would justify such intervention. In addition, intervention was not the last reasonable option to stop Iraqi atrocities. Intervention was not motivated primarily by humanitarian concerns. It was not conducted in a way that maximised compliance with international humanitarian law. It was not approved by the Security Council. And while at the time it was launched it was reasonable to believe that the Iraqi people would be better off, it was not designed or carried out with the needs of Iraqis foremost in mind.[47]

The normality of occupation

Occupying foreign countries is a somewhat typical British activity in the post-Second World War era – a British speciality, indeed – which may help to explain why Washington was keen to have London on board. Recent British experience of occupation has been largely ignored in the mainstream, but it provides some pointers for the future of Iraq. Let us briefly take one past and one current example, neither of which offers good omens.

The war in Britain's then colony of Kenya in the 1950s was essentially one over land. The Mau Mau movement demanded land for millions of landless poor; the British colonial forces defended white settlers, only a few thousand of whom owned the best land in the country. The declassified files I have seen paint a frightening picture of terrible human-rights atrocities by the colonial authorities in their attempt to defeat the opposition forces.

This war, like the war in Iraq, was invariably depicted as one of civilisation versus barbarity. In reality, although atrocities were committed on both sides, the worst abuses were committed by the British forces and their local allies. Former members of the Mau Mau movement are currently trying to sue the British government for compensation 'on behalf of the 90,000 people imprisoned and tortured in detention camps, 10,000 people who had land confiscated and a further half a million who were forced into protected villages'.[48]

British repression in Kenya consisted of 'resettlement' operations that forced 90,000 people of the Kikuyu ethnic group into detention camps surrounded by barbed wire and troops, and the compulsory 'villageisation' of the Kikuyu reserves. Livestock was confiscated and many people were subjected to forced labour. 'Villageisation' meant the destruction of formerly scattered homesteads and the erection of houses in fortified camps to replace them. This was a traumatic break from the traditional Kikuyu way of life. Even when not accompanied, as it often was, by 23-hour curfews, it resulted in widespread famine and death. In total, up to 150,000 Africans may have lost their lives due to the war, most dying of disease and starvation in the 'protected villages'. Their deaths were ignored by foreign-policy planners and the mainstream media alike.

The declassified files make clear that Britain also used the war against Mau Mau as a cover for halting the rise of other popular, nationalist forces that threatened British control of Kenya. The colonial authorities imprisoned nationalist leader Jomo Kenyatta on the charge that he was leading the Mau Mau: at the time, British officials knew this was not so. Faced with the nationalist threat to continued British control of land and general agitation for full independence, this was an early example of wiping out the threat of independent development – a key strategy of British, as well as US, planners throughout the post-war era. The pretext presented at the time, the Soviet threat, was often fabricated or exaggerated – and was non-existent in the case of Kenya. British motives in the war and occupation of Kenya were both political (to continue to determine the future of Kenya after independence) and commercial (to ensure that the country's resources lay in the correct hands).

The opposition in Kenya were invariably depicted in public as demonic and bloodthirsty or Soviet stooges. As the files show, Whitehall planners well understood this to be false, and they privately recognised the war was against nationalist forces. In Malaya at the same time, a similarly brutal occupation depicted Britain's opponents as 'communist terrorists' and the official rationale for the war was to stop Chinese expansion. In private, however, the Foreign Office understood the war as 'very much in defence of [the] rubber industry', then partly in British hands.[49] The parallels with Iraq are difficult to overlook.

Consider also a current occupation by Britain and the US which has been largely excluded from attention. The Chagos islands – formally known as the British Indian Ocean Territory – include Diego Garcia, a US military base from which US bombers have attacked Iraq and Afghanistan, and where al Qaeda suspects may be being held in circumstances even more clandestine than those in Cuba.

Beginning in 1968, the entire population of Chagossians was flung off their homeland islands to make way for a US military base. Some were tricked into leaving on the promise of a free voyage; others were physically removed. The islanders have long campaigned for compensation and the right to return, outside of significant international attention. But the Blair government set itself against the Chagossians and its sustained legal campaign was rewarded in 2003 with a High Court ruling that the Chagossians' claim has 'no reasonable grounds'. The Chagossians are currently appealing.

The giant lie at the heart of British policy was that the Chagossians were never permanent inhabitants of the islands but simply 'contract labourers'. In 1969, Foreign Secretary Michael Stewart wrote to Harold Wilson that 'we could continue to refer to the inhabitants generally as essentially migrant contract labourers and their families'; therefore, it would be helpful 'if we can present any move as a change of employment for contract workers ... rather than as a population resettlement'. This set the scene; seven successive British governments have maintained the fiction.

Until recently, visitors to the Foreign Office website were told that there were 'no indigenous inhabitants' on the islands. Then the wording suddenly changed and now acknowledges that there was a 'settled population'. Nearly four decades since the beginning of the depopulation, the truth was quietly admitted.

Yet the policy has not changed. The Blair government continues to fight the Chagossians in court and in other, less transparent ways. In a landmark decision in November 2000, the High Court ruled that 'the wholesale removal' of the islanders was an 'abject legal failure' and that they could return to the small outlying islands in the group but not the largest island, Diego Garcia. This was a nightmare for British and US planners, and Whitehall immediately seemed intent on defying it. It dragged out the process of researching island resettlement, and then concluded that resettlement was unfeasible anyway. A Foreign Office memo to a parliamentary inquiry stated that resettlement of the outlying islands would be 'impractical and inconsistent with the existing defence facilities'. It added that 'our position on the future of the territory will be determined by our strategic and other interests and our treaty commitments to the USA'. The memo said nothing about the government's obligations to the rights of the islanders.

The government was in effect already preventing the Chagossians from returning to their islands, when it delivered a stunning blow in June 2004. Instead of using the normal

legislative process, it resorted to a remnant of the royal preroga-
tive and announced two 'orders in council' to bar the
Chagossians from returning even to the outlying islands.
Announcing the decision in parliament, Foreign Office minister
Bill Rammell said that as a result of the new orders 'no person
has the right of abode in the territory or has unrestricted access
to any part of it'. He also said that 'these two orders restore the
legal position to what it has been understood to be before the
High Court decision of 3 November 2000'.[50] This showed, even
more clearly than in the case of Iraq, how the government had
captured the legal process and was using it for political ends, a situation only usually pertaining in totalitarian states.

Examples of past and present occupations bode ill for the
future of Iraq. Yet such grotesque occupations are no more
unusual than promoting 'regime change', another virtually
permanent Anglo-American activity, with similar consequences. The current mainstream debate over the tension
between state sovereignty and intervention, and changing the
so-called traditional 'presumption against intervening in
foreign countries', must surely be a joke: Attempting to
overthrow unwanted governments is a systematic feature of
British foreign policy.

Consider, for example, the long list of governments that
Britain has itself directly overthrown or tried to overthrow: Iran
(1953), British Guiana (1953 and 1963), Egypt (1956), Indonesia
(1957–1958, 1965), Yemen (1962–1970), Oman (1970), Libya
(1996), Yugoslavia (1999), Afghanistan (2001). There are also
numerous cases where Britain has welcomed the overthrow of
governments by the US, such as: Guatemala (1954), Iraq (1963),
Vietnam (1963), Dominican Republic (1965), Chile (1973),
Nicaragua (1980s) and Panama (1989).

Even a cursory understanding of past and current occupations and regime change by Britain and the US provides good
insight into the supposed commitment to 'democracy' and
'human rights' in Iraq.

2

THE IRRELEVANCE OF
INTERNATIONAL LAW

The March 2003 invasion of Iraq was an act of international aggression, an apparent violation of the Nuremberg principles applied to German leaders after the Second World War. It stands as the supreme international crime for which Blair and other ministers might be judged as war criminals.

The British government repeatedly asserts that its actions in Iraq were intended to 'uphold UN resolutions'; at the same time, its invasion was a wholesale violation of the UN charter. Faced with massive opposition to war at home and around the world, British officials tried to get UN cover for their actions. They attempted to secure a Security Council resolution specifically authorising war; the process involved the intense lobbying of other countries and even allegedly spying on other UN members. It appears that Blair had pushed George W. Bush to secure UN acquiescence in an attack on Iraq rather than immediately acting unilaterally – on the understanding that if the UN failed to authorise a US attack, the US would act anyway, and Britain would support it.

The UN was given an ultimatum clearly outlined by Blair in an interview in October 2002. He said that Iraq:

is best dealt with through the United Nations . . . but nobody should be in any doubt that if it isn't dealt with in that way, it has got to be dealt with differently.[1]

Former International Development Secretary Clare Short said following her resignation that the 'search for a diplomatic solution' to the crisis over Iraq was a charade. The effort was made to go through the UN 'for the sake of international public opinion' and 'they wanted to be free to act, having tried the UN, when they wanted to act'. Crucially, she also stated that 'this way of making the decision led to the lack of proper preparation for afterwards and I think that a lot of the chaos, disorder and mess in Iraq flowed from not having made the decision properly and made the preparations properly'.[2]

The Blair government had also prepared itself for further ignoring the UN in case France or Russia vetoed a second resolution, by inventing a term outside international law called an 'unreasonable veto', that would allow it to proceed to war. Once it became clear that other states would not support a resolution authorising war, British officials publicly blamed France, whose refusal to support war at that time was merely consistent with almost every other state in the UN. Many parts of the mainstream media wilfully participated in the fabrication of a convenient French scapegoat.

All the evidence indicates that the invasion was illegal, and that the government understood it to be so. The implications of this are massive: they effectively state that international law is seen as irrelevant.

The illegal invasion

The view of UN Secretary General Kofi Annan, just before military action started, was that 'if the US and others were to go outside the Security Council and take unilateral action they would not be in conformity with the [UN] charter'.[3]

Former UN Humanitarian Coordinator for Iraq, Dennis Halliday, has similarly said that the invasion of Iraq 'constitutes blatant aggression by the United States and Britain outside the bounds of the United Nations without any resolution under chapter 7 of the charter in support'. He added that 'it's an extraordinary adventure for two permanent members of the UN Security Council to undertake a war in complete breach of the charter'.[4]

An overwhelming majority of international lawyers appear to agree that the war could not have been legal, since the UN charter permits military action only if conducted in self-defence or if specifically authorised by the Security Council. Even Richard Perle, a leading US neo-conservative and then adviser to President Bush, said, 'I think in this case international law stood in the way of doing the right thing', admitting that 'international law . . . would have required us to leave Saddam Hussein alone'.[5]

The evidence suggests that the British government knew that the invasion was illegal. Doubts about the legality of the war were expressed by the entire Foreign Office legal establishment, the press has reported. The deputy head of the Foreign Office's legal team, Elizabeth Wilmshurst, resigned and later said that 'I did not agree that the use of force against Iraq was lawful'.[6] The *Guardian*'s Richard Norton-Taylor, who has extensive security and intelligence connections, wrote that 'not a single government lawyer or senior official in Whitehall has told me that the war, in their view, was legal'.[7]

Also, consider the government's statements on UN resolution 1441, passed by the Security Council in November 2002. Much of the debate on legality has focused on whether this resolution was sufficient to legalise a military attack. It merely authorised 'serious consequences' if Iraq failed to comply, not specifically the use of force, and required the Security Council to have further discussions if Iraq were to breach the resolution. Indeed, if it had been understood by many of the states who voted for this resolution that it was authorising force, it would not have passed, since most of the world was opposed to the Anglo-American position.

An even clearer indication that resolution 1441 did not authorise war is that both Blair and Straw had said so. Blair's statement on resolution 1441 on 8 November 2002 noted:

> In the event of Saddam refusing to cooperate or being in breach, there will be a further discussion, as we always said there would be. To those who fear this resolution is just an automatic trigger point, without any further discussion, paragraph 12 of the resolution makes it clear that this is not the case.[8]

Just before the invasion, on 12 March 2003, however, Blair told the House of Commons: 'As the Foreign Secretary has pointed out, resolution 1441 gives the legal basis for this [war]'.[9]

Jack Straw also said elsewhere that although resolution 1441 did not provide the trigger for war, neither was a second resolution required. He told a parliamentary inquiry on 4 March 2003 that 'in those circumstances where you have got a further material breach you then have the Council meeting for an assessment of the situation'. Straw added that 'but what the Council has to do . . . is to consider the situation, not necessarily to pass a second resolution'. Then he added that 'it is for the Security Council to confirm whether there has been a material breach' under resolution 1441.[10]

After the invasion Straw told the committee that:

> It was equally accepted by us that there was no 'automaticity' in 1441. In other words there had to be a process leading towards any military action in the event of non-compliance by Iraq, which process we followed.[11]

The 'process' Britain and the US 'followed' was of course one of proceeding to war; there was no substantive discussion in the Security Council that gave backing to the war lobby.

Until just before the invasion, Attorney General Lord Goldsmith's view was that a second Security Council resolution authorising force was required.[12] Only five days after this view was reported in the *Guardian*, Goldsmith announced on 17 March that the war would be legal. Hand-picked by Blair for his role, Goldsmith appears to have acquiesced in the demands of his political master. At the time of writing, the government has long resisted calls to publish his official advice. Whitehall dropped the case against former GCHQ employee Katherine Gun after the defence made clear it was pushing to make available in court the government's legal case for the war.

Goldsmith argued that the authority to use force was based on the combined effects of resolutions 678, 687 and 1141 and that since Iraq was failing to comply with resolution 1441 then 'the authority to use force under resolution 678 has revived and so continues today'. Yet, on the same day, Jack Straw wrote a letter to the Foreign Affairs Committee saying the opposite:

> It is important to stress that SCR 1441 did not revive the 678 authorisation immediately upon its adoption. There was no 'automaticity'. The resolution afforded Iraq a final opportunity to comply and it provided for any failure by Iraq to be considered by the Security Council.[13]

Again, there *was* no substantive consideration – and Straw's letter must therefore constitute a further admission by the government that it understood the war was illegal.

As argued by Keir Starmer QC, a barrister specialising in international human-rights law, resolution 678 of November 1990 authorised force simply to eject Iraq from Kuwait. Resolution 687, passed at the end of military action against Iraq in April 1991, does not authorise the use of force; it does require Iraq to destroy all WMD but this is for the Security Council, not the US and Britain, to decide. Former chief UN weapons inspector Hans Blix has also said that the war was illegal and that while it was possible to argue that Iraq was in breach of UN resolutions since 1991, the 'ownership' of those resolutions rested with the entire UN Security Council, not the US and Britain.[14]

The Butler report makes clear that when the government was considering the option of military action against Iraq in March 2002, its advice was that 'regime change of itself would have no basis in international law'. It could only be justified if Iraq were to be held in breach of resolution 687. Yet officials noted that for the Security Council to take this view 'such proof would need to be incontrovertible and of large-scale activity' – which it never was.[15]

The Attorney General's judgement appears to be a last-minute fix based on an interpretation of international law so shaky as to be close to comical. It demonstrates above all the degree to which the personalised autocracy can demand the obedience of all organs of the state, including even its legal functions – perhaps the most worrying development of all.

The evident illegality of the invasion is compounded by another myth: that the government's aim was not 'regime change' but simply forcing Iraq to comply with UN resolutions on disarmament. As soon as the invasion began, Blair stated repeatedly that 'regime change' was the goal. Indeed, he told the whole country this on 20 March 2003, in a televised address: 'Tonight British servicemen and women are engaged from air, land and sea. Their mission: to remove Saddam Hussein from power and disarm Iraq of its weapons of mass destruction'. Five days later he told a press conference that 'our objective remains as it is, to remove Saddam's regime'.[16] The government's change in position was defended only by the implication that the only way of disarming Iraq was to remove the regime; a nonsensical argument given the refusal to allow Iraq the further chances to cooperate with the weapons inspectors which Hans Blix requested.

Mark Littman QC notes that, at the Nuremberg trials, the international tribunal stated 'that to initiate a war of aggression . . . is not only an international crime, it is the supreme international crime'. It was for this crime that German Foreign Minister Von Ribbentrop was tried and hanged. Littman notes that 'members of any government actively involved in bringing about an unlawful war against Iraq would be well advised to be cautious as to the countries they visit during the remainder of their lives'.[17]

Various groups are lodging complaints to the International Criminal Court (ICC). The Athens Bar Association, a group of Greek lawyers with a membership of 20,000, has accused Blair and other ministers of crimes against humanity. A panel of international lawyers and academics has also called on the ICC to investigate Britain for alleged war crimes, especially for the use by the British military of cluster bombs in civilian areas.[18] There is certainly enough evidence for the British Prime Minister and other members of Cabinet to answer a case made against them as war criminals.

The law of the jungle?

The British government has in effect said that in future it will not be bound by international law. In its response to a House of Commons Defence Committee report, the government stated that:

> The government concurs with the importance the Committee attributes to operating within international law. We will always act in accordance with legal obligations but also effectively to defend the UK's people and interests and secure international peace and stability.[19]

The key words are 'but also': they stipulate a willingness to act outside international law. This follows various violations of international law under Blair, such as the attacks on Yugoslavia in 1999 and on Iraq in 1998, both without UN authorisation.

Then in March 2004, Blair announced the government's clearest intention yet to rewrite international law so as to make military intervention easier in future. Had Iran or even France expounded this, the British media may have found something to worry about; instead, it was received as a sign of the British

Prime Minister's high morals. The only dissenters in the UK press were a few commentators who criticised the intentions, mildly, for being unrealistic.

Blair stated that the world needed new rules for intervention on 'humanitarian grounds' beyond the current UN charter, since 'the only clear case in international relations for armed intervention' is 'self-defence, response to aggression'. 'This may be the law, but should it be?', Blair asked. After September 11, he claimed, the need for intervention had risen to address the global terrorist threat and 'now is not the time to err on the side of caution'. 'Containment will not work in the face of the global threat that confronts us'. Blair added:

> I am not saying that every situation leads to military action . . . But surely we have a duty and a right to prevent the threat materialising; and we surely have a responsibility to act when a nation's people are subjected to a regime such as Saddam's.[20]

It is possible to take these assertions seriously only if we suspend all knowledge about Britain's place in the real world. For one thing, Britain is a major supporter of many regimes 'such as Saddam's'. With regard to Indonesia, Nigeria, Colombia or Russia it is not military intervention that may be required to address humanitarian needs but simply withdrawals of support. For another, the Anglo-American invasion of Iraq has created a breeding ground for terrorists which the government now claims to be serious about confronting. Blair mentioned in this same speech 'the terrorists pouring into Iraq'; in the following paragraph, he boasted that Saddam's removal had 'diminished' this threat.

Countering the UN threat

Britain's undermining of the UN in the invasion of Iraq is far from unusual. In the mainstream, the official view is that British governments provide enduring support to the UN. The opposite is true: it is clear from the historical record that the UN has traditionally been seen as a major threat.

Britain's ambassador to the UN, Patrick Dean, lamented to the Foreign Secretary in 1963 about 'an international climate which makes unilateral protection of interests by military means increasingly complicated and difficult'. He was then complaining of the widespread opposition at the UN towards British policies on Rhodesia and British Guiana. Britain, he stated, had a 'diversity of interests of every kind all over the world' but these 'are less and less capable of protection by her own physical strength'.[21]

In the last half of the cold war, 1965–1990, Britain cast more than twice as many vetoes in the UN Security Council as the Soviet Union – 27 to 13 – mainly to protect the racist regimes in Rhodesia and South Africa from full international sanctions (the US applied 69 vetoes over the same period). The last veto cast by the Soviet Union before it collapsed was in 1984; over the next six years Britain cast 10 Security Council vetoes (the US, 32). I have yet to see any mention of this consistent British obstruction of the UN in mainstream analysis, which prefers stories about the cold war, or simply the Soviet veto, hobbling the UN.

In the 1950s, the UN was seen by British planners as 'an instrument which can be used to promote the United Kingdom's prestige and influence'. But a danger could arise given 'the possibility, under the system of "one state, one vote", for small nations to exert undue influence', which 'may endanger the ability of the United Kingdom and Commonwealth to preserve their essential interests from United Nations interference', the Foreign Office noted.[22]

A Foreign Office paper of 1964 states that 'a specific British objective' towards the UN is:

> to use it as a channel of influence in the pursuit of British policies and for this purpose to maintain our existing privileged position as one of the five permanent members of the UN Security Council.[23]

The Foreign Secretary in the Heath government, Alec Douglas-Home, wrote in 1970 that Britain's position as a permanent member of the Security Council 'gives us special opportunities for using the United Nations as a forum to exert our influence'. He then considered three policy options: first, to make the UN the major element in British foreign policy; second, a policy of minimal contribution and involvement in the UN; and third, a policy based on recognising the 'practical limitations' of the UN but also 'its importance to the achievement of our foreign policy goals'. The first two options were rejected – the first since, according to Douglas-Home, other nations would not follow suit and the UN was unable anyway to become more effective. The third option was therefore the favoured one.

This meant that the UN was not an organisation 'which we can hope to use across the board to promote our interests'; this will happen 'only occasionally and in certain fields'. It also meant that Britain should focus its efforts as part of the UN to achieving British objectives 'and not to the long term hope that it will develop into a more effective world force'. On matters where 'our essential national interests are affected', Britain should 'make clear in advance' that it would be ready to use its veto.[24]

This policy continues today. For the past 50 years, the essence of British strategy has been to ensure the UN's failure to prevent or condemn Britain's, or its allies', acts of aggression. From 1980 to 1988, for example, Britain and the US vetoed 12 separate UN Security Council resolutions condemning apartheid South Africa – Britain vetoing 11 of these, the US all 12. After its brutal invasion of Angola, South Africa was protected from full international pariah status when the US vetoed, and Britain abstained on, a resolution in 1981. Britain used its veto in May 1986 against a draft resolution condemning South Africa's attacks on Botswana, Zambia and Zimbabwe, and the following month Britain and the US vetoed a resolution condemning South Africa for further attacks on Angola.

When Indonesia invaded East Timor in 1975, leading to the deaths of around 200,000 people in one of the bloodiest operations in post-war history, Britain in effect supported Jakarta at the UN. Declassified files show that the British planned before the invasion not to condemn the Indonesians and that 'if there is a row in the United Nations . . . we should keep our heads down and avoid taking sides'.[25] Between 1975 and 1982 there were two Security Council resolutions and eight General Assembly resolutions condemning the invasion and urging Indonesian withdrawal. Britain did vote in favour of the two Security Council resolutions, though these were weakly worded and simply 'called upon' Jakarta to withdraw. London abstained on, or voted against, all the General Assembly resolutions, while it provided arms to Indonesia and deepened aid, trade and diplomatic relations.

When the US organised an invasion of Guatemala in 1954 to overthrow the reformist nationalist government of Jacobo Arbenz, the Guatemalans took their case to the UN. A Guatemalan request for the Security Council to consider its complaints about external aggression was rejected partly due to abstentions from Britain and France, acting in support of US policy.

US aggression against Nicaragua in the 1980s resulted in condemnations from around the globe, while the US delivered seven UN vetoes between 1982 and 1986. On all of them, Britain declared its de facto support for Washington by abstaining. Thus Britain could not bring itself to condemn the mining of Nicaraguan ports by the US or support the ruling of the International Court of Justice which found the US aggression against Nicaragua to be illegal and which demanded the US comply with international law.

Similarly, when the US invaded Panama in 1989 it was not only Washington but also London that vetoed a draft resolution calling on the US to withdraw.

For the first decades of the post-war world, the British government fought tooth and nail to keep the UN out of its colonial affairs. In 1950, for example, the Colonial Office noted that such 'ignorant or prejudiced outside interference would do uncalculable harm'. It also explicitly stated its fear that the colonial powers would have to become 'accountable to the United Nations', something which necessarily had to be avoided.[26]

In the early 1960s, Britain undertook a covert, 'dirty' war in Yemen to destabilise a new, popular republican government (see Chapter 16). A British ministerial meeting of December 1963 concluded that 'any proposal that the United Nations should be invited to find a solution for the problem should be resisted since it would be detrimental to our position' in neighbouring Aden. The UN, explained Sir Roger Allen, deputy undersecretary at the Foreign Office, consisted only of 'trouble makers' and would reflect only the position of the Egyptians, then Britain's rival in the region.[27]

British policies have long been condemned at the UN and invariably ignored and deflected by Whitehall planners. After the British intervention in Oman in the 1960s to support the extremely repressive Sultan's regime against a rebellion (also detailed in Chapter 16), the UN's ad hoc committee produced a report in January 1966 concluding that Oman was a 'serious international problem' arising from 'imperialistic policies and foreign intervention'. Afro-Asian delegates in the Fourth Committee, which dealt with colonial issues, tabled a motion stating that 'the colonial policies of the UK in its various forms prevents the people of the territory from exercising their rights to self-determination and independence', and calling on Britain to cease repressive activity and withdraw troops. This resolution was passed by large majorities in both the Fourth Committee and the General Assembly and was subsequently ignored by London, which got on with the business of backing its client.[28]

When Britain invaded Egypt in October 1956, international condemnation provoked London's first Security Council vetoes. Britain refused any serious attempts to resolve the dispute with Egypt through the UN since 'neither the Security

Council nor the General Assembly could give us what we wanted', Foreign Office minister Anthony Nutting later explained. According to Geoff Simons' study of the UN, Prime Minister at the time, Anthony Eden 'was prepared to have the crisis discussed in the Security Council but only as a prelude to independent British action'. He notes that UN Secretary General, Dag Hammarskjold, did his best to ensure the success of talks at the UN 'but there was a substantial British interest in their failure, and fail they did', thus paving the way for military aggression.[29]

During the civil war in Nigeria between 1967 and 1970, London backed the Lagos government's brutal repression of the secessionist region of Biafra (see Chapter 10). This support included the prevention of any significant UN involvement in the war. Britain was 'strongly opposed to any suggestion of taking the Nigerian question to the United Nations', the Commonwealth Secretary told US officials at the time.[30]

The files also show that due to public opposition to Britain's policy of arming the Nigerian government during its aggression, British officials went through the motions at the UN of taking soundings on an arms embargo. The files make clear that this was done entirely for public relations, to demonstrate that an arms embargo was a 'non-starter' and so enable Britain to continue arming the regime. 'The Prime Minister's purpose in suggesting these soundings was presumably to strengthen our parliamentary position', a Foreign Office official noted.[31]

Western policy at the UN well before Iraq was described by former adviser to the Secretary General, Erskine Childers. He noted that the Western powers have long used 'economic bribery and intimidation' to get their way at the World Bank and IMF but that this had now been extended to the UN:

> Whenever the Western powers are determined to get a given vote through either the Security Council . . . or the General Assembly . . . governments are warned. If they

45

do not 'behave' they will not get debt relief, World Bank capital projects, easier IMF adjustment conditionalities or urgently needed hard currency IMF credit to pay oil bills. Reduction or cut-off in bilateral aid is an additional threat.[32]

This general contempt for the UN throughout the post-war era, starkly illustrated in the invasion of Iraq, reveals a fundamental issue at the heart of Britain's foreign policy: that most of the world has traditionally been opposed to Britain's major policies. This is the opposite of what our mainstream political culture generally claims – that Britain and the West are the guardians of the highest universal ideals and that it is others who are the barbarians.

3

DECEIVING THE PUBLIC: THE IRAQ PROPAGANDA CAMPAIGN

Politics has been described as many things but in Britain currently a good summary is that it is the art of deceiving the public. Clare Short, after resigning her position as International Development Secretary, told a parliamentary inquiry of 'a series of half-truths, exaggerations and reassurances that were not the case to get us into conflict [with Iraq] by the spring' of 2003.[1] This is, in my view, an understatement: all the evidence suggests that – at least over Iraq – the public has been subjected by the government to a campaign of managed deception.

'Dark actors playing games'[2]

In June 2003 it was revealed that the British government had for twelve years been promoting an operation designed to produce misleading intelligence that Iraq had weapons of mass destruction. Operation Rockingham had been established by the Defence Intelligence Staff in 1991 to provide information proving that Saddam had an ongoing WMD programme and quashing evidence that stockpiles had been destroyed or wound down.[3]

According to Scott Ritter, a former chief UN weapons inspector, Operation Rockingham and MI6:

institutionalised a process of 'cherry picking' intelligence produced by the UN inspections in Iraq that skewed UK intelligence about Iraqi WMD towards a predordained outcome that was more in line with British government policy than it was reflective of ground truth.

He added that 'they had to sustain the allegation that Iraq had WMD [when] Unscom [the UN weapons inspectors] was showing the opposite'.[4] This 'intelligence' was supplied to the Joint Intelligence Committee, the body that drew up the September 2002 dossier alleging Iraq's ongoing WMD programmes.

One of the tactics used in the operation, according to Ritter, was leaking false information on weapons to inspectors and then when the search for them proved fruitless, using that as 'proof' of the weapons' existence. He cited an example from 1993 when information led to inspections of a suspected ballistic-missile site; when the inspectors found nothing 'our act of searching allowed the US and UK to say that the missiles existed', he said. The government revealed in January 2004 that Operation Rockingham continued into 2002/3 with a budget of £79,000.[5]

Another operation – called Mass Appeal – was revealed by the press in late 2003. This was launched in the late 1990s by MI6 and aimed to gain public support for sanctions and war against Iraq and involved planting stories in the media about Iraqi WMD. Scott Ritter was personally involved in this operation in 1997–1998 after being approached by MI6. He said that 'the aim was to convince the public that Iraq was a far greater threat than it actually was', and that the operation involved the manipulation of intelligence material right up to the invasion of Iraq.

Poland, India and South Africa were initially chosen as targets for these media stories, with the intention that they would then feed back into Britain and the US. Ritter notes that 'stories ran in the media about secret underground facilities in Iraq and ongoing [WMD] programmes. They were sourced to Western intelligence and all of them were garbage'. He also said that 'they took this information and peddled it off to the media, internationally and domestically, allowing inaccurate intelligence data to appear on the front pages'.[6]

US investigative journalist Seymour Hersh notes that the British propaganda programme was known to a few senior officials in Washington. 'We were getting ready for action in Iraq, and we wanted the Brits to prepare', he quotes a former Clinton administration official saying. A former US intelligence officer told him that at least one member of the UN inspections team who supported the US and British position arranged for dozens of unverified intelligence reports and tips to be funnelled to MI6 operatives and quietly passed to newspapers in London and elsewhere. The source said: 'it was intelligence that was crap, and that we couldn't move on, but the Brits wanted to plant stories in England and around the world'. Hersh notes there was a series of clandestine meetings with MI6 at which documents were provided and quiet meetings were held in safe houses in the Washington area.[7]

British propaganda campaigns on Iraq were established well before the new phase began in late 2002. In the run up to the invasion, the government established a Coalition Information Centre technically based in the Foreign Office Information Directorate but chaired by Alastair Campbell and run from Downing Street. Campbell also chaired another cross-Whitehall committee, the Iraq Communication Group. It was these organs that played a key part in controlling the campaign that misled the public about Iraq's WMD and which oversaw the production of the dossiers.[8]

In March 2004, the all-party House of Commons Defence Committee produced a report showing that 'the Ministry of Defence began working on its media strategy [on Iraq] in September 2002 in consultation with the Americans'. This strategy plan 'was an integral part of the overall military plan' and was 'coordinated across Whitehall with a daily inter-departmental media coordination meeting chaired by No. 10'. In all, some 200 additional press officers were deployed by the Ministry of Defence 'to support the media campaign effort'.

The system of embedding journalists within the military in operations in Iraq – described by the Defence Secretary as 'one of the more novel aspects of the media campaign' – 'helped secure public opinion in the UK', the Defence Committee notes. It quotes the British land force commander, General Brims, stating that 'from my point of view . . . none of them [the embedded journalists] let the side down'. Air Vice Marshall Torpy, the commander of the air force in the invasion of Iraq, said that his staff were 'very satisfied with the coverage that they got'. The all-party Defence Committee entirely approves of these operations and recommends they should be significantly stepped up in future.[9]

Media stories which may have been based on disinformation put out by British officials during the Iraq operation, included: a supposed 'uprising' in Basra; the death of Saddam; three giant cargo ships said to contain WMD (carried in the *Independent*); Saddam killing Iraq's 'missile chief' to thwart the UN inspectors (carried in the *Sunday Telegraph*); 'Saddam's Thai gem spree hints at getaway plan' (covered in the *Sunday Times*); and a story from 'American and British war planners' that Iraq was preparing a 'scorched earth policy ahead of any US military attack' to 'engineer a devastating humanitarian crisis against his own people' (carried in the *Observer*).[10]

The propaganda campaign has continued into the occupation period. In November 2003 the *Guardian* revealed that the government was conducting a 'media offensive' with a code name of 'Big October' to convert the public to supporting the outcome of the Iraq war. Leaked documents showed that the Ministry of Defence had drawn up the strategy in September, a time when Britain and the US were facing increasing opposition; they stated that 'information operations are seen as a tool to help keep the situation manageable'. One document specified that 'the MoD's main target is the UK public and media while [the main target] of the Basra headquarters for British troops is the Iraqi people'. The two main issues to stress through the British media were: 'security in Iraq – try to push the perception that Iraq is becoming more secure', and 'utilities and reconstruction – try to demonstrate that services and utilities are as good if not better than before the war'.[11]

Iraq was not perceived as a serious threat

Two myths widely conveyed in the mainstream media are, first, that there was simply a huge 'failure of intelligence' over Iraq and, second, that ministers acted in good faith in presenting to the public their view of the threat posed by Iraq, but simply got it wrong. These myths combine to let the government off the hook and protect the decision-making system.

When the Butler report was published, the *Economist* wrote an editorial about Bush and Blair entitled 'sincere deceivers'. It noted that 'in making the case for last year's invasion of Iraq, they were honest about what they believed'. 'Such salesmanship' about the threat from Iraq 'was understandable' given 'widespread scepticism about whether war was the right solution'. Similarly, a *New Statesman* editorial noted that Blair 'got it wrong', adding that 'Mr Blair was almost certainly sincere when he said he was "in no doubt" that the threat from the Iraqi dictator was "serious and current"'. Blair therefore made a 'catastrophic misjudgement' and 'failed to do his job'.[12]

The reality is quite the opposite. It is clear from both the Hutton and Butler inquiries that the intelligence given to ministers was regularly vague and uncertain about an Iraqi threat. The Butler report notes that after the departure of the UN weapons inspectors in 1998, 'information sources were sparse, particularly on Iraq's chemical and biological weapons programmes'. 'The number of primary human intelligence sources remained few' while MI6 'did not generally have agents with first-hand, inside knowledge of Iraq's nuclear, chemical, biological or ballistic missile programmes. As a result, intelligence reports were mainly inferential'.

Joint Intelligence Committee reports were variously saying that intelligence on Iraqi WMD was 'patchy', 'unclear', 'limited' or 'poor' while noting that 'there is very little intelligence' and 'our picture is limited'. A JIC report produced a few weeks before the release of the government's September 2002 dossier stated that it 'knew little about Iraq's CBW [chemical biological weapons] work since late 1998'.[13]

In March 2003 the Joint Intelligence Committee provided an assessment stating, according to the government, that:

> Intelligence on the timing of when Iraq might use CBW was inconsistent and that the intelligence on deployment was sparse. Intelligence indicating that chemical weapons remained disassembled and that Saddam had not yet ordered their assembly was highlighted.

The JIC also pointed out that other intelligence suggested that Iraq's 750km range ballistic missiles remained disassembled and that it would take 'several days to assemble them once orders to do so had been issued'. The government also noted the 'uncertainty of the assessments and the lack of detailed intelligence' provided by the JIC.[14]

In July 2003, the Ministry of Defence produced a report called *Operations in Iraq: First Reflections*, which noted that 'very little was known about how [Iraqi forces] planned to oppose the coalition or whether they had the will to fight'. The regime might 'possibly' use WMD 'if it could make the capabilities available for operational use'.[15]

This admission that very little was known of Iraqi capabilities, in tune with the JIC reports noted above, is in stark contrast to the certainties of the Iraq threat contained in the September 2002 dossier and elsewhere, presented to the public at the time.

According to former Foreign Secretary Robin Cook, Tony Blair probably knew two weeks before the war that Iraq had no functioning WMD. Cook recalls a briefing on 20 February 2003 from John Scarlett, the chairman of the JIC. Cook notes that:

> When I put to him my conclusion that Saddam had no long range weapons of mass destruction but may have battlefield chemical weapons, he readily agreed. When I asked him why we believed Saddam would not use these weapons against our troops on the battlefield, he surprised me by claiming that, in order to evade detection by the UN inspectors, Saddam had taken apart the shells and dispersed them – with the result that it would be difficult to deploy them under attack. Not only did Saddam have no weapons of mass destruction in the real meaning of that phrase, neither did he have useable battlefield weapons.

Cook states that he put these points to Blair on 5 March, noting that he 'gave me the same reply as John Scarlett, that the battlefield weapons had been disassembled and stored separately. I was therefore mystified a year later to hear him say he had never understood that the intelligence agencies did not believe Saddam had long range weapons of mass destruction'.[16]

Indeed, Blair had already said, almost a year before, in May 2002, that 'there is no doubt in my mind' that Iraq had concealed its weapons and that it would be 'far more difficult for them to reconstitute that material to use in a situation of conflict'.[17]

Although the intelligence presented to ministers was vague and uncertain, the JIC still miraculously came to the conclusion that Iraq was likely to possess some forms of WMD – and it is this which has been interpreted as an intelligence 'failure'. Yet the critical issue here is that, as the Butler report makes clear, Iraqi use of WMD was seen as a threat only in response to an invasion. The intelligence was telling ministers that Iraq was otherwise little or no threat.

A JIC report from September 2002 notes that 'faced with the likelihood of military defeat and being removed from power, Saddam is unlikely to be deterred from using chemical and biological weapons by any diplomatic or military means'. It also noted that 'the use of chemical and biological weapons prior to any military attack would boost support for US-led action and is unlikely'. Yet when this intelligence came to be inserted into the September 2002 dossier, it simply read: 'It [the intelligence] shows that he does not regard them [WMD] only as weapons of last resort'.[18] This raises a further issue for those who accept that ministers really did believe Iraq possessed WMD – that they were still prepared to authorise an invasion knowing that this was the most likely provocation for Iraq to use them.

After the invasion of Iraq, Foreign Secretary Jack Straw told a parliamentary inquiry that before the war neither he nor Blair 'had ever used the words "immediate or imminent" threat' to describe Iraq, but that they had spoken of 'a current and serious threat, which is very different'. Straw added: 'Impending, soon to happen, as it were, about to happen today or tomorrow, we did not use that because plainly the evidence did not justify that'.[19] In other words, we could have waited for weapons inspections, potentially avoiding the deaths of thousands of people.

One email which emerged from the Hutton inquiry well-reported at the time showed that Jonathan Powell, Blair's chief of staff, raised serious doubts about a draft of the September dossier:

> The document does nothing to demonstrate a threat, let alone an imminent threat from Saddam . . . we will need to make it clear in launching the document that we do not claim that we have evidence that he is an imminent threat.[20]

Powell also stated that the drafters 'need to make it clear that Saddam could not attack *at the moment*. The thesis is he could be a threat to the UK in the future if we do not check him'.[21] Yet a week later, Blair launched the document, together with a warning that Iraq could deploy WMD within 45 minutes of an order to do so.

The lack of a credible threat from Iraq was also outlined in a report from the Pentagon's Defence Intelligence Agency, leaked to the media in June 2003. A summary obtained by CNN stated that 'there is no reliable information on whether Iraq is producing and stockpiling chemical weapons or where Iraq has or will establish its chemical warfare agent production facilities'. This report was produced in September 2002, the same month as the British dossier.[22]

Robin Cook has plausibly commented that many of the most stark assertions in the September 2002 dossier were not repeated in the debates in March on the eve of the invasion – by this time, there was no reference to weapons being ready in 45 minutes, to Iraq seeking to procure uranium from Niger or to a nuclear-weapons programme that had been reconstituted. His argument is that if the government had not already known in September 2002 that Iraq presented no real threat, it certainly did by March 2003, when it went to war.[23]

It should also be said that the September 2002 dossier – the key public plank of the British government's whole case against Iraq – provided no actual evidence of a threat from Iraq. The *Guardian* reported at the time that 'British government officials have privately admitted that they do not have any "killer evidence" about weapons of mass destruction. If they had, they would have already passed it to the inspectors'. On the day before Blair announced that the dossier would soon be published, a Whitehall source was quoted as saying that the dossier was based on information found up to 1998, when the inspectors withdrew from Iraq, and that there was 'very little new to put into it'.[24]

Also worth remembering is that the September 2002 dossier was not the first produced by the government to prepare the country for military intervention. Before the bombing of

Afghanistan, the government produced a report called 'Responsibility for the terrorist atrocities in the United States, 11 September 2001', making the case against al Qaeda. This includes various mentions of al Qaeda's alleged 'substantial exploitation of the illegal drugs trade from Afghanistan'. It also said that 'in the spring of 1993 operatives of al Qaeda participated in the attack on US military personnel serving in Somalia'.[25] These are false accusations that ended up in the pot, like many of the fabrications on Iraq.

Observer journalist Jason Burke comments in his book on al Qaeda that:

> The British intelligence specialists must have known that the dossier they gave to the prime minister to reveal to parliament and the British public to justify involvement in a major conflict included demonstrably false material but felt the war in Afghanistan needed to be fought and the public needed to be convinced of it.[26]

The government's media propaganda on Afghanistan continued well after the bombing phase and the collapse of the Taliban. In March 2002, for example, the *Observer* published a story under a headline 'Story of find in Afghan cave "was made up" to justify sending marines'. The paper stated that:

> Britain was accused last night of falsely claiming that Al Qaeda terrorists had built a 'biological and chemical weapons' laboratory in Afghanistan to justify the deployment of 1,700 Royal Marines to fight there. The allegation follows a Downing Street briefing by a senior official to newspapers on Friday which claimed US forces had discovered a biological weapons laboratory in a cave in eastern Afghanistan . . . The claim, carried by a number of newspapers yesterday, was denied emphatically last night by Pentagon and State Department sources.[27]

This precedent suggests that similarly false claims about Iraq were to be expected. That many journalists still played along shows the degree to which mainstream news reporting is characterised by wilful self-deception.

The case for going to war was fabricated

Amazingly, various parliamentary committees and the Hutton inquiry cleared the government of 'sexing up' intelligence. In the real world, all the evidence suggests that the case for going to war was not just 'sexed up' but consciously fabricated; it needed to be, given the understanding of the level of threat posed by Iraq. Blair's cabal was so bent on promoting its perceived interests through invasion, that the result was a public deception strategy that sought to justify it. This shows how far removed from the national interest is that of the narrow policy-making elite.

Clare Short told a parliamentary inquiry that 'the suggestion that there was the risk of chemical and biological weapons being weaponised and threatening us in the short term was spin. That didn't come from the security services'. When asked whether she thought that ministers had exaggerated the use of intelligence material, she replied: 'That is my suggestion, yes'. This was done in order 'to make it [the threat] more immediate, more imminent, requiring urgent action'.[28]

From the Hutton inquiry emerged various emails from Downing Street officials, described by the *Guardian* as 'a frantic attempt to produce a dossier that will justify aggressive action against Saddam Hussein. Within the space of a fortnight and with almost no new evidence – other than the now infamous "45 minute warning" – Mr Blair's aides turned British policy towards Iraq upside down'.[29]

One Downing Street press official wrote that:

> Much of the evidence we have is largely circumstantial so we need to convey to our readers that the cumulation of these facts demonstrates an intent on Saddam's part

– the more they can be led to this conclusion themselves rather than have to accept judgements from us,
the better.[30]

He also wrote that 'the more we advertise that unsupported
assertions (eg Saddam attaches great importance to the possession of WMD) come from intelligence the better'. This should
'add to the feeling that we are presenting real evidence'. A
Downing Street press officer similarly wrote: 'Can we show why
we think he [Saddam] intends to use them [WMD] aggressively,
rather than in self-defence?' The *Guardian* also reported that
Julian Miller, John Scarlett's deputy, was having meetings with
Downing Street media staff to ensure that everyone was 'on the
right track'.[31]

In the material intended for public consumption, the government transformed possibilities about Iraqi capabilities into
certainties and removed vital caveats. To give three examples in
the process of drafting the September dossier:

• The dossier stated that Iraq 'continued to produce chemical
and biological weapons'. Yet the JIC 'did not know what had
been produced and in what quantities', according to the
parliamentary Intelligence and Security Committee.
• A draft of Blair's foreword to the dossier read: 'The case I
make is not that Saddam could launch a nuclear attack on
London or another part of the UK (he could not)'. This was
omitted from the final document.
• An email from Jonathan Powell commenting on a draft of the
dossier stated that the claim that Saddam would use chemical
or biological weapons only if his regime was under threat
posed 'a bit of a problem'. So the passage was redrafted and
all reference to Saddam's defensive use of such weapons was
taken out, leaving the impression that Britain was 45 minutes
from attack.[32]

Brian Jones, a former senior Defence Intelligence Staff (DIS)
official, stated that 'the expert intelligence analysts of the DIS

were overruled in the preparation of the dossier' which resulted 'in a presentation that was misleading about Iraq's capabilities'. It is 'the intelligence community leadership . . . that had the final say on the assessment presented in the dossier', he noted. Jones told the Hutton inquiry that his staff had told him 'that there was no evidence that significant production had taken place either of chemical warfare agent or chemical weapons'. But 'the impression I had was . . . the shutters were coming down on this particular paper [i.e., the September dossier], that the discussion and the argument had been concluded'. An MoD civil servant similarly said that 'the perception was that the dossier had been round the houses several times in order to try to find a form of words which would strengthen certain political objectives'.[33]

The case against Iraq was indeed 'sexed up' both by No. 10 staff and some senior 'intelligence' officials. According to the *Guardian's* Richard Norton-Taylor, John Scarlett was 'hopelessly seduced by Blair's coterie. Under Scarlett's control, drafters of the dossier put things in at Downing Street's suggestion. They also took things out'. Robin Cook noted that 'John Scarlett was only too consciously aware that the Prime Minister expected him to come up with a justification for war'.[34]

Alastair Campbell suggested more than a dozen separate changes to the draft dossier on Iraq; Scarlett responded by saying the language had been 'tightened'. Crucially, Campbell suggested that the word 'may' was weak and be substituted for the word 'are' so that when the dossier was published the assertion was that Iraq possessed weapons that '*are* deployable within 45 minutes of an order to use them'.[35]

Campbell also suggested another significant change to the dossier. The September 5th draft stated that after the lifting of sanctions 'we assess that Iraq would need at least five years to produce a [nuclear] weapon. Progress would be much quicker if Iraq were able to buy fissile material'. In a memo on September 17th Campbell wrote to John Scarlett that the Prime Minister 'like me, was worried about the way you have expressed the nuclear issue . . . Can we not go back, on timings, to "radiological device" in months; nuclear bomb in 1–2 years with help; 5 years with no sanctions'. The final document stated that: 'Iraq could produce a nuclear weapon in between one and two years'.[36]

45 minutes

Perhaps the most amazing thing about the 45-minute claim is that anyone fell for such transparent hype. David Kelly apparently 'just laughed about the 45 minute claim', believing it 'risible'.[37] If journalists had done the same thing, the government's case for invading Iraq might have collapsed.

Defence Secretary Geoff Hoon admitted that when the dossier was published he knew that the claim that Iraq could launch weapons within 45 minutes referred only to 'battlefield munitions' such as shells; i.e., that they could be used by Iraq only in response to an invasion. Many press reports (dutifully reporting propaganda as fact) assumed that the claim related to strategic or long-range missiles; one paper suggested they could reach bases in Cyprus. Clare Short told a parliamentary inquiry that in the numerous verbal and written briefings she received from the intelligence services, the 45-minute allegation was never a feature.[38]

It was JIC chairman John Scarlett who told the Hutton inquiry that the claim was meant to refer only to short-range battlefield weapons. According to the *Guardian*'s citation of well-placed sources, both Scarlett and Sir Richard Dearlove, head of MI6, assumed that the 45-minute warning referred to short-range battlefield weapons when they read the intelligence report at the end of August.[39] Hutton's report would have us believe that Blair, reputedly an avid consumer of 'intelligence', did not know this.

When asked in parliament on how many occasions between January and May 2003 the 45-minute claim was raised with him, the Prime Minister replied: 'as far as I am aware, none'.

This tallies with what Geoff Hoon told the Defence Committee inquiry, that in the run-up to the invasion he briefed the Prime Minister regularly and:

> Had this [i.e., the 45-minute claim] been a significant issue in terms of the decision to take the country to war, I am sure that this issue would have arisen in conversation between us, but, as I emphasise, it was not a significant issue.[40]

Hoon is probably being honest – it was never a significant issue since it was understood to be false; it appears to have been intended simply for public relations. The Butler report referred to 'suspicions' that the claim had been included in the September dossier because of its 'eye-catching character'.[41]

We also know that the 'intelligence' on this claim, which miraculously appeared at the end of August 2002, just before the government began drawing up its dossier, was extremely vague. The source – an Iraqi brigadier-general – said that Iraq had a command, control and communication system that would have enabled Saddam or his close associates to contact commanders in the field within 45 minutes authorising the use of WMD. This does not mean deploying WMD or even having them ready. Rather, there was 'no specific intelligence of their [Iraqi] plans as to how/when/with what they would do', the press reported.[42]

Moreover, the Iraqi general who is thought to have acted as this source – Nizar al-Khazraji – was living in exile in Denmark and received his information from another Iraqi officer serving in the army. Al-Khazraji had neither any means of checking the assertion himself nor any documentary evidence. Furthermore, he was considered by the CIA to be a possible replacement for Saddam if the army staged a coup, and so had a vested interest in the invasion taking place.[43]

If the 45-minute claim had been perceived as real, one might have expected the March 2003 JIC report to refer to it, rather than stating that any chemical weapons 'remained disassembled'. We might also have expected the government to refer to it in the debates on the eve of war.

Today reporter Andrew Gilligan's broadcast on 29 May 2003 – the source of the fierce argument between No. 10 and the BBC – was largely accurate, and surely one of the best media discoveries on Iraq, which may explain the attack on him and the BBC by Alastair Campbell. Gilligan correctly noted that the dossier had been 'sexed up' against the wishes of some intelligence officers, and that his unnamed source, David Kelly, refuted the government's 45-minute warning. (Kelly also told *Newsnight* reporter Susan Watts that the 45-minute claim 'just got out of all proportion' and that 'they were desperate for information'.)[44]

Kelly was not the only source for Gilligan's story. The editor of the *Today* programme, Kevin Marsh, had two other sources: Sir Richard Dearlove, the head of MI6, along with two of his colleagues; and Clare Short. According to *The Times*, Marsh interviewed Dearlove and interpreted his words:

> as meaning that the intelligence did not support the case for war against Iraq . . . that hard evidence of weapons of mass destruction in Iraq would never be found. This, it is said, struck him [Marsh] as an odd conclusion if, at the time the September dossier was published, these weapons were being held at 45 minutes' readiness.

Then, also before Gilligan's report, Marsh met Clare Short who told him that 'no intelligence had been produced which conclusively demonstrated that Iraq was an imminent threat'. According to *The Times*, 'her words helped to persuade the programme to believe Mr Gilligan's apparent scoop: that Downing Street inserted a claim, against the wishes of experts, that Iraq could launch weapons of mass destruction within 45 minutes'.[45]

Gilligan's assertion that the government 'probably knew' that the 45-minute claim was false but still included it in the report is also essentially correct. He appears to have been wrong in suggesting that Alastair Campbell was responsible for inserting the claim. But the dossier's first mention that Iraq had WMD ready for use within 45 minutes appears in a paragraph concerned with Iraq's 'goal of regional domination' and just after the claim that Saddam 'has been able to extend the range of his ballistic missile programme'.[46] Thus the government at worst encouraged, and at best did nothing to correct, the view that the 45-minute claim referred to long-range weapons. Yet Hoon, Scarlett and Dearlove all knew it referred to battlefield rather than long-range strategic weapons.

The link with al Qaeda and the February 2003 dossier

A further unsound claim by the government intimated links between Saddam's regime and al Qaeda. Before this campaign began, Foreign Office minister Ben Bradshaw had told parliament in both January and April 2002 that 'I have seen no evidence which demonstrates that an al Qaeda network exists in Iraq'. By late 2002, however, this was the wrong story; now the new Foreign Office minister Mike O'Brien was saying that 'we believe that there are al Qaeda operatives in Iraq'. On 5 February 2003, Tony Blair told the House of Commons that :

> It would be wrong to say that there is no evidence of any links between al Qaeda and the Iraqi regime. There is evidence of such links. Exactly how far they go is uncertain . . . There is intelligence coming through to us the entire time about this . . . It is not correct to say that there is no evidence of any links between the Iraqi regime and al Qaeda.[47]

Later, government ministers denied ever having made such direct links between Baghdad and al Qaeda. Yet, contradicting this, even in June 2004, a Downing Street spokeswoman was claiming that the Prime Minister 'has always said Saddam created a permissive environment for terrorism and we know that the people affiliated to al Qaeda operated in Iraq during the regime'. The Butler report concluded that in the intelligence presented to ministers 'the JIC made clear that, although there were contacts between the Iraqi regime and al Qaeda, there was no evidence of cooperation'.[48]

This suggestion of a link was scuppered by intelligence sources quoted in the press who, asked whether Saddam had any connections with al Qaeda, said 'quite the opposite'.[49] Downing Street then hit on an ingenious new formula: 'Terrorism and rogue regimes are part of the same picture', Jack Straw started saying around the turn of 2002/2003, a framing often repeated by Blair. The reason was that 'the most likely sources of technology and know-how for such terrorist organisations are rogue regimes', Straw said.

The alleged al Qaeda link was simply a case of making-it-up-as-you-go-along, perhaps the clumsiest of the propaganda fabrications in this period.

A close rival for this accolade, however, was the second government report released in February 2003, which has become known as the 'dodgy dossier' (though in content it hardly seems dodgier than the first). Blair misled parliament in passing this off as 'an intelligence report'; it was later revealed that much of the document had been directly copied from a source on the Internet. Indeed, the dossier was not checked by any of the intelligence agencies before publication.[50]

The authors of the dossier were close to Alastair Campbell, who oversaw the project, which was intended mainly as a briefing for the media. The dossier exaggerates the original text in a number of places, changing, for example, Iraq's 'aiding opposition groups in hostile regimes' to 'supporting terrorist organisations in hostile regimes'.[51]

Uranium from Niger

The government claimed in the September dossier that Iraq was seeking to procure uranium from Niger for use in its nuclear programme. On 7 July 2003 the *Guardian*, under a headline of 'Britain "knew uranium claims were false"', wrote that 'British officials knew there had been no secret trade in uranium from Africa to Iraq seven months before such claims were raised in the September dossier released by Downing Street', according to the retired US ambassador who investigated the issue for the CIA. The *Guardian* repeated the following week that 'Joe Wilson, an envoy sent by the US to Niger to check the documents, has said that Britain knew there was no secret trade in uranium months before publishing the claim in the September dossier'.[52]

Note that this report carries the same message as Gilligan's – that the government knew something was false but invoked it anyway. That there has been so much less furore about this claim is further evidence of how the media in effect allow the government to frame their agenda.

In March 2003, Mohamed El Baradei, the director general of the International Atomic Energy Agency (IAEA), told the UN Security Council that the Niger uranium documents were fakes. US investigative journalist Seymour Hersh, noting the British propaganda campaign on Iraq in the late 1990s, writes that these documents were initially circulated by the British, although it cannot be ascertained whether MI6 actually forged them. One member of the IAEA told Hersh that 'these documents are so bad that I cannot imagine that they came from a serious intelligence agency'. One letter was signed by a minister in Niger who had been out of office for the past 11 years. Meanwhile, the government has admitted that 'just before the dossier was published, the CIA offered a comment noting that they did not regard the reference to the supply of uranium from Africa as credible', but Britain went ahead anyway based on its own 'reliable intelligence', which, it says, came from more than a single source.[53]

Even this might all be beside the point. As Professor Norman Dombey of the University of Sussex has pointed out, 'so what if Iraq sought the supply of uranium from Africa? Iraq already has hundreds of tons of uranium at its disposal. Without enrichment facilities this material is useless for nuclear weapons'.[54]

The Butler report rejects most of this evidence and concludes that the government had intelligence from several quarters that indicated that the Iraqi visit to Niger was for the purpose of acquiring uranium. Yet it fails to mention evidence from Joseph Wilson and its only reference to the CIA is to state: 'The CIA advised caution about any suggestion that Iraq had succeeded in acquiring uranium from Africa, but agreed that there was evidence that it had been sought'.[55]

Once the invasion had taken place, and the pretext of an Iraqi threat had served its purpose, ministers began to backtrack on their earlier claims. In an interview in April 2003, Blair said that 'we were never going to be able to find them [WMD] until the conflict is at a stage where the Iraqi scientists and experts working on these programmes are prepared to talk about them'.[56] Jack Straw's comment that the government never regarded Saddam as an imminent threat has been detailed above. Straw said at one point that it was 'not crucially important' to find weapons of mass destruction, despite their elimination being the official rationale for the operation.[57]

Straw also told a parliamentary inquiry that 'I do not happen to regard the 45 minute statement having the significance which has been attached to it' – and this despite Blair's emphasis on the claim in the foreword to the dossier and associated media briefings. Straw was also asked whether he still stood by the 45-minute claim. Rather than simply replying 'yes' Straw first said 'it was not my claim. I stand by the integrity of the JIC'. The most he could say was 'I accept the claim but did not make it'.[58]

Invading Iraq will if anything increase terrorism

At one level, it was obvious that invading Iraq would increase the likelihood of terrorism. The use of Anglo-American brute force in the occupation of Iraq, coupled with de facto support for

Israeli aggression in the West Bank, was always going to provide a spur to a second generation of terrorists – in much the same way that Anglo-American covert support for the mujahidin fighters in 1980s Afghanistan helped to create the first.

On 10 February 2003, five weeks before the invasion began, a secret JIC report stated that any terrorist threat would increase by invading Iraq:

> Al Qaeda and associated groups continued to represent by far the greatest threat to Western interests and that threat would be heightened by military action against Iraq . . . Any collapse of the Iraq regime would increase the risk of chemical and biological warfare technology or agents finding their way into the hands of terrorists, including al Qaeda.[59]

Over the 10 days following this assessment, 18 senior politicians were briefed by JIC chairman, John Scarlett, about Iraq.[60] It seems likely that the increased threat to Britain resulting from an invasion of Iraq was known to a wide set of people; the same politicians, that is, who now pose as our saviours in protecting the country from the scourge of terrorism.

In December 2003, the government wrote in a memorandum to the Foreign Affairs Committee that 'coalition action in Iraq, and other regional issues, has sustained and may have increased terrorist motivation', although added that 'we have no direct evidence that it has increased al Qaeda recruitment'. The Foreign Affairs Committee concluded in a report published in February 2004 that 'the war in Iraq has possibly made terrorist attacks against British nationals and British interests more likely in the short term'.[61]

4

THE NEW MINISTRY OF OFFENCE

It is rarely difficult to discover plausible reasons for government actions; the invasion of Iraq is no exception. A good starting point is to ignore official explanations and the media commentary they provoke and to look at what the government is saying elsewhere. Two important documents have recently been produced by the government which help to explain possible reasons for the invasion. Both have been virtually ignored in the mainstream media. Together they offer a worrying insight into the current thinking of British foreign-policy planners.

Securing foreign energy supplies

As Tony Blair, Jack Straw and others were swearing that war with Iraq could not possibly have anything to do with oil, the government published a document in February 2003, just weeks before the invasion began, showing how concerned it is with securing foreign energy supplies.

The document is the Department of Trade and Industry's white paper called *Our energy future – Creating a low carbon economy*. Tony Blair's foreword to the document notes that Britain faces 'new challenges' and that 'our energy supplies will

THE NEW MINISTRY OF OFFENCE

increasingly depend on imported gas and oil from Europe and beyond'. The document then outlines the central dilemma that 'as a country we have been a net exporter of energy . . . but this will change.' Britain, it says, is set to become a net importer of gas by around 2006 and of oil by around 2010:

> By 2010 we are likely to be importing around three-quarters of our primary energy needs. And by that time half the world's gas and oil will be coming from countries that are currently perceived as relatively unstable, either in political or economic terms.

Therefore, the report continues, 'moving from being largely self-sufficient to being a net importer of gas and oil requires us to take a longer term strategic international approach to energy reliability'.

One solution emphasised strongly in the report is to diversify sources of energy and 'avoid the UK being reliant on too few international sources of oil and gas'. The key gas-supplying countries and regions will be Russia, the Middle East, North and West Africa, and the Caspian Sea region. For oil, which accounts for 40 per cent of global energy consumption, the major producers will be Saudi Arabia, other Gulf states, South and Central America, Africa, Russia and the Caspian region. Of particular importance to ensuring diversity of oil sources, the report notes, are non-OPEC suppliers such as Russia, the Caspian region and West Africa. Therefore, 'we will continue to promote good relations with existing and new suppliers in the Middle East, Russia, the Caspian and Africa'.

Overall, the report states that 'we need to give greater prominence to strategic energy issues in foreign policy' across the government. 'Our aims are to maintain strong relations with exporting countries' while 'in promoting diversity we will also work to minimise the risk of disruption to supplies from regional disputes'.[1]

This document goes a long way to explaining the close

relationships between London and the regimes discussed in part three of this book, notably Russia, Colombia, Indonesia and Nigeria – with all of whom Britain is maintaining 'good relations', while they exterminate sections of their populations. All are important producers of oil and gas offering alternative sources of supply to the Middle East. Russia, which has the world's largest gas reserves, is especially important following the recent signing by BP and Shell of investment agreements in the Russian energy sector worth billions of pounds.

Nor is it fanciful to suggest that a factor in the British intervention in Sierra Leone – universally described as 'humanitarian' – was to ensure regional 'stability' (i.e., pro-Western governments) partly to ensure continued access to oil in Nigeria and elsewhere in West Africa (see Chapter 7). As regards the Caspian, the desire to secure Western control over the region's oil and gas reserves, in rivalry with Russia, was a likely factor in the Anglo-American bombing of Afghanistan, as I argued in *Web of Deceit*.

US strategy could hardly be clearer. In 2003 the Pentagon announced that it was moving 5,000–6,000 troops from bases in Germany to new bases in various countries in Africa. The express purpose was to protect US oil interests in Nigeria, which in future could account for 25 per cent of US oil imports. Undersecretary of State for African Affairs, Walter Kansteiner, had previously said that African oil 'has become a national security strategic interest'. The Bush administration's national energy policy, released in May 2001, predicted that West Africa would become 'one of the fastest growing sources of oil and gas for the American market'. Currently the region supplies around 12 per cent of US crude-oil imports; the US National Intelligence Council estimates that this share will rise to 25 per cent by 2015.[2]

US officials, including Secretary of State Colin Powell, have recently visited African oil-producing countries such as Gabon, Sao Tome and Angola while the US has stepped up military ties to Nigeria at the same time as pressing it to pull out of OPEC. The political advantage of these states to the US (and also to Britain) is that none of them, apart from Nigeria, belongs to OPEC. As Robert Diwan, a managing director of the Petroleum Finance Company has noted, 'there is a long term strategy from the US government to weaken OPEC's hold on the market and one way to do that is to peel off certain countries'. US oil companies were set to invest around £10 billion in African oil in 2003.[3]

Documents leaked to the *Guardian* in late 2003 provided further evidence of a joint Anglo-American strategy to 'secure African oil'. A US report to the President and Prime Minister noted that:

> We have identified a number of key oil and gas producers in the West Africa area on which our two governments and major oil and gas companies could cooperate to improve investment conditions, good governance, social and political stability, and thus underpin long term security of supply.

These areas included Nigeria, Sao Tome, Equatorial Guinea and Angola. British officials were charged with developing 'investment issues facing Africa that could be ripe for US-UK coordinated attention'.

The report also stated that Britain and the US 'have noted the huge energy potential of Russia, Central Asia and the Caspian' and that 'in our discussions on how to move forward in approaching Russia and the Caspian/Central Asian countries, we have concluded that we have similar political, economic, social and energy objectives'.[4]

Many post-war British interventions and policies are rooted in the need to exercise continued control over, or access to, energy supplies. The recent government documents signify a new phase in the ongoing policy defined in the declassified British files.

The issue of control of oil, rather than simply access, is more clearly the motivation for the US, which currently satisfies three-quarters of its energy demand from domestic sources.

But control of oil has also been a critical factor for Whitehall, particularly given British companies' huge role in the international oil industry and their vast investments in many countries. As Foreign Secretary Rab Butler told the Prime Minister in April 1964:

> It is not that we are frightened of oil being cut off by unfriendly local governments, but the profitability of the oil companies' operations and the supply of oil to consumer countries including our own on acceptable terms, is most important for our economy and our balance of payments. This depends in part on the diversity of political control of the main sources of oil (eg, if Iraq controlled Kuwait, we might all be held to ransom). This would be especially dangerous for the UK for we draw 60% of our oil requirements from the area.[5]

Similarly, the Treasury noted in 1956 that, given Britain's dependence on oil:

> It is highly desirable that we should not have to rely on oil which is increasingly controlled by other powers, including even the USA, whose interests are not necessarily identical with our own. Further, the large investments of British companies in the Western hemisphere provide a partial insurance against the interruption of supplies from the Middle East.[6]

A Cabinet Office report of 1960 noted that 'there is a particular United Kingdom interest at stake' in the Middle East, namely 'the profits made by the United Kingdom oil companies from their operations in the area'. The overall strategy was therefore to be 'continued control of sources of oil with consequential profits to United Kingdom' [sic].[7]

The files show the huge profits made in the past by British oil companies in the Middle East. The Treasury noted in 1956 that the benefit to the British balance of payments generated by

British oil companies was around £200 million a year in recent years. In 1964 the Foreign Office similarly noted that 'our balance of payments depends significantly on oil operations' in the region. It calculated that British oil companies continued to earn the balance of payments £200 million per year 'and might be much more'. No wonder that the British strategy was 'to preserve as long as possible the advantageous arrangements under which we obtain our oil from the Middle East'.[8]

The Foreign Office noted in March 1967 that oil supplied 40 per cent of the world's energy needs and that the international trade in oil was controlled by eight companies, two of which, Shell and BP, were British. It stated that 'the United Kingdom has a stake in the international oil industry second only to that of the United States'. The overseas book value of British investments was £2,000 million. Also:

> From our massive stake in the international oil industry,
> we enjoy two major advantages for the balance of pay-
> ments: our oil costs a good deal less in overseas payments
> than it would if we bought it all from foreign companies;
> we get large invisible earnings from the business of
> producing and selling oil in other countries.

The Foreign Office estimated that the 'earnings' for the balance of payments in the second category alone were £142 million in 1961, £179 million in 1962, £201 million in 1963, £115 million in 1964 and £158 million in 1965. It also stated in this secret report that 'this information has never been officially published and the calculations and estimates are highly confidential'.[9]

The level of secrecy is unsurprising: these profits resulted from British control of local resources, and were thus a form of plunder of poverty-stricken populations. This was recognised by foreign-policy planners, as was the need to continue the state of affairs. Explicit British policy was to oppose any suggestion that oil resources be used primarily for the benefit of local populations; the threat of nationalism has always been regarded as the most dangerous one in the Middle East.

Control over Middle Eastern oil was (and is) to be secured through close relations with the repressive feudal families of the Gulf sheikhdoms, in turn aided by British arms exports and military training. Then as now, policy was 'to ensure the maintenance of our oil supplies by defending the rulers of the oil states, particularly Kuwait', as the Cabinet Secretary said in 1963.[10] The 'energy future' document recently produced by the Blair government is merely the latest attempt to promote these basic British goals.

Iraq as mission one

In December 2003 the government produced another extraordinary public document, this time outlining its military strategy. It counts as one of the most worrying pieces of government literature I have ever seen, even including the declassified files. Nine months after the invasion of Iraq, the New Labour government delivered a very clear message: from now on, it will be more of the same.

The document is a Defence white paper, entitled *Delivering security in a changing world* – a formulation worthy of Orwell. It surpasses the military strategy outlined in the government's Strategic Defence Review (SDR) produced in 1998, which stated that the priority in future will be 'force projection' and that 'in the post cold war world we must be prepared to go to the crisis rather than have the crisis come to us'. This involved plans to buy two larger aircraft carriers 'to power more flexibly [sic] around the world'.

Other new weapons systems would be a new generation of attack helicopters, submarines equipped with cruise missiles, and fighter and bomber aircraft. It stated that 'for the next decade at least' the air defence of Britain would be a low priority but 'long-range air attack will continue to be important both as an integral part of warfighting and as a coercive instrument to support political objectives'. A key aspect was the government's retention of nuclear weapons with which Britain should be 'retaining an option for a limited strike' and which would be able 'to deter any threat to our vital interests'.[11]

A new chapter added to the SDR in July 2002 noted 'the emphasis on expeditionary operations', and the need for 'rapidly deployable intervention forces' and 'force projection and strike capabilities'. Noting that the government spending review in 2002 envisaged 'the biggest sustained real increase in defence spending plans for 20 years', the report states that:

> Experience since 1998, and since the 11 September attacks, suggests that we may need to deploy forces further afield than Europe, the Gulf and the Mediterranean (which the SDR identified as the primary focus of our interests) more often than we had envisaged.

In this, 'we wish to work more closely with our most important ally, the US'. Out of the spending increase, around £1 billion was intended for equipment and capabilities for the 'additional challenges'.

One especially revealing passage demonstrates very clearly the utility of the 'war against terrorism' for achieving these British military goals:

> The capability priorities which have emerged from our work on countering international terrorism are entirely consistent with the requirements generated by other likely demands on our forces. They reinforce the thrust of our existing plans. Extra strategic lift and communications, for example, have much wider utility across a range of operations beyond counter terrorism. So it makes sense to think of these as components of all rapid reaction forces, rather than as dedicated counter-terrorism capabilities.

Translated: the new intervention capabilities we say are needed for the 'war against terrorism' can be used for the wider need to intervene.[12]

This strategy was applied in the invasion of Iraq. The MoD report, *Operations in Iraq: Lessons for the future*, states that:

> The operation in Iraq demonstrated the extent to which the UK armed forces have evolved successfully to deliver the expeditionary capabilities envisaged in the 1998 Strategic Defence Review and the 2002 New Chapter.[13]

The latest document, the December 2003 white paper, says that British intervention capability needs to go beyond even that envisaged in these two earlier documents. It states that 'we must extend our ability to project force further afield than the SDR envisaged' including in 'crises occurring across sub-Saharan Africa and South Asia' and arising from 'the wider threat from international terrorism'. 'The threat from international terrorism', it notes, 'now requires the capability to deliver a military response globally'. It calls for the British military to conduct 'expeditionary operations' while 'rapidly deployable forces' are needed for 'a range of environments across the world'. 'Priority must be given to meeting a wider range of expeditionary tasks, at greater range from the United Kingdom and with ever-increasing strategic, operational and tactical tempo'.

The forces needed include cruise missiles which 'offer a versatile capability for projecting land and air power ashore', and two new aircraft carriers and combat aircraft which will 'offer a step increase in our ability to project air power from the sea'. These are key elements in a 'modern expeditionary strategy'. It reiterates 'the need to confront international terrorism abroad rather than waiting for attacks within the UK'.

In all this, the report states that 'our armed forces will need to be interoperable with US command and control structures'. At the same time, it notes that 'we do not believe the world community should accept the acquisition of nuclear weapons by further states' – only the exclusive club of which Britain is a member has this right.

The report continues:

> Whereas in the past it was possible to regard military force as a separate element in crisis resolution, it is now evident that the successful management of international security problems will require ever more integrated planning of military, diplomatic and economic instruments.

Translated: we will increasingly threaten those who do not do what we say with the prospect of military force.

Elsewhere, the report highlights the importance of 'effects based operations', which means:

> that military force exists to serve political or strategic ends . . . Our conventional military superiority now allows us more choice in how we deliver the effect we wish to achieve.

While terrorism is meant to provide the rationale for this increased force-projection capability, the report notes in a section called 'UK policy aims' that:

> more widely the UK has a range of global interests including economic well-being based around trade, overseas and foreign investment and the continuing free flow of natural resources.[14]

At the same time as the MoD was producing this strategy paper, the Foreign Office released a report on 'UK international priorities', stating that 'our ability to project armed force will be a key instrument of our foreign policy' and that 'early action to prevent conflict' played an important part in this. The context was the identification of 'eight international strategic priorities' for British foreign policy, one of which was 'security of UK and global energy supplies'. It was also reported that the Prime Minister's strategy unit, based in the Cabinet Office, was conducting a review of 'how to create a consensus on the legitimacy of external interventions' in 'failed states'.[15]

This strategy of enhanced intervention is confirmed in various speeches given by Defence Secretary Geoff Hoon, who has said that the British military is being equipped 'for more frequent operations' and 'higher numbers of concurrent smaller operations' in regions beyond Europe. Indeed, Hoon has observed that since the SDR in 1998 there has been 'a new operation arising on average about once a year'.[16]

It was Britain not the US that first committed itself to the strategy that is mislabelled 'pre-emption'. A better description would be 'preventive': it means that military force will be undertaken not in response to an imminent threat, but before a threat materialises. The first is a kind of self-defence; the 'threat' posited in the latter is open to interpretation and can easily be used to justify offence, as in the invasion of Iraq.

Indeed, these documents amount to a reconfiguration of British military strategy to an overt focus on offensive operations; Britain now has a Ministry of Offence. 'Defence' was always a misnomer intended largely for public relations: Britain has always had a strong intervention capability and has conducted numerous offensive operations which have had nothing to do with defending Britain or the interests of the public. But now this is barely even being hidden. Geoff Hoon has said that 'long experience indicates that a wholly defensive posture will not be enough'; the key 'is to take the fight to the terrorist'.[17] This 'terrorist' threat is the cover for greater and more frequent interventions. While the media have been sidetracked by issues such as who named David Kelly when and at what meeting, the Defence Secretary has been pushing ahead with plans for a new 'expeditionary strategy' that envisages more Iraqs all over the world. Presumably, only the current humiliation in Iraq, together with public opposition, is holding the Blair cabal back.

The intellectual justification for this new phase in imperial strategy comes from 'liberal imperialists' such as Robert

Cooper, a senior British diplomat close to Tony Blair. Cooper has written, apparently without irony, that 'the challenge to the postmodern world is to get used to the idea of double standards'. 'Among ourselves', he believes, 'we operate on the basis of laws and open cooperative security' . . .

> But when dealing with more old-fashioned kinds of states outside the postmodern continent of Europe, we need to revert to the rougher methods of an earlier era – force, pre-emptive attack, deception, whatever is necessary to deal with those who still live in the nineteenth century world of every state for itself. Among ourselves, we keep the law but when we are operating in the jungle, we must also use the laws of the jungle.[18]

The comparison of declassified files and recent government publications suggests that basic strategies alter very little over time; only the pretexts change. The February 2003 report on securing foreign energy supplies and the December 2003 strategy for enhanced global intervention are two sides of the same coin. The earlier document is a clearly stated rationale for the latter – a new period of global intervention, which provides a more plausible motivation for the invasion of Iraq than the proclamations about 'humanitarian intervention', terrorism and WMD parroted by many media commentators and academic analysts.

5

MASSACRES IN IRAQ: THE SECRET HISTORY

Britain has long been complicit in aggression and human-rights abuses in Iraq. Indeed, many of the roots of the current crisis in the country can be found in the horrific events of the 1960s. Formerly secret British files tell the story of British backing for repression and killings by regimes in Baghdad well before the arrival of Saddam Hussein. They reveal stunning levels of complicity in aggression against the Kurds, including in the use of chemical weapons – policies which are the roots of the later Western support extended to Saddam.

At the moment, London and Washington are bent on maintaining in power a friendly regime in Baghdad. It is a policy with a long historical precedent, and a background which does not bode well for the future of Iraq.

The fall of the monarchy

The British-backed monarchical regime of King Faisal and Prime Minister Nuri El Said was overthrown in an Arab nationalist revolution on 14 July 1958, which established a republic under Brigadier Abdul Karim Qasim. Said and the royal family were killed and the British embassy, long known to be the power behind the throne, was sacked by a mob with the loss of one British life. British embassy officials described it as 'popular revolution' based on 'pent-up passions of hatred and frustration, nourished on unsatisfied nationalist emotion, hostility to autocratic government, resentment at Western predominance, disgust at unrelieved poverty'.[1]

The regime Britain had supported for so long was one of the most unpopular in the history of the Middle East. The British were well aware of its repressive features. A Foreign Office brief noted, for example, that 'wealth and power have remained concentrated in the hands of a few rich landowners and tribal sheikhs centred round [sic] the Court'.[2]

Three months before the revolution, Sir Michael Wright, Britain's ambassador in Baghdad, had told Foreign Secretary Selwyn Lloyd that 'the constitutional position in Iraq is very like what it was in the United Kingdom at the accession of George III'. Political power resided in the palace, the King appointed and dismissed prime ministers at will while 'the opposition may not hold public meetings or express opposition to the regime itself in the press'. Wright also noted that 'the efficiency of the Iraqi security service has increased materially in the last year, thanks largely to British assistance with training and equipment'; the situation had been one of 'complete political suppression'. Wright then outlined his opposition to democracy by saying that 'a complete relaxation of present controls on freedom of expression coupled with completely free elections' would 'produce chaos and possibly a revolution'; his recommendations extended no further than to allow the formation of political parties.[3]

In one stroke, the popular nationalist revolution removed a pro-British regime and a key pillar of British imperial policy in the Middle East. Still worse, Qasim was conceded by Whitehall to be personally 'extremely popular'.[4] His rule was certainly autocratic and his police force often savage in its repression, but compared to the previous Said regime, Qasim's was relatively benign. Although in the early days, Qasim was tolerated by Britain, he soon joined the ranks of Sukarno in Indonesia,

Jagan in British Guiana and Nasser in Egypt as popular, nationalist enemies to British interests in the Third World.

The threats posed by Qasim were aptly summed up by a British member of the Iraq Petroleum Corporation, which controlled Iraq's oil, in a memo to the Foreign Office just months before the regime was overthrown. Qasim, he wrote:

> wished to give Iraq what he considered political independence, dignity and unity, in brotherly cooperation with other Arabs and in neutrality between the world power blocs; he wished to increase and distribute the national wealth, partly on grounds of nationalist and socialist principle, partly out of simply [sic] sympathy for the poor; on the basis of economic prosperity and justice he wished to found a new society and a new democracy; and he wished to use this strong, democratic, Arabist Iraq as an instrument to free and elevate other Arabs and Afro-Asians and to assist the destruction of 'imperialism', by which he largely meant British influence in the underdeveloped countries.[5]

Qasim's policy on oil is the subject of a huge amount of correspondence in the declassified files and a major reason why Whitehall wanted him removed. The background was that in 1961 Qasim announced that the Iraqi government wanted to take more than 50 per cent of the profits from oil exports; he had also complained that the British companies were fixing the oil prices. In a law in December, he purported to deprive the IPC of about 99.5 per cent of its concession, the expropriated areas including valuable proven oil fields. A draft law setting up a new Iraqi National Oil Corporation had been published in October 1962 but had not come into force by the time of the coup that removed Qasim in February 1963.

Also of major concern to Britain was Iraq's claim to Kuwait. In 1961, Britain landed troops in Kuwait supposedly to defend it from an imminent Iraqi attack. The declassified files, however, show that British planners fabricated the Iraqi threat to justify a British intervention in order to secure the reliance of the leaders of the oil-rich state on British 'protection', as described in *Web of Deceit*.[6]

The 1963 massacres

The Qasim regime fell, its leader executed, on 8 February 1963 in a coup under General Abdul Arif and Prime Minister General Abdul al-Bakr of the Baath party, which thus secured power for the first time. The coup was the result of substantial CIA backing and organisation and was masterminded by William Lakeland, stationed as an attaché at the US embassy in Baghdad. The US had previously actively conspired to murder Qasim and the CIA's Health Alteration Committee, as it was called, once sent Qasim a monogrammed, poisoned handker-chief, though it either failed to work or to reach its intended victim.

According to author Said Aburish, the US had insisted beforehand on implementing a detailed plan to eliminate the Iraqi Communist party as a force in Iraqi politics, meaning physical extermination of its members. The CIA provided the February coup leaders with a list of names, around 5,000 of whom were hunted down and murdered. They included senior army officers as well as lawyers, professors, teachers and doctors. There were pregnant women and old men among them, many of whom were tortured in front of their children. The eliminations mostly took place on an individual basis, house-to-house visits by hit squads who knew where their victims were and who carried out on-the-spot executions. 'The coup is a gain for our side', Robert Komer, a member of the National Security Council, told President Kennedy immediately after.[7]

Saddam Hussein, then a junior Baath party member, was closely involved in the coup. As an Iraqi exile in Cairo he and other plotters had since 1961 benefited from contacts with the CIA arranged by the Iraqi section of Egyptian intelligence. During the coup Saddam had rushed back from Cairo and was personally involved in the torture of leftists during the massacres.[8]

Britain had also long wanted to see the fall of Qasim. The declassified files contain mentions of British willingness to be involved in his ousting, and several of the files from this period have not been declassified. It appears that Britain may have known of the coup in advance, but there is no direct evidence that Britain was in contact with the plotters.

Five months before the February coup, a note by a Foreign Office official refers to the British ambassador's view 'that the sooner Qasim falls the better and that we should not be too choosy about doing things to help towards this end'. The ambassador, Sir Roger Allen, was also reported to be supporting 'a forward policy against Qasim'. One note from Allen five weeks before the coup refers to a plot against Qasim, stating that 'we have been assured that the plot is carefully worked out in detail and that the names of all those destined for key positions has been chosen'; but this note does not suggest that General Arif, who eventually led the coup, would be its figurehead. Allen also notes the importance of his staff in Baghdad not 'appearing to be aware or mixed up in plotting and I have recently emphasised again to members of the staff, including the new Air Attache, that we must always act with the greatest caution'.[9]

Eleven days before the coup, Ambassador Allen was told by the US chargé d'affaires in Baghdad that 'it was time to start building up a credit with Qasim's opponents, against the day when there would be a change of government here'. Allen concluded that 'for the first time since I have been here, I have the feeling that the end may just possibly come in the foreseeable future'. This does seem like a tip-off, at least, from the US, whose embassy was closely conniving with the plotters. Indeed, one day after the coup, on 9 February, Roger Allen cabled the Foreign Office that the new Minister of Defence 'was expected to become Air Force Commander in the event of a coup' – indicating some kind of advance knowledge.[10]

What is indisputable is that British officials in Baghdad and London knew of the massacres and welcomed the new regime carrying them out. The files make clear that Roger Allen and another embassy official were monitoring Iraqi radio reports on the first two days of the coup. Messages from the new regime called on people to 'help wipe out all those who belong to the Communists and finish them off'. They urged people to 'destroy the criminals' and to 'kill them all, kill all the criminals'. These announcements were all repeated several times. Allen told the Foreign Office on 11 February that 'the radio has been exhorting people to hound down the communists. Such fighting as had taken place seems to have been directed at any rate in part against communist sympathisers'. He sent a transcript of all these messages to the Foreign Office on 15 February.[11]

Britain's military attaché in the Baghdad embassy said in a despatch of 19 February that on 9 February there had been 'firing throughout the city' and the 'rounding up of communists', adding: 'since the embassy is in a communist stronghold area, considerable small arms firing was heard throughout most of the day'. On 10 February the embassy was telling the Foreign Office of the 'rounding up of Communists' and 'some sporadic shooting in various parts of the city'. On the same day, the Foreign Office noted that 'strong action is being taken against the Communists'.[12]

On 11 February, the embassy was reporting 'some firing' in outlying districts where there were believed to be Communists, with 'stories of heavy casualties, presumably among civilians, but these are not confirmed'.[13]

By 26 February, the embassy was saying that the new government was trying 'to crush organised communism in Iraq' and that there were rumours that 'all the top communists have been seized and that fifty have been quietly executed', although adding that 'there may be no truth in this'.[14]

The following month, a letter from the Iraq Petroleum Corporation to the Foreign Office referred to 'the hunt for communists' and that 'it remains to be seen how far they will be physically destroyed'. Writing six weeks after the coup, a Foreign Office official refers to a 'bloodbath' and 'we should not wish to be seen publicly to advocate such methods of suppressing communism'. 'Such harshness', the official noted, 'may well have been necessary as a short term expedient'.[15]

'The communist menace was tackled with determination', Britain's ambassador to Iraq reflected in a note to Alec Douglas-Home in May, adding that the Iraqi government said there were now 14,000 political prisoners and that 'the prisons are still overflowing with political detainees'. By June, Foreign Office official Percy Cradock – later to become chair of the Joint Intelligence Committee – noted that 'the Iraqi regime is continuing its severe repression of communists', with 39 executions recently announced.[16]

It was recognised by the Foreign Office that the massacre of the Communists was an entirely offensive operation. It noted on 9 February, for example, that killings were occurring at 'a time when there is no indication of a Communist threat or of any effective opposition to the new government'.[17]

British officials in effect supported these massacres. Roger Allen told the Foreign Office a week after the coup that 'the process of winkling out Communists in Baghdad and the towns is continuing' but that 'a Communist problem will remain':

> The present government is doing what it can, and therefore it is my belief that we should support it and help it in the long term to establish itself so that this communist threat may gradually diminish.

The new government, he wrote, 'probably suits our interests pretty well'. In a different despatch on the same day he wrote that since 'communist opposition is likely to continue' and that, in his view, there was no alternative to this government, 'it is therefore essential for it to get consolidated quickly'. It will 'need all the support and money it can get'.[18]

By this time the Foreign Office had already sent round a memo to various embassies explaining the British attitude to the coup. It said that the new regime 'has already taken strenuous action against local communists' and that 'repression of the local communists' will probably be maintained, while one of its other key problems will be 'the pacification of the Kurds'. 'We wish the new regime well', the memo stated, after referring to the deterioration of British relations with the previous Qasim regime.[19]

An internal Foreign Office brief also commented that the new rulers 'have shown courage and steadfastness in hatching and executing their plot' and that they should be 'somewhat friendlier to the West'.[20]

Allen met the Foreign Minister of the new military regime two days after the coup. There is no mention in his record of having raised the subject of the killings; the meeting is described as 'extremely friendly'.[21] Indeed, there is no mention in any of the files that I have seen of any concern whatever about the killings – the only response they prompted from the British government was support for those conducting them.

Thus officials noted that they should 'examine all possible means of profiting from the present anti-communist climate in Iraq' and to make 'a major effort to establish links with the new rulers'. The Foreign Office recommended various ways 'to make gestures' to the new regime, including 'to be helpful over the supply of arms' and to 'provide military training courses if the Iraqis want them'. This memo was written on the same day that Allen sent the Foreign Office the radio transcripts urging Iraqis to 'kill the criminals'.[22]

The embassy in Baghdad similarly recommended 'some kind of warm-hearted gestures' to 'those who had suffered in the process of dismantling Communism in Iraq' – that is, to those who had suffered in overcoming the Communists, not those who were victims of the massacres. This would be done in 'appreciation of the anti-communist effort here'.[23]

London's policy was to provide diplomatic recognition to the new regime right away and to establish 'a business relationship' with it. It was also to 'make friendly contact as soon as possible with the Baathist and nationalist leaders' and to invite members of the National Guard (that is, the organisation which had helped to carry out the massacres) to London. But this needed to be done 'under some other heading' to keep it secret, so as to avoid being seen publicly to identify with any particular group. The policy was shared with the US, where a senior state department official told the Foreign Office that if the coup 'resulted in a regime of Baathist complexion its policies were more likely to be acceptable to the United States government'.[24]

It was hoped that one advantage of the new regime was 'a chance for a new period in the oil companies' relations with the government' and to replace Qasim's previous oil policies, which had clearly been threatening the Western oil corporations' domination of the Iraq Petroleum Corporation.[25]

A week after the coup, Roger Allen was happily reporting that things are 'almost back to normal', hoping that the 'period of frustration' under Qasim was now over 'and that there will be scope for relatively constructive work here'. This was in full recognition that 'the problem of the communists and the slum dwellers is not yet, however, by any means removed' – therefore, the repression of Communists by the regime would presumably continue. By April, Allen could refer to 'our record of friendship for the new regime'.[26]

The Foreign Office also mentioned the need to 'keep track' of a new organisation set up by Labour MPs called the British Committee for the Defence of Human Rights in Iraq, which had the idea of visiting Iraq and investigating the killings. The embassy also 'warned' the Foreign Office of similar human-rights activities by Lord Bertrand Russell, described as a 'source of irritation' in Anglo-Iraqi relations.[27]

Another advantage to the British was the new regime's stance towards Kuwait. After Qasim was overthrown the British advised Kuwait to pre-empt any future threat to their independence by the new regime by bribing it. The Kuwaitis paid the new Baath government £50 million which, according to Said

Aburish, goes a long way towards explaining Saddam's attempt to intimidate Kuwait in 1990–1991, before invading, and force it to pay him money to meet Iraq's financial needs.[28]

Arming aggression

British complicity in violence in Iraq goes well beyond the February coup, however. Also in 1963, Britain supported the same Iraqi government's aggression against the Kurds. The precedent set by this episode plays an important part in understanding how Saddam Hussein got away with a campaign of such horrific violence against the Kurds in the 1980s.

On 10 June 1963, the Iraqi military began a vicious attack on the Kurds, whose struggle for autonomy against Baghdad had been stepped up in 1961. The Kurds were also calling for a share in Iraqi oil and the exclusion of Arab troops from Kurdistan, the northern region of Iraq.

British officials noted the 'Iraqi intention to carry out terror campaign' [sic]. Within ten days of operations, they wrote: 'the army are now apparently engaged in the clearing out and destruction of Kurdish villages in the Kirkuk neighbourhood'. With two-thirds of the Iraqi army deployed in the north, the Foreign Office reported that 'the Iraq [sic] government is now clearly making an all-out effort to settle the Kurdish problem once and for all'. 'Ruthless tactics' were being employed by the Iraqi military, including air strikes.[29]

The British embassy in Baghdad reported to London on 22 June:

> The brutality of the methods used by the army is likely to mar Arab/Kurdish relations for some time to come. The army has succeeded in clearing the Kurdish villages in lowland areas around vulnerable points . . . The method adopted is to take the villages one by one, shelling them from a safe distance with tank guns and field artillery, giving sometimes little or no warning to

the inhabitants. After a safe interval the National Guard or government-paid Kurds move in to loot . . . In some cases, eg in the Kurdish quarters of Kirkuk, bulldozers have been used to knock down houses. The result is that the men take to the hills, women and children are often left to fend for themselves and the village is left abandoned and, for the time being, quiet.[30]

The Foreign Office recognised there were certain dangers in this campaign for British interests. These were: that 'unsuccessful hostilities could jeopardise the present Iraq regime'; that fighting might increase the opportunities for Russian trouble-making in Kurdistan; that the Kurdish unrest could spread to Turkey, Iran and Syria; and there was also a risk of damage to the IPC's oil installations and of interruptions in the flow of oil. Glaringly absent from this Foreign Office list was the effect the fighting would have on the Kurdish people.[31] The files indicate that the ambassador encouraged Baghdad to negotiate a settlement with the Kurds, but once the campaign was launched, Britain provided outright support for the Iraqi government.

Before Baghdad began operations, Britain had already approved major arms exports which they knew would be used against the Kurds. Douglas-Home 'is anxious that in general Iraq's arms requirements should be met as quickly as possible', one file reads. On 11 April, ministers approved the export of 250 Saracen armoured personnel carriers which, it was recognised, were 'possibly for use if needed against the Kurds'. Also approved were exports of artillery ammunition, 22 Hunter fighter aircraft and rockets for Iraq's existing Hunters, 'again possibly for use against the Kurds'. 'There are considerable commercial advantages to be gained', a ministerial committee commented, and 'the scope for military exports is considerable' – the deal was worth £6 million.[32]

Officials decided to delay the supply of some of the rockets since:

We must give the Iraqis some of their requirements in order to enable them to hold their own vis-à-vis the Kurds, but it may be inadvisable to give them too generous supplies, since this might only encourage them to be more intransigeant [sic] with the Kurds and, if fighting breaks out and there are indiscriminate rocket attacks, there might be parliamentary and public criticism.[33]

After Baghdad attacked Kurdistan, the British government further deliberated on whether to deliver the rockets, a 'sensitive item' since they 'are intended for use against the Kurds'. In the files, there is no consideration of the humanitarian consequences, merely the effect on public relations: 'The news of the fighting may provoke public criticism of our decision to supply Iraq with arms', a briefing for the Cabinet reads.[34]

Two weeks into the campaign, the Foreign Office wrote that 'we are ready to do our best to meet Iraqi requirements in the field of arms and training', though ministers were still keen to delay the supply of rockets, for which the Iraqis were pressing. In July, ministers approved the export of 500 of these 'high explosive rockets'. A senior Iraqi air-force commander, Brigadier Hilmi, had told the British ambassador that he 'needed these weapons now in order to bring their war against the insurgents to a quick and successful conclusion'. When told that Britain would be delivering the rockets, Hilmi was 'genuinely grateful', according to the ambassador, who further commented that the commander 'would be delighted at our gesture'.[35]

A Foreign Office brief to embassies explaining British policy said that 'we have throughout thought it possible that any arms we supply might be used against the Kurds, but we have had to weigh this argument against other factors', which were to develop good relations with the new Iraqi rulers and to wean them away from Soviet military supplies.[36]

By the end of August 1963,the Iraqi air force had collected 500 Hunter rockets, a further 1,000 were to be delivered on 1 September and another 500 on 1 October. A further 18,000 were to be provided later. Following this, approvals were given to supply 280,000 rounds of ammunition for Saracen armoured cars, mortar bombs, 25-pounder shells, armed helicopters and sterling sub-machine guns.[37]

Britain also agreed to requests to send a team to Iraq to mend the guns on Centurion tanks which had been supplied by Britain. The 'one tricky political point', the Foreign Office observed, was the continuation of Iraqi operations against the Kurds. British officers could not be seen to be going near the areas of fighting; therefore, 'if tanks guns [sic] break down in the North, the tanks would simply have to be brought to Baghdad and repaired there'.[38]

There is no doubt that ministers knew exactly what they were authorising. In October, for example, a Foreign Office official approved the export of demolition slabs on the understanding that these 'will probably be used not only to destroy captured Kurdish strong points but also for the demolition of Kurdish villages'.[39] This complicity in the destruction of Kurdish villages was the forebear of the same British policies with regard to Iraqi aggression in the 1980s and Turkish terror against Kurds in the 1990s.

Indeed, British officials were aware that the Iraqi aggression they were supporting may have constituted genocide. The Foreign Office noted in a minute in September that 'Iraq's methods have been brutal and might sustain a charge of attempting to destroy or reduce the Kurds as a racial minority'. The British embassy in Baghdad had told the Foreign Office on 6 July that:

> the Kurds tend to be shot rather than taken prisoner. We have had some indications from officials that this may be deliberate policy ... We have since heard reports of an intention drastically to reduce the Kurdish

population in the North and to resettle the area with Arabs and of at least one Arab officer's disgust with the methods employed as inhuman and ill-advised in the long term. There is no doubt at all of the government's deliberate destruction of villages . . . The government of Iraq . . . have resorted to the use of force without the normal civilised safeguards against undue loss of civilian life and perhaps even with some intention of reducing the size of the Kurdish minority in Iraq, or at least cowing it permanently.[40]

The date of this memo is important: most of the British arms exports to Iraq for use against Kurds were approved after this date; policy was thus similar to the increased British support given to the Saddam regime after the chemical-warfare attacks on Kurdistan in March 1988.

Another similarity between 1963 and 1988 was British attempts to ensure there would be no international action taken against Iraq. In 1963, British officials worked to ensure that the UN would not discuss allegations of genocide in Iraq. A draft Foreign Office brief dated 12 September 1963 is entitled: 'The policy of genocide carried out by the government of the republic of Iraq against the Kurdish people: Reasons for opposing inscription'. This brief provides instructions for Britain's delegation to the UN, saying: 'it is obviously HMG's wish to get rid of this item as quickly as possible'.[41]

Foreign Office official William Morris suggested that if the question of genocide did come up at the UN 'our best line would be to abstain from voting' and to 'avoid saying anything at all if we possibly can'. Morris also explained that raising the charge of genocide meant the UN concerning itself with the internal affairs of member states, which was contrary to its charter and 'would be most unwelcome to us in the context of any trouble in our dependent territories'.[42]

British arms exports and training could also help in 'internal security', i.e., supporting the military regime in domestic repression. British help in mending Iraq's Centurion tanks was acknowledged to be specifically for this purpose: 'the two Centurion regiments form the backbone of their internal security in Baghdad'. The supply of Hunter aircraft went ahead in the knowledge that 'it may strengthen the ability of Iraqis to be masters in their own house (the Iraqi air force played an important part in overthrowing Qasim and achieving control of Baghdad)'.[43]

Indeed, during the February coup British-supplied Hunter aircraft had been used to attack the Ministry of Defence building where Qasim had taken refuge, a scenario repeated ten years later in Chile when British-supplied Hunters were also used successfully to attack the palace where democratically elected president Salvador Allende was holding out (see Chapter 14).

The offensive against the Kurds continued throughout 1963, before in effect reaching a stalemate. In April 1965, the Iraqis resumed what was to be another year-long offensive with similar levels of brutality, until an agreement was signed in June 1966 giving the Kurds some autonomy. The British embassy noted in July 1965 that 'Kurdish casualties have been mainly among the civilian population who are again being subjected to considerable suffering through indiscriminate air attack'; indiscriminate air attack, that is, from the Iraqi air force's 27 Hawker Hunters, thousands of rockets and other ammunition supplied by the Douglas-Home and Wilson governments. It was also known that napalm was being 'evidently dropped from the Iraqi Hunters'. Villages continued to be razed to the ground along with 'the forcible de-Kurdisation' of some areas in Kurdistan.[44]

British arms exports continued to flow with the change from the Conservative to the Labour government in 1964. The latter defied a mid-1965 call in parliament to stop arms exports to Baghdad while noting that 'Her Majesty's Government had no intention of withholding normal assistance to the Iraq government in the form of arms supplies'.[45] Huge orders were by then in the pipeline, including 17,000 Hunter rockets to be delivered from July, again in the knowledge that they would be used against Kurds. The Wilson government also agreed to supply the Iraqis with 40 Lightning fighter aircraft.

A June 1965 Foreign Office brief noted that 'we have maintained our arms supplies to Iraq, even during periods of Kurdish fighting' for the reasons of maintaining links with the military, described as 'the Iraqi governing class', to reduce Iraqi arms supplies from the Soviet Union and Nasser's Egypt, and since 'they bring us considerable commercial benefit'. Meanwhile, 'we have no official dealings with the Kurds and give them no assistance'.[46]

The declassified files also reveal that the Wilson government provided a more terrifying precedent to the rulers in Baghdad: Saddam Hussein was not the first Iraqi leader to use chemical weapons against the Kurds. This had also occurred in the middle 1960s.[47]

In August and September 1965, Mustafa Barzani, president of the largest Kurdish group in Iraqi Kurdistan, claimed to the British Prime Minister that Iraq had purchased 'large quantities of toxic gases for use against Kurdish inhabitants'. Barzani appealed to Wilson to stop arming Baghdad and to intercede with the regime to 'prevent the latter carrying out their alleged intention of launching gas attacks against the Kurds'.[48] No British reply was sent to this letter, or to others sent by Barzani; the British refused to have any formal contacts with the Kurds.

This refusal came despite the understanding that the Kurds had good intelligence connections in the Baghdad regime. It also came in the knowledge that in September 1964 the Iraqi Ministry of Defence had approached the British, West German, US and Soviet governments with a preliminary enquiry for an order of 60,000 gas masks 'for urgent delivery'. Finally, British officials received 'an account which we believe to be reliable, of the Army's plan for putting an end to the Kurdish problem'.[49]

Moreover, the British embassy wrote in September that:

The Iraqis would have little humanitarian compunction about using gas if things were (as they are) going badly for them. They would probably believe they could hush up the incidents and might not worry very much about world opinion. They are certainly showing a strong current interest in chemical warfare. We believe they may well have stocks of some gas (probably of the riot control variety) and likely looking cylinders have actually been seen.

Although the memo went on to say that it was difficult to see the Iraqis using gas in current circumstances, it also stated that, 'on the other hand there is ample evidence that the Kurds are genuinely worried at the possibility that gas will be used'.[50] The interesting revelation from this is British unwillingness to intercede with Baghdad anyway even given major concerns and evidence.

The Baathist regime that came to power in Iraq for the first time in February 1963 was itself overthrown in another military coup in November. By this time, Britain had reduced much of its earlier backing for the regime; but the record clearly states that this was not for humanitarian reasons.

'They began well', the British ambassador said in December 1963 after the regime had been replaced. The problem was that the Baathists eventually pursued similar policies to Qasim, including an Arab nationalist attempt to unite Syria, Egypt and Iraq in the United Arab Republic. Before long, the new regime had 'alarmed the business community with their hints of nationalisation of industry, banking and trade'.[51]

It was not until 1968 that the Baath party, following a succession of governments through the 1960s, took power again – and this time held it until the invasion of Iraq in 2003. The 1968 coup brought into power the Baathist General Ahmed al-Bakr, who had been Prime Minister after the February 1963 coup. Saddam Hussein became Vice President, before taking over from al-Bakr in 1979. The 1968 coup was also backed by the CIA, which immediately developed close relations with the ruling Baathists.

The Baath regime of 1968 was also immediately welcomed by Britain: 'The new regime may look to the United Kingdom for military training and equipment and we should lose no time in appointing a defence attache', the ambassador in Baghdad wrote. The regime's new Defence Minister, General Tikriti, was invited to the Farnborough Air Show and was told by the ambassador that 'it seemed to me we now had an opportunity to restore Anglo/Iraqi relations to something of their former intimacy'. In reply, 'General Tikriti said that during the Baathist regime of 1963 he had greatly appreciated the cooperative attitude of HMG'.[52]

From these roots emerged the Saddam regime, and Britain's support for it.

PART II

PROPAGANDA, REALITY

6

PSYCHOLOGICAL WARFARE BEYOND IRAQ

The government's propaganda campaign over Iraq is not a one-off, but part of a wider strategy to mislead the public over its foreign-policy objectives. It is the culmination of the lessons learned from numerous British military interventions. Indeed, this strategy goes beyond propaganda; it is more properly called 'perception management' – a polite term for thought control. It is designed to counter the major threat to Britain's foreign policy: the public.

The campaign has two major elements. First, the constant rhetoric about moral motives and the most noble of intentions, which permeates every speech and public comment by British ministers. All governments have, of course, done this; but New Labour has taken proclamations about its moral purpose to new heights. Second, and the subject of this chapter, are specific 'information operations', which are viewed as an increasingly critical part of government policy, including military interventions.

Information operations

The leading independent critic of such 'information operations' in Britain is Professor David Miller of Strathclyde University.

Miller refers to the strategy as one of 'information dominance' which amounts to a 'philosophy of total propaganda control'. Such operations are already a formal part of US military strategy. According to the Pentagon, the US must be able 'to conduct prompt, sustained and synchronised operations with combinations of forces tailored to specific situations and with access to and freedom to operate in all domains – space, sea, land, air and information'.

The US army defines information operations as

> The employment of the core capabilities of electronic warfare, computer network operations, psychological operations, military deception, and operations security . . . to affect or defend information and information systems, and to influence decision making.

Miller argues that such a strategy goes beyond traditional conceptions of propaganda – which involve crafting a message and distributing it through the media – to incorporating, gathering, processing and deploying information via computers, intelligence and military command and control systems. The US already has 15 'information dominance centers' in the US, Kuwait and Baghdad.

One aspect of the strategy is the system of 'embedding' journalists with the military, as in Iraq, to make journalists dependent on the military and ensuring that 'friendly information' is reported. Another is direct attacks on journalists reporting 'unfriendly information'. This has now become a permanent feature of the recent Anglo-US wars, as demonstrated by strikes against Reuters and al-Jazeera offices in Baghdad in the 2003 invasion, against the al-Jazeera office in Kabul during the bombing of Afghanistan, and the attacks on the Serbian television building in Belgrade during the bombing of Yugoslavia in 1999.[1]

According to David Miller, the British government has significantly stepped up its machinery of 'information operations' in recent years, and has 'comprehensively overhauled' its 'internal and external propaganda apparatus', outside of any significant media or parliamentary scrutiny. In 2002, the British army stated that in future conflicts, 'maintaining moral as well as information dominance will rank as important as physical protection'. Two years earlier, armed-forces minister John Spellar had commented that 'we shall depend increasingly, not on simple numerical superiority in firepower, but on information dominance'.[2]

The Foreign Office has rebranded its propaganda work as 'public diplomacy'. Following a review of its activities in this area, it concluded that the government needed an 'overarching public diplomacy strategy' that would shape 'the core messages that we wish to put across to our target audiences'. Such a strategy is considerably aided by the Foreign Policy Centre, a think tank established by New Labour. Its director Mark Leonard is one of the most passionate intellectual articulators of this new form of propaganda. One of the major threats identified by Leonard, for example, is 'the rise of global NGOs and protest movements' which 'have changed the nature of power and put even greater constraints on the freedom of action of national governments' – have increased, that is, the danger that the public might influence policy.[3]

The Foreign Office's 'public diplomacy' operation now costs £340 million per year for operations based in London alone, excluding those undertaken in embassies around the world. The operation is 'entirely outside of democratic control' and works 'on the basis that anything goes so long as it is calculated that it can be got away with'.[4]

More traditional activities – such as unattributably planting information in the domestic and foreign press – continue under the headings 'grey' and 'black' propaganda operations. These stories then get recycled, and are used by governments as 'proof' of otherwise unsubstantiated claims.[5]

Britain's leading analyst of MI6, Stephen Dorril, has written that 'intelligence agencies continually create alarmist disinformation'. Examples from the past include: the story of 'red mercury', the mysterious substance that was meant to be a source of cheap nuclear weapons for terrorists; the nuclear artillery shells that supposedly went missing from Soviet southern states; and the 'Islamic bomb' which terrorists were meant to be building to be in use by 1995.

'Since 11 September', Dorril argues, 'the intelligence agencies with the aid of gullible journalists, editors desperate for endless copy and politicians on a crusade have constructed a truly global conspiracy theory'. At the top is Osama bin Laden, a mastermind as in every Ian Fleming fantasy, who is meant to control a vast network of thousands of terrorists across the world intent on murdering us in our beds. Numerous scare stories continue to be spread about al Qaeda's supposed plans.[6] The threat from terrorists is real, but as with the 'Soviet threat' throughout the cold war, details are exaggerated and often deliberately fabricated as part of a strategy to achieve domestic and foreign-policy goals.

For example, in April 2004 we were told that the security services had foiled a fiendish plot by international terrorists to detonate a dangerous chemical weapon in London, based on a substance called osmium tetroxide. Brian Jones, former head of the branch of the Defence Intelligence Staff responsible for analysing intelligence on chemical warfare, wrote that he had never heard of this substance. 'It all begins to sound like so much froth', he added: 'at first, it crosses my mind that this information could have entered the public domain as a result of an ill-conceived attempt to boost the reputation of one or other of the hard-pressed intelligence and security agencies'. Or it could have been 'inspired by the Home Office to support their policy initiatives'. Either way, Jones concludes that it is 'frightening' that those leading the counter-terrorism effort 'either do not understand the requirement' or 'are prepared to see the public misled as a short term expedient to achieve policy goals'.[7]

Investigative journalist David Leigh has recently written that 'British journalists – and British journals – are being manipulated by the secret intelligence agencies' in three ways: the first is by attempting to recruit journalists to spy on other people or for spies themselves to go under journalist cover; the second is when intelligence officers pose as journalists to write tendentious articles under false names; the third is when propaganda stories are planted on willing journalists who disguise the origin from their readers. On this latter aspect, Leigh identifies 'a very active programme by the secret agencies' to promote 'information operations'. He cites the example of the *Spectator* publishing a pseudonymous article by an MI6 officer on the subject of Bosnia in 1994.[8]

The government has stated that, following Iraq, propaganda will increase. A Ministry of Defence report entitled *Operations in Iraq: Lessons for the future*, published in December 2003, says that in future British military strategy 'will place greater emphasis on information and media operations, which are critical to success'. In a section called the 'key lessons' of the Iraq campaign, number one is: 'An information campaign, to be successful, needs to start as early as possible and continue into the post-conflict phase of an operation'.

Another lesson is that:

> Targeting of indigenous media infrastructure, where justified under international law, needs to take account of the respective needs of the information campaign and the overall military campaign.

The report also notes the success of the strategy of embedding journalists with the US-British military, stating that 'commercial analysis of the print output they produced during the combat phase shows that 90% of embedded correspondents' reporting was either positive or neutral.'[9]

The all-party House of Commons Defence Committee agrees on the importance in the future of 'information' and media operations, illustrating the degree to which elected MPs represent the interests of the public. In a report on the 'lessons of Iraq' published in March 2004, the committee stated that:

Our evidence suggests that if information operations
are to be successful, it is essential that they should start
in the period when diplomatic efforts are still being
made, albeit backed by the coercive threat of military
force through overt preparations.

It added that 'we believe that the British information operations
campaign' on Iraq 'did not begin early enough' and it was
'disappointing that the coalition is widely perceived to have
"come second" in perception management'. 'Information
operations are an activity which can be expected to become of
increasing importance in future operations'. This includes
media operations where:

The early establishment of a robust media operations
capability in theatre must be a priority for any operation
. . . Overall the embedding of journalists with combat
units worked well. The experience is likely to be seen as
a precedent for future operations.[10]

Indeed, 'information operations' – ostensibly run by the
military and targeted at the military enemy – and 'media
operations' – targeted at the international and domestic public
– are in reality somewhat enmeshed. Air Marshal Mike Heath,
ex-Director of the British military's Targeting and Information
Operations section, has said that during the invasion of Iraq the
information operation strategy was 'very closely tied to media
operations' with staff meeting the Campbell group in No. 10 on
a daily basis.[11]

The past as precedent

Current psychological-warfare operations have been honed
through long experience of past military interventions, with
their modern roots going back at least as far as the Second
World War. The Ministry of Information had been set up in
1939; as Paul Lashmar and James Oliver comment in their

study of British propaganda, its prime task was 'to generate propaganda aimed at the British people'. Its activities included government information policy, publicity campaigns and censorship. During the Second World War the BBC became 'an instrument of state information policy'.

After the war, the Labour government created the Information Research Department (IRD) within the Foreign Office specifically to disseminate propaganda about the Soviets and other enemies, which continued until it was closed down in the late 1970s. Stories about the Soviet threat were planted in the British and international media and IRD activities ranged widely across the globe, especially in Britain's colonies. The strategy was not so much to spread outright lies but carefully selected material which distorted the picture in favour of British foreign-policy objectives.

Lashmar and Oliver conclude that while it may have appeared 'that a diverse range of media were separately coming to the same conclusions about communism and the nature of the cold war, in fact much of the media was singing from a hymn sheet which was provided by IRD'. IRD's strategy included targeting a range of domestic organisations; for example, one body called the Psychological Warfare Consultations Committee was established to carry out 'psychological operations against any peace movements' and 'planned intelligence service operations against progressive organisations in England'.

One particular IRD operation helped to overthrow President Sukarno in Indonesia in 1965. This was part of a wider British-backed campaign to replace the regime; the result was up to a million deaths in a bloodbath by the Indonesian army and its allies.[12] The operation was managed by an IRD expert working closely with Britain's ambassador in Jakarta, whose brief from London was 'to do whatever I could to get rid of Sukarno'. It involved a campaign of manipulating the world's press by placing stories to blacken the PKI, the Indonesian Communist party which the Indonesian generals set out to destroy, and asserting that Indonesia was on the verge of a Communist dictatorship.[13]

Government propaganda towards the British public is a permanent aspect of major operations, especially military interventions, in every British foreign policy I have looked at. Preventing the public from seeing a true picture of policy and concealing evidence are all normal features of strategy. The rest of this chapter uses the Vietnam war to provide a snapshot of media management.

As with Iraq in 2003, the biggest problem for the government was massive public opposition to escalating US aggression and Britain's support for it. Prime Minister Harold Wilson told President Johnson in December 1967 that he was under:

> heavy political pressure and this was now not simply from left-wing opinion. There was in Britain now a wide-based opposition to the Vietnam war, including organs of opinion in the centre and right.[14]

The threat from the public had been previously recognised by the British ambassador in Saigon, who noted that 'mischievous publicity' about the war and the campaign of teach-ins and lobbies 'is having an effect on the policy of Her Majesty's Government'. He continued:

> If the pressure continues, as it shows every sign of doing, I fear that it will become increasingly difficult to resist and that we shall find ourselves forced into policies and attitudes which are contrary to the real national interest.

Translated: the public might force a change in elite policy. He concluded by asking whether 'something cannot be done to counter this campaign by making the facts about Vietnam better known to the British public'.[15]

By June 1965, Foreign Office official James Cable had also become aware that there was 'every sign of an organised campaign' against the war in Britain. He stated that:

> All this has not yet affected our basic support for American policy in Vietnam, but it has generated a

certain preference for discretion in the outward manifestations of this support.[16]

The government had no intention of being swayed by mere
public opinion; rather, it would have to keep its policy of
strongly backing the war more secret.

The same official also provided a briefing note to ministers
on 'defending the government's policy on the controversial and
increasingly critical issue of Vietnam', adding: 'I think there
could be considerable advantage in the same points being
made, over and over again, by a number of different supporters
of the government'.[17] Prolonged repetition of often nonsensical
positions is now a standard feature of government propaganda.

By early 1966, another official was writing that 'we have
taken certain specific measures to see that British opinion is
informed'. This included producing various publications,
organising seminars 'to guide discussion among intellectuals
to a responsible awareness' of Vietnam and organising an
opinion poll 'to help analyse the views and misconceptions held
by the public and to indicate what might therefore be done to
counteract them', such as individual briefings to journalists.[18]

The British embassy noted in 1969 that 'we distribute IRD
material to some twenty people in Saigon. This includes some
politicians, highly placed civil servants, newspaper editors and
foreign journalists'. The task of policy overall was 'to ensure
accurate reporting of events here'.[19]

Throughout the early 1960s the British embassy in Saigon
housed an 'information' expert as part of the British advisory
mission. He advised the extremely repressive and unpopular
Diem regime in South Vietnam on improving its 'various
information services' and launching a propaganda campaign
that would promote 'publicity for the government's achievements'; no small task. It also involved 'clarification of what is
meant by psychological warfare and, at the same time, a much
closer definition of the targets and aims of "unattributable"
propaganda and similar subterfuges'.[20]

The Foreign Office also once said that it would 'keep News Dept fed with information about N. Vietnamese misdeeds' to bring these to 'public notice'. The British ambassador in Saigon, Harry Hohler, asked the Foreign Office news department if 'there is anything you can do' in talking to the media in London 'to make them understand' Vietnam better and especially to deflect criticism of Diem and his family. He also lamented in February 1962 that 'our own parliament is now beginning to show interest in Vietnam' and feared 'more attention here from visiting British journalists who have been mercifully few and far between of late'.[21]

7

'HUMANITARIAN INTERVENTION': THE FRAUDULENT PRETEXT

One of the major aims of propaganda and 'information operations' is to convince the public that the government is acting from the highest of moral motives. In modern times, military interventions cannot be justified by – and soldiers sent to die for – sordid objectives such as grabbing oil. Rather, our leaders need to be depicted as the High Defenders of Civilisation. The basic duplicity which underlies this pretence is no recent phenomenon, however. My research on the declassified record of foreign policy reveals that the reasons publicly given for British military interventions are never those understood by planners in private.

Iraq in 2003 is not the first time that British policy-makers have fabricated a threat to justify intervention in that region; the same happened in 1961. Then, British planners feared that Kuwait, a newly independent country where Britain had major oil interests, would sever ties from London. Kuwait had signed an agreement for Britain to defend it if requested, but the solidity of this agreement was questionable. British fears were that 'as the international personality of Kuwait grows, she will wish in various ways to show that she is no longer dependent upon us'. Therefore, 'we must continue to use the opportunities which our protective role will afford to ensure so far as we can that Kuwait does not materially upset the existing financial arrangements or cease to be a good holder of sterling'.

Iraqi leader Abdul Qasim publicly claimed Kuwait as part of Iraq in June 1961 (reiterating a long-standing Iraqi claim). Foreign Office officials in London, together with the British embassy in Baghdad, fabricated a story that Iraq had ordered a tank regiment to speed south towards Kuwait. The files show that British officials in Basra, near the Kuwait border, saw no such threat; Whitehall did not even take Qasim's grandstanding seriously. However, a terrified Kuwait emir, told by British officials that Iraq was about to invade, permitted the landing of British troops. A Ministry of Defence report 11 days later finally admitted it was 'unlikely' that Iraq had ever posed a threat.[1]

If we turn to more recent pretexts for intervention, the bombing of Yugoslavia in 1999 is conventionally held up as an example of 'humanitarian intervention'; NATO forces, especially Britain and the US, are conventionally said to have come to the rescue of Kosovars being persecuted by Milosevic's Yugoslavia.

The year before NATO began its bombing campaign, in March 1999 around 2,000 people had been killed – largely the result of the civil war between Yugoslav forces and the Kosovo Liberation Army (KLA). The mass refugee exodus from Kosovo – the result of an horrific campaign of systematic ethnic cleansing by Milosevic – began only after the NATO bombing had commenced. The situation in Kosovo was indeed serious before this, with terrible repression by Yugoslav forces and a large number of internally displaced people, but Yugoslav forces took advantage of the NATO bombing to implement this more terrifying campaign.

The all-party House of Commons Defence Committee concluded after the bombing campaign that 'all the evidence suggests that plans to initiate [NATO's] air campaign hastened the onset of the disaster'. There is also evidence that NATO leaders knew from intelligence reports that Milosevic might launch such a campaign if they attacked, but went ahead anyway.

By the end of 2000, more than 200,000 Serbs had been forced to flee Kosovo, most of them in the first few weeks of the NATO troop deployments, as agreed in the peace accord. Killings, the burning of Serbian homes and violence against Serbs then ensued. Massive human-rights abuses were taking place under the very noses of NATO troops. No massive military intervention was required to act in defence of these human rights; simple arrest procedures might have been sufficient. But in this case, the human-rights abuses were allowed to continue (as they did, incidentally, in Chechnya and Indonesia at the same time).

Given NATO's humanitarian failure in this instance, it is worth considering alternative reasons for the bombing campaign. One motivation mentioned by Blair was that NATO's 'credibility' had been at stake over Kosovo. This was at a time when NATO was searching for a new mission as its 50th birthday approached in late April 1999. 'If NATO fails in Kosovo, the next dictator to be threatened with military force may well not believe our resolve to carry the threat through', Blair said. Yugoslavia needed to be blasted, he implied, to teach others a lesson. Other strategic Western objectives at the time were enlarging both the EU and NATO eastwards. Milosevic's Yugoslavia, with a reconstituted Communist party in power and with strong independent, nationalist tendencies, was effectively a barrier to these policies. The NATO assault could be seen as an attempt to return eastern Europe to a client region of the West. These are, at the very least, considerations – ones which have rarely been mentioned in mainstream media.

Sierra Leone and Zimbabwe

There are two recent cases aside from Kosovo regularly upheld as 'proving' the government's seriousness about humanitarian intervention and speaking out against human-rights abuses – Sierra Leone and Zimbabwe.

There can be little doubt that British military intervention in Sierra Leone in May 2000 had a positive short-term impact. This makes it very unusual in the history of British post-war foreign policy.

Foreign Secretary Jack Straw contended that Britain intervened 'because we wanted to uphold the values of the UN charter, to restore the rule of law and respect for human rights, and to establish the conditions for democracy'[2] – a view parroted by most commentators. But the wider context reveals a somewhat different picture.

The May 2000 British deployment provided a more secure environment for the UN to reinforce its troop presence and staved off an advance into Freetown by the Sierra Leonean rebels, the Revolutionary United Front (RUF). The RUF were a truly gruesome force, having routinely terrorised the country by hacking off the limbs of around 100,000 people. The intervention was understandably broadly welcomed by the population of the capital. The small British deployment – only around 1,000 troops – shows how easy it can sometimes be for external actors to provide much-needed short-term security for victims of conflict.

There had, however, been several opportunities to demonstrate a commitment to human rights before May 2000. In January 1999, for example, the RUF killed around 9,000 people, terrorising the population as it temporarily entered Freetown; there was no British intervention at this point. Rather, in July 1999, the international community, including Britain, forged a 'peace agreement' that actually brought the RUF into the Sierra Leone government and even made RUF leader, Foday Sankoh, the Vice President. Foreign Office minister Peter Hain told parliament shortly after that 'we welcomed the signature on 7 July of the Lome peace agreement between the government of Sierra Leone and the Revolutionary United Front'.[3] This agreement was widely condemned by human-rights groups as likely to lead to further abuses, which duly occurred. Britain also voted for the establishment of a UN peacekeeping force, but refused to participate in it; the result was widely recognised as an ill-equipped force.

Then in February 2000, UN Secretary General Kofi Annan pleaded with members of the Security Council to increase the size and mandate of the UN force in Sierra Leone, reiterating that it was ill-equipped to deal with the situation. Britain, along with the rest of the Security Council, voted for this but neither it nor any of the other countries with the best-equipped militaries offered substantial numbers of troops.

It was this inaction in February that contributed to the deteriorating situation in May. By this time, the UN force numbered only 8,500, rather than the mandated strength of 11,100. The RUF had by now taken 500 UN peacekeepers hostage and was on the verge of retaking Freetown. It was then that Britain intervened – in a unilateral operation outside of the UN command. It appears that this operation had been intended only to secure the airport and evacuate British nationals; it stayed on and stabilised the capital, allowing UN reinforcements.

British inaction before May 2000, especially given its responsibilities as a permanent member of the Security Council, is rather striking. If Britain had been serious about human rights, perhaps it might not have exported 7,500 rifles to Sierra Leone as part of a £10 million package in 1999. The country was already awash with weapons, whose availability contributed to the phenomenon of child soldiers. If Britain were serious about human rights now, perhaps it would try to weed out from, rather than absorb into, the reconstituted army it is currently training those past human-rights abusers.

Most important of all, perhaps Britain might become serious about addressing the poverty that is the root of the conflict in Sierra Leone. A major plank of the Blair government's view of the world is to impose failed policies of economic 'liberalisation' on the country, along with the rest of Africa; this is essentially a condition of British aid. In early 2002, Human Rights Watch commented that, although the human-rights situation had improved, 'the poverty and corruption which gave rise to the decade-long conflict remains much the same'. David Keen, of the London School of Economics, has commented that 'Britain's portrayal of the conflict as a struggle between good and evil served as an excuse for continuing corruption and the neglect of rural grievances'.[4]

There are more plausible explanations for the intervention, to me, or at the very least, reasons to strongly question the official story. Rather like Blair's statement that NATO needed to maintain its 'credibility' by acting over Kosovo, Britain is seen as demonstrating a 'great power' status by intervening in Africa. A Downing Street source, for example, specifically referred to the May 2000 intervention in Sierra Leone as showing Britain's 'leadership'.[5] This is characteristic of Blair: posing as the saviour of Africa through grandstanding public gestures rather than effecting the simplest of policy changes that would actually make a long-term difference. The British unilateral action outside of the UN demonstrates its status as an independent actor in the world; it makes the point that London can trump the UN. West Africa is a region where historically Britain has been keen to play the 'over the horizon' great-power role, not least in rivalry with France.

There is also the issue of reinstalling a pro-British regime in West Africa, where Britain has important and growing interests in maintaining 'stability', notably in Nigeria. The latter's oil resources are the chief prize in the region. The spread of the conflict that has engulfed Liberia and bordering countries threatens to upset British plans for Nigerian oil. Intervention in Sierra Leone went some way to ensuring the kind of 'stability' most in Britain's interests.

Then there is Zimbabwe, a case regularly invoked as demonstrating New Labour's commitment to human rights. That Mugabe's Zimbabwe is a repressive authoritarian regime that thuggishly silences its opponents and has a horrendous human-rights record, is a statement of fact. But this human-rights record is no worse than many British allies and is in fact noticeably better than one other major African state, Nigeria, which enjoys close relations with London while Whitehall remains virtually silent on human-rights atrocities (see chapter 10). The dozens of deaths at the hands of Mugabe's security forces – grim enough, to be sure – compares to around 10,000 deaths in Nigeria since 1999, in many of which the Nigerian police and army are directly complicit.

Unlike Nigeria (or Russia, Israel, Colombia, Turkey and others) which enjoys the protection of Britain, Zimbabwe has been the object of consistent criticism from London ostensibly about human rights. While Britain has played a leading role in imposing EU sanctions on Zimbabwe (in February 2002), it has played an equally vigorous role in blocking calls for EU sanctions against, for example, Israel.

On Zimbabwe, the media follows the policy of the state, as normal, and Mugabe is now a byword for violence – the subject of numerous articles and documentaries – while the public could be forgiven for never having heard of Nigerian President Olesegun Obasanjo.

What explains the British policy of speaking out against Mugabe's human-rights abuses? The chronology of Britain's pressure on the Mugabe regime helps to provide a few possible explanations.

Britain publicly stepped up pressure against Zimbabwe in April/May 2000. This involved condemning the regime's violence against opponents and raising the prospect of a cut-off in EU aid; it culminated in the announcement of a British arms embargo. Before this period, throughout 1998 and 1999, Britain had been providing various military equipment to Zimbabwe while human-rights violations had already become serious and even after Zimbabwe had openly intervened in the civil war in the Democratic Republic of Congo (DRC) in August 1998. Zimbabwe was using British-supplied Hawk aircraft to devastating effect – they were 'deployed in the DRC from time to time', Foreign Office minister Peter Hain said in April 2000. Amnesty International commented that in 1998 'Zimbabwean warplanes repeatedly bombed civilian targets and troops killed civilians during indiscriminate shelling' in the DRC. Yet the government carried on approving the export of spare parts for the Hawk aircraft until May 2000. At least 150 arms export licences for equipment were approved from August 1997 to January 2000.[6]

Human rights in Zimbabwe certainly deteriorated in 2000, especially around the April election campaign, when opponents were brutally intimidated. Yet in January 1998, for example, the Zimbabwean police and army had shot around 20 people, with at least 9 dying. Violations had worsened in 1999 with torture becoming widespread and increasing attacks by the regime on the media, the opposition and the judiciary. Throughout this time, not only did Britain continue to arm the regime but it retained a small military training mission in the country (which was withdrawn only in March 2001).

Without access to the planning files we cannot be sure precisely why Britain stepped up pressure in spring 2000. Two factors, however, cannot be ignored: the breakdown of talks between Zimbabwe and the IMF in late 1999; and the introduction of Mugabe's 'fast track' strategy of seizing white-owned farms in February/March 2000.

Foreign Secretary Robin Cook's speech to parliament on 3 May 2000 announcing the arms embargo is replete with concerns about land seizures and Zimbabwe's opposition to 'a fair programme of land reform'. Among Cook's demands was that such reform be 'based on a fair price to the farmer'; something not unreasonable, perhaps, but in the context of Zimbabwe's recent past, somewhat revealing of Whitehall's priorities.[7]

In November 1997 the Zimbabwean government had announced the compulsory acquisition of 1,471 farms. The 'fast track' land-seizure programme, however, has involved all manner of human-rights violations, more against poor, rural, black people than white farm owners. There is little doubt of the urgent need for radical land reform in the country. By the beginning of the 'fast track' programme, around 4,500 mainly white large-scale commercial farmers still held 28 per cent of the total land; at the same time, more than one million black families, or around 6 million people, eked out an existence in overcrowded, arid, 'communal' areas, representing around 41 per cent of the land – essentially the land allocated to Africans by the British colonial government. This situation created 'a significant land hunger in Zimbabwe', in the words of Human Rights Watch.[8]

In the first decade after independence in 1980, the government redistributed over 3 million hectares of land, resettling more than 50,000 families. In the second decade, however, less than one million hectares was acquired for redistribution and less than 20,000 families resettled as the pace of land reform declined. Meanwhile, population density in the 'communal' areas increased.[9]

Historically, Britain has gone to huge lengths to protect the property interests of white farmers in Africa. In the 'decolonisation' process in Kenya in the 1950s, for example, British plans for land reform ensured that the settlers' ownership of the best land would continue after independence. In Zimbabwe, the price of independence was also a status quo on the land. During the independence negotiations, Britain secured the agreement of Zimbabwe's resistance leaders to preserve for ten years the pattern of land ownership that benefited the white farmers. This agreement included provisions that the new government would not engage in any compulsory land acquisition and that when land was acquired the government would pay adequate and prompt compensation. It is believed that Britain promised the Zimbabweans to raise hundreds of millions of pounds for long-term land reform as part of the deal to end the war.[10] In the event, Britain provided only £44 million in aid after independence for land reform, and also imposed conditions on how that money could be spent. Conservative governments under Thatcher and Major insisted on government purchases of land from willing settlers at full market prices.

When Labour came to power in 1997, the new International Development Secretary, Clare Short, told the Zimbabwean government that 'we do not accept that Britain has a special responsibility to meet the costs of land purchase in Zimbabwe'.[11] After an international donors' conference on land reform in 1998, relations between the donors and the Zimbabwean government broke down and the latter accused the donors of not putting up the funds they had pledged and of protecting the interests of white agribusiness.

It is also worth considering the fear that Zimbabwe's land-seizure programme might be replicated elsewhere. In South Africa, for example, 13 per cent of the population own 80 per cent of the land. Since the African National Congress government came to power, only a tiny percentage of the land has been redistributed, but one opinion poll showed that 54 per cent of South Africans supported the land occupations in Zimbabwe. The *Financial Times* has referred to the 'Zimbabwe contagion', meaning the danger of the conflict in Zimbabwe spreading elsewhere and undermining the prospects for foreign investment.[12]

A related threat posed by the Mugabe regime is its refusal to implement the orders of the Washington-based institutions, the IMF and the World Bank. Zimbabwe's adoption of a Structural Adjustment Programme in 1991 led to rises in inflation and the contraction of manufacturing and employment. By 1997 Zimbabwe was in the throes of a serious economic crisis. The IMF demanded further cutbacks in government spending as well as an end to Zimbabwe's intervention in the DRC, which was costing £1 million a day. When Zimbabwe refused, the IMF cut off aid.

The Blair government is one of the world's leading champions of global economic 'liberalisation'. Countries failing to promote the required model – of trade liberalisation and privatisation under World Bank/IMF guidance – are routinely pressurised through the denial of aid and debt relief. Zimbabwe is one such example, although not a favourable model by any means. When

Cook announced the arms embargo on Zimbabwe in May 2000, he repeated the government's position that for the Mugabe government to receive new IMF aid, 'it must meet the full conditionality of any IMF support'.[13]

When, in 1998, Britain withdrew its support for Indonesia after 30 years, ministers suddenly discovered a history of human-rights abuse; they even referred to the regime as a dictatorship. The real concern was that Suharto was failing to implement an IMF programme. The stance over Zimbabwe is strikingly similar, while the media has almost universally swallowed the argument that human rights are the only motive of the British government.

If the British government were in any way interested in promoting 'humanitarian intervention' as a strategy or doctrine, or interested in upholding human rights in anything like a serious way, then it might undertake the simplest of steps with regard to some of its key allies engaged in state terror and repression – reducing total support from London, for example. It is to this that we turn in part 3, but before doing so, let us consider what planners have been articulating in private about their actual goals.

8

FROM THE HORSE'S MOUTH: WHITEHALL'S REAL GOALS

Britain has a highly secretive state that withholds many government planning files even after the 30-year rule which is meant to declassify most of them. Censorship of key passages and names in the declassified documents is also routine and widespread. Yet the documents that can be viewed – from the Foreign Office, Treasury, Ministry of Defence, the Prime Minister's office and others – are available to any member of the public who chooses to visit the National Archives.

It is an indictment of British academics and, to a lesser extent, journalists, how little of this private planning is ever revealed to the public and much of what does emerge is of marginal importance, ignoring more significant issues. Most commentators choose to ignore the private record, preferring to take at their word what officials say in public. The secret files might never be able to provide the full picture of government planning, but they do provide the single most comprehensive one that is available. Indeed, a fairly clear picture emerges from these files as to what British governments really want in their foreign policy.

Whitehall's economic and political goals

A July 1970 report entitled 'Priorities in our foreign policy' states that Britain needs 'to act in support of our commercial and financial interests throughout the world':

> We must contribute within our economic capability to international stability and the protection of our interests in the rest of the world from which so many of our raw materials derive . . . We shall need to pay particular attention to the Middle East, Southeast Asia and Southern Africa.[1]

The basic aim is to ensure that other countries establish economic climates favourable to British, and Western, companies. A Foreign Office report from 1968 recognises that the primary goal of foreign policy is to make Britain economically strong, meaning that 'we should bend our energies to help produce a world economic climate in which our external trade, our income from invisibles and our balance of payments can prosper'. The key to this is 'freer' global trade and 'increasing our efforts to open up new markets in Europe, Latin America and the Far East'.[2]

Ensuring a favourable investment climate was especially important for countries where Britain had important oil interests. The Cabinet Office noted in 1958, for example, that one of Britain's aims was 'to maintain political conditions favourable to our trading requirements throughout the world, and especially in the Middle East'. An interdepartmental Whitehall group noted in 1968 the 'need in developing countries for an economic and political climate attractive to expatriate capital, and the advantages of the status quo both to security and to low prices'.[3]

'The broad aim', the Foreign Office noted in 1968, 'is to inhibit undue governmental interference in the international oil trade': Britain should 'oppose, or at least attempt to moderate' resolutions in the United Nations that would encourage governments to 'expropriate or acquire too direct a control over Western oil investments'.[4]

British planners were at pains to counter the trend towards nationalisation since 'expropriation nearly always results in a measure of loss for the UK interests involved'. This policy was promoted in the knowledge that nationalisation embodied 'the hope that a large share of the profits may be retained locally and increased funds be made available for local investment'.[5] Thus British policy-makers were perfectly aware that in opposing nationalisation they were also opposing likely improvements in the welfare of the people of those countries.

This aim of ensuring favourable investment climates for big business – and countering governments who do not – has been the primary goal of numerous post-war British and US military interventions, in Iran, Kenya, Indonesia, British Guiana, Central America and elsewhere. This is also the root of Britain's global economic policy, promoted in bilateral 'aid' programmes, the World Bank and International Monetary Fund's 'structural adjustment' programmes and in the shaping of the rules of the World Trade Organisation. The consequences of promoting privatisation and economic liberalisation have often been devastating for hundreds of millions of people around the world. The most basic of British goals bears significant responsibility for maintaining, often deepening, global poverty.

The files indicate that strategies to address Third World poverty are to be opposed except where they enhance British business interests. The Foreign Office noted in 1968, for example, that:

> We should for the time being adopt a 'heads down' attitude in regard to proposals which, however, desirable in themselves, would throw a significantly greater strain upon our balance of payments, eg commodity schemes directed primarily to raise prices rather than at stability of markets.[6]

Another report from the same year, 1968, noted that Britain should assist economic development in the poorest countries 'especially those which are or can be expected to become important sources of raw materials or important markets for British goods and services'.[7]

Britain's 'aid' programme was thus seen as 'a weapon in the armoury of foreign policy', in the words of the Foreign Office in 1958. Ten years later, it similarly stated that:

> We must ensure that our aid programme supports not only the developmental needs of recipient countries but also our own commercial and foreign policies . . . Wherever possible we should try to shape our aid programme to fit more appropriately the pattern of our trade and investment interests in different countries.[8]

This role for 'aid' has been long understood by planners: the forerunner of the modern aid programme was the Colonial Development Corporation, which was established after the Second World War 'to promote and undertake the expansion of the supplies for colonial foodstuffs, raw materials and other commodities', a 1947 Cabinet memorandum reads.[9]

Critical to achieving these basic economic goals is Britain's political power – or 'prestige' or 'status' as it is variously referred to in the planning files. Promoting British prestige is often seen as an end in itself; indeed British planners have traditionally been obsessed with their standing in the world, and this factor has often been more important than economic goals in deciding policy.

The Foreign Office commented in 1958, for example, that 'there is no alternative to remaining a Power with interests in many parts of the world' for two reasons. The first is that 'the UK is not self-sufficient' and 'must maintain and expand our level of trade or lose our standard of life'. The second is that 'our prosperity is closely linked to the maintenance of the sterling area [the large part of the world where the pound was then the dominant currency] and to the status of the pound'. Both of these depended on 'our ability to preserve our influence in the world'.[10]

As the Foreign Office observed in 1968:

> For the foreseeable future our direct economic world-wide interests will require us to do what we can to maintain and increase our existing influence outside Europe. Indeed, in terms of stark economic interest, we cannot afford to lose such influence.[11]

In 1950, at a time when Britain was increasingly being forced to 'decolonise', the Foreign Office had warned:

> If the United Kingdom were voluntarily to abandon her position or political influence in selected areas, she would probably find herself not only without economic access to those areas but unable, through loss of prestige, to prevent a further involuntary decline in her influence elsewhere and consequently a general decline in the strength of the Western powers.[12]

Eight years later, in 1958, the Foreign Office similarly warned of the dangers of decolonisation occurring too quickly:

> Our remaining colonial territories are likely to be in many, if not most years, net contributors to our gold and dollar reserves. Premature withdrawal would lead to collapse of markets and sources of supply for the United Kingdom.

However, 'timely grants of independence would not endanger economic links with the United Kingdom' which were seen as 'sacrifices to maximise long term investment in colonies'.[13]

Maintaining such 'great power' status will only come at a price. The Cabinet Office noted in 1960, for example, that:

> There are many desirable ways of using our resources at home, especially the improvement of our standard of living through better social services and the

increasing of our wealth through productive investment. But we cannot exert influence in the world
unless we devote resources sufficient to underwrite
our external responsibilities.[14]

Therefore, the price for the British elite to maintain its global
prestige will be paid by the general public.

Possessing nuclear weapons is another way Britain maintain
their status in the world. The Cabinet Office in 1960, for
example, noted that in the 1950s 'our influence throughout the
world was enhanced' by 'being a nuclear power with a
significant potential both in weapons and delivery systems'. It
noted that 'unilateral nuclear disarmament is, of course, within
our power' but this would threaten Britain's security and 'would
undermine our standing in the Atlantic Alliance and in the
world as a whole'.[15] It was largely to uphold the British position
with the US that Attlee's Labour government acquired nuclear
weapons after the war.

The twin goals of ensuring favourable investment climates
and maintaining 'great power' status have been especially
important in three regions – the Middle East, South-east Asia
and Southern Africa.

In the Middle East, oil has of course been of paramount
importance; the Foreign Office had described the region's oil in
1947 as 'a vital prize for any power interested in world influence
or domination'. Prime Minister Harold Wilson's private
secretary, Oliver Wright, wrote in 1964 that:

We have really only two interests in the Middle East.
The first is access on reasonable terms to Middle East
oil. The second is overflying rights across the Middle
East barrier so that we may get to the other parts of the
world where our presence is necessary.[16]

In the Middle East as elsewhere the British strategy under
'decolonisation' was to ensure that power passed to local
clients. In this way, control over oil could be maintained. The

Cabinet Office observed in 1958, for example, that in the Middle East many countries have

> evolved to a point which makes it impossible to subject them to further tutelage . . . The basic task which confronts the United Kingdom in the Middle East is thus to pass smoothly from the previous patron–client relationship, suitable to our former strategic needs, to a new and more equally balanced commercial relationship which will preserve for as long as possible the continued supply of oil as a mutually advantageous basis of trade.[17]

Not only Arab countries but also Iran were important for oil. Indeed, Iran had a particular importance, as the Joint Intelligence Committee noted in 1961:

> Iran is the only source of Middle Eastern oil which is not under the control of an Arab government, and present production could be considerably increased in an emergency. This strengthens the West's hand vis-à-vis the Arab oil producing countries.[18]

Noticeably absent from the government's planning record is mention of the concerns of the people of the region. Nowhere that I have seen in any of these files, covering three decades, are the interests or wishes of the inhabitants of the Middle East even considered.

South-east Asia was also recognised as critical, mainly owing to British investments in the region, notably Malaya. The war in Malaya in the 1950s was described by the Foreign Office as 'very much in defence of [the] rubber industry'. It was fought at a time when Malaya was the largest net earner of dollars in the sterling area, due mainly to its rubber and tin exports, then partly in the hands of British companies. By 1962, British companies had invested £810 million in South-east Asia. A Foreign Office paper noted two other interests in the region – that sea and air routes from Britain to Australia and New

Zealand pass through it, and that it was a 'conspicuous battlefield in the cold war'.[19]

Southern Africa, and especially South Africa, has always been of primary importance to British planners as a field for commercial investment – a priority which was never seriously upset through the long decades of apartheid. A Foreign Office paper from 1964 notes that in 1961 the return on British investment in the region was £124 million, 26 per cent of the global total. A Cabinet Office study of 1959 summed up the role of Southern Africa:

> General interests of the West will be: (1) excluding Sino-Soviet infiltration and keeping local governments and populations on our side or, at least, benevolently neutral; (2) developing trade and guarding access to raw materials.[20]

A 1967 Cabinet Office report referred to the international debates over the racist regimes in Rhodesia and South Africa, and stated that 'apart from this our major interests in both Middle and Southern Africa in the long run are economic and are substantial'. 'Our only political interest' in the region, it added, 'is to do what we can to create conditions . . . in which we can pursue our important economic interests to the best advantage'. This meant that 'we should positively seek to create in Middle African states an atmosphere conducive to British trade and investment and to the presence of British nationals'.

As regards apartheid South Africa, 'we should continue to make it clear . . . that we cannot contemplate economic or political warfare with South Africa'. Rather, South Africa 'is likely to remain impregnable for a long time to come and must therefore be left to evolve in whatever way her own internal pressures dictate', while 'we are prepared to do business with South Africa and the Portuguese colonies', referring to Mozambique and Angola. The most important issue overall was to 'have regard to the protection of our investments and other economic interests'.[21]

If anyone believes that the interests of mere Africans have ever had anything to do with British policy towards Africa, they should read these files.

Seeing Africa primarily as a source of raw materials and a field for investment was a direct continuation of pre-war and immediate post-war policy. Foreign Secretary Ernest Bevin noted in 1948, for example, that the basic need was 'to develop the African continent and to make its resources available to all' (i.e., Britain). This echoed the view of Field Marshall Montgomery, who the previous year had noted the 'immense possibilities that exist in British Africa for development' and 'the use to which such development could be put to enable Great Britain to maintain her standard of living, and to survive'. 'These lands contain everything we need', he wrote, such as minerals, food and labour. But, he said, 'there must be a grand design for African development as a whole'. Britain needed to develop the continent since the African 'is a complete savage and is quite incapable of the developing the country [sic] himself'.[22]

Latin America was portrayed even more starkly as simply a source of raw materials. A 1958 Foreign Office paper stipulated two British aims:

(1) Promotion of trade and good relations. Latin America is an important source of raw materials for the United Kingdom and in some cases might become a vital one if the delivery of supplies from other parts of the world were to be interrupted, eg, oil, tin, copper and meat; (2) The retention in the Western camp of an economically rich area which has comparatively secure communications and is at present opposed to communist penetration.[23]

The importance of America and Europe

Two fundamental pillars of British foreign policy today are the special relationship with the US and the role inside the

European Union. The first has been a core feature of Whitehall's planning since the early 1940s; the second since at least the early 1960s when British planners made the decision to join the then EEC.

In 1968 the Foreign Office wrote that:

> If we want to exercise a major influence in shaping world events and are prepared to meet the costs we need to be influential with a much larger power system than we ourselves possess. The only practical possibilities open to us are to wield influence with Western Europe or the United States or both.[24]

Since Britain's imperial decline had led to diminishing ability to impose itself unilaterally around the globe, London essentially joined forces with the world's superpower to preserve British interests and Western dominance. British officials opted for a special relationship with the US during the Second World War, both to survive and as part of a vision for the post-war world. By 1945 they were talking of acting as a 'junior partner in an orbit of power predominantly under American aegis'.[25] The idea of Britain and European allies acting as a 'third force' between the US and Soviet Union – which planners had dabbled with in the late 1940s – was soon rejected. The price of playing second lieutenant to Washington – which involved the US displacing Britain from parts of the globe – was one that British planners (albeit often reluctantly) agreed to pay for the benefit of maintaining a residual great-power status and commercial interests.

US post-war planning envisaged nothing short of control of the entire non-Soviet world, and especially the global economy, well documented by several US analysts. In 1949 the Foreign Office noted the 'importance of our maintaining control of the periphery [around the Soviet Union] which runs round from Oslo to Tokyo'. 'This policy', it noted, 'should be concerted with the United States'.[26] These British planners, rooted in imperial ideology, cannot be accused of under-ambition: the whole planet is an object to be controlled; they are restricted only by the means available and the extent of opposition.

'Our partnership with the United States is an existing source of world power . . . and our status in the world will largely depend on their readiness to treat us as their closest ally', the Cabinet Office wrote in 1960. 'From our point of view the alliance with the United States is the most important single factor in our foreign policy', the Foreign Office wrote four years later. It added that 'the possibility of a hostile United States reaction is as considerable a deterrent to our adopting a given policy as the certainty of United States support is an encouragement'. The special relationship goes so deep that 'even the exasperation we occasionally feel for each other's habits and views is a family affair'.[27]

The essential component of the special relationship, as I have argued in *Web of Deceit* and elsewhere, is British support for US aggression (and vice versa, especially in the earlier post-war period). Another feature of the special relationship is a de facto division of the world into US and British zones of influence.

British planners analysed the various regions of the world according to the extent of British interests, in a major 1958 report. They concluded that to achieve British and Western aims, 'in some parts the main burden must fall upon the United States', but in others Britain had to act itself to promote its aims. There were three key areas of the world: Europe and the Middle East; South-east Asia and Africa; and the Far East and Latin America. The latter was a US preserve and 'we can therefore afford to leave them to the US, whose resources are great enough to manage them'. At the other end of the scale came Europe and the Middle East, where Britain had major specific interests. And 'in between' were South-east Asia and Africa, which Britain 'cannot afford to abandon or transfer to another power'.[28]

Britain thus needed to preserve some unilateral means of intervention in the first two areas, for which the US usually provided strong support (US opposition to the British invasion of Egypt in 1956 being a notable exception). In 1947, Foreign Secretary Bevin proposed to the US a review of the situation in the Middle East 'for the purpose of arriving at a gentleman's understanding in regard to a common policy and joint responsibility throughout the area'.[29] Although in some cases – for example, Iran – the US sought to replace Britain's primary external role with its own, in many others it was happy to leave the controlling role to Britain. The Gulf states, for example, remained a British preserve with Britain continuing to have important unilateral interests in Iraq and Jordan.

In the earlier post-war period, the US also looked to Britain to continue its colonial role in Africa and South-east Asia, generally approving of British (and other European) 'development' plans and the reassertion of European political control. The idea of the US as an opponent of post-war European colonialism is simply false. A 1957 National Security Council report on Africa, for example, declared that the US wanted sub-Saharan Africa to develop 'in an orderly manner' towards independence 'in cooperation with the European powers now in control of large areas of the continent'.[30]

The US has always seen its junior partner as a collaborator in global intervention. Secretary of State Dean Rusk once told Harold Wilson that 'the US did not want to be the only country ready to intervene in any trouble spot in the world. We hoped the British would continue to uphold their world-wide responsibilities'. 'The US attaches the greatest importance to Britain's retaining a world power role', Rusk told Foreign Secretary Michael Stewart in Anglo-American talks in January 1966. He added that 'the British world role has, in a sense, a multiplier effect because of its influence on other nations'. The 'maintenance of British commitments around the world' was 'an essential element in the total Anglo-American relationship', Undersecretary of State George Ball told Wilson in September 1965. These discussions were taking place while the British were considering withdrawing from military bases 'East of Suez', against which the US was strongly lobbying London.[31]

The dangers of Britain acting as a US stooge – a not irrelevant issue in current circumstances – receive some recognition in the files. A Foreign Office paper from 1958 notes that 'the United Kingdom is already greatly dependent upon United States support' but 'we must never allow this to develop to the point where we seem to be little more than an instrument of United States policy'.[32] Some things, apparently, do change with time.

By the 1960s at least, Whitehall planners tended to view membership of the European Community as enhancing rather than undermining the special relationship with the US. As the Foreign Office observed in 1968, 'if we fail to become part of a more united Europe', Britain's links with the US 'will not be enough to prevent us becoming increasingly peripheral to US concerns'. It was believed that 'we can regain sufficient influence in world affairs to protect our interests overseas and those of other Western European countries' by joining the EEC. The Foreign Office Planning Staff stated in 1968 that 'it is the hope of bringing our economic influence to bear more effectively in the political field that constitutes the principal motive of our application to join the EEC'.[33]

The aim of British planners has always been to ensure that a cohesive Atlantic Alliance operates under US hegemony – a role which planners and the media currently refer to as a 'bridge' between the US and EU. The Foreign Office wrote in 1972 that

> The UK will, in its own interests, take on at times the role of a Trojan Horse . . . [in the EEC] . . . but its effectiveness in this role will depend on . . . not appearing to act as a US stooge.[34]

The US appears to have understood the British role in the same way. Undersecretary of State George Ball told President Johnson in 1966 that Britain should be 'applying her talents and resources to the leadership of Western Europe' and that the US should be encouraging British membership of the EEC. Crucially, this British role would 'provide the balance' in

Europe that 'might tend to check the dangerous tendencies which French nationalism is already producing'.[35]

Today, the danger to British and US interests is less nationalism in the EU than federalism, and especially federalism that challenges US hegemony in the Atlantic Alliance; it is this that the British Trojan Horse continues to fend off, partly on behalf of its US ally, notably in debates about an EU military capability.

One question often asked today is why don't British planners throw in their lot with the EU entirely and, some would also argue, attempt to make the EU a counter-balance to the US. The question is naive (under current political structures): it ignores the fact that Whitehall has traditionally regarded the special relationship with the US as its single greatest source of power. And it also forgets the fact that the British role in the EU is precisely to play a supportive role to the US.

The files contain a further reason why Britain rejected the idea of a 'third force Europe' as it was called in a long report by the Foreign Secretary in 1968: that if a 'Third Force Europe' really succeeded there would be a considerable risk that Germany would be the dominant power in it'.[36]

Principal threats

The major threat to British foreign policy – aside from the public at home and the UN – has been independent nationalist forces. These movements have challenged Western control over their resources and the basic British economic goals outlined above. Many nationalist forces in the past were relatively benign, and Britain's opposition to them shows how London has traditionally set itself against groups and governments wanting to address the poverty endemic in many countries of the world.

In 1958 the Cabinet Office noted 'the emergence of fervid nationalism as a driving force in the Middle East and Asia' and lamented that it was leading to:

attacks on our colonial, strategic and commercial
interests which we have been unable to resist by force,
partly because of trends in home and world opinion,
and partly by the prohibitive cost of conquering and
occupying territory.[37]

The 'principal current problem' was understood in a US
intelligence report as confrontation 'between Arab nationalism
and Western strategic and commercial interests'. Such Arab
nationalism 'threatened the ability of the Western powers to
control developments', the US State Department later commented, in an analysis that seems relevant to Iraq today. This
threat was compounded by the then leader of Third World
nationalism, Egyptian President Nasser, who was understood
by Britain's Joint Intelligence Committee to have 'secured
widespread popular . . . support in the Middle East and has a
certain popularity in parts of Africa'.[38]

Policy was thus to counter such forces, often under the public
pretext of countering the Soviet Union. By 1958 – a tumultuous
year for Britain and the US in the Middle East, when the pro-
British Iraqi regime was overthrown by a nationalist government that joined with Syria and Egypt in countering Anglo-
American hegemony over the region – British files refer to 'an
unwritten commitment to the United States to join with them
in . . . stopping Soviet and "neutralist" influence spreading'.[39]
The latter half of the 1950s was a high point in covert planning
to undermine and oust heretic governments, perhaps
comparable to the present period where widespread regime
change is also on the agenda.

A particular threat was posed by the Cuban revolution of
1959, which overthrew the Batista dictatorship and brought
Fidel Castro to power. British officials were terrified that the
revolution would spread:

A new explosive form of radical nationalism has
appeared in Cuba which may well influence policies of
other governments and possibly cause further

revolutions . . . There is a danger that Cuba's neutralist anti-American example may be followed by some other Latin American states.[40]

A year later the Cuban threat had grown. The Joint Intelligence Committee wrote that:

Castroism still retains much of its popular appeal. If, in the longer term, the Cuban revolution succeeds in achieving a stable regime which appears to meet the aspirations of the depressed classes, there will be a serious risk that it will inspire similar revolutions elsewhere in Latin America.[41]

Britain set itself against the Cuban revolution knowing that it offered much to the people of Latin America. Rather than Castroism, Britain preferred the 'orderly and stable development of Latin America' which was important to Britain not only 'as a member of the Western Alliance but also from the point of view of the protection of the extensive British national interests in the area'.[42]

By 1970 the JIC was noting Cuba's 'dramatic social improvements, eg in the virtual eradication of illiteracy and unemployment and in the fields of health and education'. These features 'set Cuba apart from its neighbours'; where it was closer to them was in the 'traditional Latin American pattern of authoritarian government' and the 'coercive machinery' used by the Cuban government – i.e., forms of repression also used by British allies in the region, but without any of the improvements in welfare that Cuba could offer.[43]

Favoured clients needed to be kept in power – elites who would counter popular forces in their country. A similar principle applied at home, since it was understood by planners that the British public were also sympathetic to nationalist forces overseas. This reflected deeply elitist beliefs on the part of British policy-makers. For example, a Colonial Office minute from 1946 observed that:

> A major civilising influence comes from the action of
> the elite among a community, but only if the social
> structure permits the natural elite to emerge from the
> average ruck.

In the Middle East this required alliances with 'traditional'
ruling groups which would support Western interests, a policy
often well understood by planners as supporting 'reactionary'
forces against 'progressive' ones.[44]

The very thin basis of British foreign policy is clearly revealed
in these files: that fundamental British policies invariably do
not – and are understood not to – benfit people overseas, but
harm them. They also have nothing to do with promoting the
interests of the British population as a whole, but rather the
interests of a political and economic elite in whose interest
policy is made. Basic British goals also have nothing to do with
promoting the grand principles intended for public consumption, but with maintaining Britain's political status in the
world and with organising the global economy to benefit
British, and Western, businesses.

PART III

TERROR, AGGRESSION

9

FRIENDLY TERRORISTS: NEW LABOUR'S KEY ALLIES

There are certain issues which it is not done to mention in respectable circles, and one of these is British involvement in terrorism.

If we define 'terrorism' as the systematic use of violence and intimidation for political ends, then there are two kinds of terrorism in the world today: on the one hand, the campaigns of private networks like al Qaeda; on the other, the violence promoted and sponsored by states. The latter operates on a considerably greater scale, yet its perpetrators receive little or no attention in the mainstream media – particularly when they are British allies. Indeed, on any rational indicator, during a supposed 'war against terrorism' Britain counts as one of the leading supporters of terrorism in the world. Moreover, Britain's support to states promoting terrorism has been noticeably stepped up following the invasion of Iraq.

Russia: Another special relationship

Russian atrocities in Chechnya have worsened throughout 2003 and 2004, according to human-rights groups. When Russia invaded the province in 1999, the capital, Grozny, was flattened in a ferocious attack by indiscriminate bombing that killed thousands. Since then Chechnya has been pacified with executions, torture, rape and hundreds of 'disappearances'. Overall, untold thousands of people have been killed, tens of thousands have been forced to flee and, according to the Russian press, tens of thousands of Chechen children suffer from traumas, congenital pathologies and illnesses caused by the war. While Britain was busy invading Iraq in March–April 2003, Human Rights Watch was documenting the highest rate of 'disappearances' since the beginning of the conflict in Chechnya and concluding that violations were increasing and that the situation was 'abysmal'.[1]

In June 2003 Russia expanded the conflict still further by conducting a series of operations in the neighbouring republic of Ingushetia, replicating many of the abuses committed in Chechnya itself. Ingushetia houses around 80,000 refugees who have fled the Chechen conflict; it had been a relatively safe, peaceful area until Russian forces began attempting to close the camps and force many of the refugees back to Chechnya in December 2002. The result has been 'numerous cases of arbitrary detention, ill-treatment and looting' as well as killings, according to Human Rights Watch.[2]

The Blair government has essentially backed Russian President Vladimir Putin's strategy in Chechnya all the way. While Grozny was being flattened at the beginning of 2000, Defence Secretary Geoff Hoon was speaking of engaging Russia 'in a constructive bilateral defence relationship'. Blair himself has been the most outspoken apologist for Russian terror in Chechnya and, at numerous meetings with President Putin, has consistently publicly defended Russia and praised its leader. Indeed, Blair has even boasted of this support, once conceding that 'I have always been more understanding of the Russian position [regarding Chechnya], perhaps, than many others'.[3]

Meanwhile, relations with the Russian military have deepened and none of the potential levers available to London – an annual aid programme, a large line of export credit and major trade relations – has been used to press Moscow. The government, and much of the media, have maintained the fiction that the only option to pressure Russia is all-out war.

Blair met Putin in June 2003 just as the Russian military was reactivating its campaign to widen the conflict into Ingushetia. He told parliament that he would mention Chechnya in his talks with Putin, adding that 'it's also important that we support Russia in her action against terrorism'. In a joint press conference Blair said, 'I think the leadership of President Putin offers not just tremendous hope for Russia, but also for the wider world. I would pay tribute to him as a partner and as a friend'. There was only one possible allusion to Chechnya when Blair said that the two leaders had discussed 'all those things you would expect us to cover'. Foreign Office minister Denis MacShane has even referred to *'allegations* of human rights violations' in the province.[4]

At this time Blair also reportedly claimed, without offering any evidence, that Chechens had fought in Iraq against US and British forces. He repeated this allegation in parliament in September citing 'US military sources'. A few months later, the government admitted that 'we have no evidence of Chechen terrorists being in Iraq'.[5]

This meeting took place three months after a referendum in Chechnya blatantly designed to secure a win for Moscow's position on a mandate for a new constitution for the province. It took place 'in atrocious circumstances – widespread arbitrary detention, daily disappearances and an overall atmosphere of impunity', according to Human Rights Watch. This was good enough for Blair, who praised the process by telling the Russians that 'I think it is absolutely right that you resolve [the situation] through the policy process and political dialogue that you have engaged in'.[6]

Human Rights Watch says that Blair praised the election 'as if it were a substantial step towards a stable democracy' when in fact it was 'a fiction'. Lord Judd, the Council of Europe's special rapporteur on Chechnya, resigned in protest at the conditions in which the referendum took place.[7] Elections followed in

October, also condemned by various international organisations as blatantly rigged, and which guaranteed victory for
Moscow's candidate, Akhmed Kadyrov (who was assassinated
in May 2004).

British policy has changed not a jot. Its support for 'democracy'
has always been only for the cameras: Russia had already
successfully destroyed the previous Chechen government of
Aslan Maskhadov, which had been democratically elected, and
had received no less support from Whitehall.

Britain continues to help Putin by consistently pushing the
line that Russia is engaged in 'counter-terrorist operations' in
Chechnya. Meanwhile, evidence has emerged of the Russian
security services' involvement in causing the September 1999
blasts which provided the pretext for the Russian invasion in
the first place. There is now also evidence that Russian forces in
Chechnya are deliberately planting mines and organising
provocations which are then attributed to Chechen guerrillas.[8]

By 2004, human-rights atrocities in Chechnya were once
again increasing. Russians troops were committing numerous
atrocities such as 'disappearances', torture and attacks on
civilians in various parts of the province. Of Chechnya's
population of 800,000, around 100,000 remained displaced
from their homes. According to Human Rights Watch:

> Russian forces round up thousands of men in raids,
> loot homes, physically abuse villagers and frequently
> commit extrajudicial executions. Those detained face
> beatings and other forms of torture, aimed at coercing
> confessions or information about Chechen forces.
> Federal forces routinely extort money from detainees'
> relatives as a condition for release.[9]

Britain has rejected the call for an international tribunal on
war crimes in Chechnya as 'counter-productive' – such
processes being reserved for official enemies such as Saddam.[10]
While Putin deepens a system of authoritarian control over
Russia as a whole, undermining political pluralism and media

freedom, Blair scrupulously avoids any comment, let alone action, which has the potential to offend him.

This is 'the most serious human rights crisis of the new decade in Europe', according to Human Rights Watch. Yet it is not true to say, as the *Guardian* has done, that 'in Chechnya, the West looks the other way'.[11] British policy is not to turn a blind eye to Russian terror: it is to support it.

Colombia: Stepping up support

The Colombian military and police are the worst human-rights offenders in the Western hemisphere. The line peddled by London and Washington is that these forces are engaged in a fight against drugs and terrorism perpetrated by guerrillas and drug-traffickers. The reality is that while the guerrilla groups certainly engage in terrorism and drug-trafficking, the main responsibility for both lies with the state and the right-wing paramilitaries. According to a UN report from 2000, the Colombian military tolerate and collaborate with the illegal paramilitary groups:

> The state bears the responsibility for the present proportions and complexity of the paramilitary problem. The direct and indirect aiding and abetting of paramilitarism is aggravated by the absence of any effective policy to combat it.[12]

The main targets of killings are civil society activists such as trade-union leaders, teachers, land-reform and human-rights campaigners and peasant and indigenous leaders, at least 15,000 of whom have been killed in the past ten years.

The war in Colombia is a complex one, but is essentially over the control of resources in a deeply unequal society: the elite, especially the large landowners, control most of the wealth while the majority of the population lives in poverty. Three per cent of landowners own more than 70 per cent of the land; 57 per cent of the farmers subsist on less than 3 per cent of the land. The basic role of the state is to marginalise the popular forces and ensure that Colombia's resources – notably oil – remain in the correct hands.

US strategy is to support this. Since 2000, US military aid of more than £2 billion has been poured into Colombia, which is the second largest recipient after Israel. The 'war on drugs' is a cover for supporting the Colombian state and military in its acts to counter progressive forces calling for social change. As Doug Stokes of the University of Aberystwyth has pointed out, given the close links between the Colombian military and paramilitaries, 'in effect, US military aid is going directly to the major terrorist networks throughout Colombia, who traffic cocaine into US markets to fund their activities'.[13] US training is also provided to some Colombian brigades named by Human Rights Watch as involved in paramilitary killings.

Britain has long provided aid to Colombia outside of media and parliamentary scrutiny. The SAS were sent to Colombia in 1989 and appear to have been there ever since. This was reported only briefly in the early 1990s; since then the government has refused to disclose any details.

Trade and Foreign Office minister Baroness Symons noted in October 1997 that Britain had provided £14 million in 'drugs related assistance' since 1989, 'focusing mainly on law enforcement, training, demand reduction and alternative development'. In November 1999 the government said that 'UK military assistance is provided to Colombia to meet specific requests'. Examples of this included 'some assistance to the counter-narcotics authorities', while 'advisory visits and information exchanges have taken place on operations in urban theatres, counter-guerrilla strategy, and psychiatry'. It added that 'military assistance offered to the Colombians generally includes human rights elements'. In January 2000, Foreign Office minister Keith Vaz told parliament that 'we should give as much support as possible to the government of President Pastrana' – as extensive human-rights violations and killings continued.[14]

The election of President Alvaro Uribe in August 2002 has resulted in strengthened relations with London. As a large landowner himself, Uribe was implicated in massacres of peasant and trade-union leaders when he was a state governor in the mid-1990s. Under his presidency the level of political assassinations has doubled, the press reported in late 2003. Human-rights violations by the state and its allies are higher than ever while the instruments established to investigate them have been disabled. Mass arrests of trade unionists and human-rights defenders, false charges and imprisonment and media censorship are widespread. Uribe's rhetoric about terrorism has hardened while paramilitaries continue to maintain clandestine alliances with units of the Colombian army. The government has avoided seriously challenging the paramilitaries or rooting out the corrupt government officials who work with known human-rights abusers.[15]

In this context, the British government has invoked the standard pretext for increasing support to repressive regimes – that the human-rights situation has improved. In March 2004 Foreign Office minister Bill Rammell was noting 'improvements' and 'some impressive results in some areas of fundamental rights'.[16] Only six months earlier, in September 2003, 80 human-rights organisations had accused Uribe of promoting state terror against civilians.[17]

The Blair government held a carefully orchestrated international donors' meeting in London in June 2003 that declared admiration for Uribe's progress on human rights. This ignored reports by Colombian and international NGOs that violations had increased, and by the Colombian Commission of Jurists, which reported that in Uribe's first year in government there had been nearly 7,000 political killings and 'disappearances', worse than the average throughout the preceding four-year Pastrana presidency. Britain thus opened the door for Colombia to receive a new round of international loans. Foreign Office minister Bill Rammell said that 'all government representatives present reaffirmed their strong political support for the Colombian government'.[18]

This meeting was apparently organised on Blair's personal

initiative and was fully backed by Prime Minister Aznar of Spain, the two governments operating as a pro-US axis in Europe. The details were worked out by the British embassy in Bogota in consultation with Uribe's team. The following month Rammell gave a speech to the British-Colombian Chamber of Commerce saying that 'vital to business is the need of the Colombian government to work on improving its international image, to enhance its investment prospects'.[19]

Meanwhile, British military support has also been boosted. In July 2003 the *Guardian* revealed that Britain was 'secretly stepping up military assistance to Colombia', reporting that the SAS were training the narcotics police, the Fuerza Jungla, and that military advice was being provided to the army's new counter-guerrilla mountain units. Also, there was a 'surge in the supply of military hardware and intelligence equipment' while Britain was providing assistance in setting up an intelligence centre and joint intelligence committee.

This aid made Britain the second largest military supporter of Colombia. It was also provided secretly: Whitehall refused to disclose the extent of its military involvement 'on the grounds of national security', the *Guardian* reported. The export of arms rose by 50 per cent from 2001 to 2002 with supplies including missile technology, components for combat helicopters and explosives ostensibly for anti-drugs operations. The new intelligence support builds on work begun in the early 1990s when an MI6 station head was sent to Bogota to start an anti-narcotics operation. When New Labour came into power this was expanded and coordinated by an MI6 officer in London.[20]

A string of senior British military officials have been despatched by the Blair government to Bogota to advise the Colombian military. At least ten visits were made by MoD experts from 2000 to 2003 to advise on 'counter-terrorism' (to the forces, that is, responsible for much of the terrorism in the country). Senior Colombian army officers have also attended training courses in Britain.[21]

There is a suggestion that this training will improve human

rights, but the Colombian military is responsible for its violations not by accident or through ignorance. As David Rhys-Jones of the Colombia Solidarity Campaign has pointed out, this training 'is part of a concerted and active policy to nullify the opposition and terrify the general population into further submission'. Indeed, some of Latin America's most notorious killers have been graduates of 'human rights' courses.[22] Virtually every human rights and trade union organisation in Colombia has called for British military aid to be frozen.

British support for state terror in Colombia is not entirely unconnected with BP's massive investment in the country. BP's £2 billion project in the Casanare oilfields is Britain's largest commercial investment in the whole of Latin America and controls half of Colombia's oil output. Baroness Symons said in October 1997 that 'Colombia's economy has been one of the most stable in the region' and 'it is that performance which has attracted substantial British investment to the country, to the point at which Britain is now the largest investor, even ahead of the United States'. In 2003, British investments in Colombia amounted to around $10 billion.[23]

BP chief executive Lord Browne is reported to be very close to Blair, while some of the Prime Minister's senior aides have close connections and friendships with senior BP executives. BP is also part of a group of companies in the US–Colombia business partnership which has lobbied the US administration to promote favourable US policies towards Colombia. BP is believed to have been involved in lobbying the Clinton administration to push for a military solution that became Plan Colombia.[24]

Oil operations and human-rights violations are two sides of the same coin. BP receives protection from the Colombian military and has recruited ex-SAS soldiers to protect its oilfields and infrastructure. Former SAS soldiers have reportedly secretly trained the Colombian police in counter-insurgency tactics on BP oil rigs. The Ocensa oil-pipeline company, in which BP is the major shareholder, was reported in 1998 to have bought and supplied paramilitary equipment for the protection of its pipeline to a Colombian army brigade which had been implicated in two massacres by right-wing death squads.[25] This complex nexus of actors and interests ensures that resources remain in the correct hands.

Israel: Taking sides

One of the great myths promoted by the media has been Britain's even-handedness in the Israeli-Palestinian conflict. This myth was of supreme importance in drumming up support for the invasion of Iraq – many MPs, it appears, were prepared to support the invasion in the belief that Blair would then use supposed British influence over Washington to press the US for a solution to the Arab-Israeli conflict.

It is amazing that such a theory managed to gain widespread currency. For one thing, the US has never had any intention of pressing Israel for a solution on anything except US-Israeli terms. For another, there is no evidence that London has much influence in Washington anyway, least of all in the context of Israel. But thirdly, and what I will concentrate on here, the Blair government itself has consistently acted as an apologist for Israeli actions.

The period since the invasion of Iraq has seen the continued Israeli expansion of illegal settlements and a descent into spiralling violence in the occupied territories. The toll of rising desperation has been especially gruesome for the millions of Palestinians living under Israeli occupation and for those Palestinians killed by Israeli forces, as well as for Israeli civilians murdered in horrific suicide bombings.

According to the UN, by the time of the invasion of Iraq, half the Palestinian population in the occupied territories were unemployed and two-thirds were living below the poverty line. A quarter of Palestinian children were suffering from acute or chronic malnutrition. Israel's policy of encircling Palestinian cities, together with its frequent military attacks, house demolitions and farmland clearances, have brought the Palestinian economy near to collapse. The plight of Palestinians in the occupied territories had reached such a point that even a British parliamentary committee had noticed it. A report of January 2004 notes that 'life under the occupation is becoming increasingly oppressive and increasingly inhuman'. Rates of malnutrition in Gaza and parts of the West Bank are similar to those in sub-Saharan Africa.[26]

It is instructive to view the Foreign Office's analysis of Israeli policy on settlements in the occupied territories. It notes that 42 per cent of the West Bank is now slated for settlement expansion and that:

> HMG, together with the rest of the international community, regard Israeli settlements in the territories which Israel occupied in June 1967 as illegal under international law (including under Article 49 of the Fourth Geneva Convention). Settlement activity is also politically damaging. It fuels Palestinian anger with Israel. And it strengthens the widespread belief among Palestinians that Israel is not interested in reaching a peace agreement through a two-state solution based on the 1967 borders.

The Foreign Office concludes that 'these are dark times for advocates of a lasting settlement in the Middle East'.[27]

Yet London's basic strategy has always been to blame 'both sides' for violence and to overlook the fact that one side is in illegal occupation of territory and, indeed, that Israel is responsible for far more deaths than the Palestinians. Blair's statements in particular have invariably been careful not to condemn Israel outright while the government has repeatedly adopted the Sharon line that Palestinian suicide bombings need to stop first before Israeli 'reprisals' would stop.

British arms exports were doubled from 2000 to 2001, reaching £22.5 million, in the year which marked a sharp escalation of Israeli aggression in the occupied territories. Supplies included small arms, grenade-making kits and components for a range of equipment such as armoured fighting vehicles, tanks and combat aircraft. In 2002 press reports noted that Britain was apparently blocking the export of some military items to Israel and considering them on a case by case basis. It was after this, however, that Whitehall approved the export of British spare parts to be used in US F-16 aircraft which were being used to target Palestinians. Throughout 2001/2002, 14 Israeli military officers were trained in Britain.[28]

Since the invasion of Iraq, London's policies have if anything hardened in support of Israel. On arms, the case-by-case review policy has resulted in exports falling from £22 million to £10 million. However, goods supplied include machine guns, rifles, ammunition, components for tanks and helicopters, leg irons, electric-shock belts, chemical and biological agents such as tear gas and categories covering mortars, rocket launchers, anti-tank weapons and military explosives.

Tony Blair assured parliament in February 2003 that in recent discussions with Israeli opposition leader, Amran Mitna, 'I made clear that there is no arms embargo on Israel. We continue to support Israel's right to defend itself'. Given the use to which Israel puts 'defence' equipment, this was a clear message of support. An official in the DTI's Trade Partners unit has similarly said that 'there was no question of treating applications for Israel more harshly or rigorously than [other countries]'. This is at least consistent since the illegal occupation, violence and terrorism which define Israeli military policy are indeed no worse than the practices of many other recipients of British arms.[29]

The British arming of Israel continues even as unarmed British citizens are shot in the occupied territories, three of them between December 2002 and May 2003. The Foreign Office has reportedly taken an extremely softly-softly approach to raising these killings with the Israelis.[30]

In early 2004 the British government gave assurances to the Israeli Defence Minister, Shaul Mofaz, that he would be immune from arrest for crimes against humanity on his visit to

London. Mofaz was the army chief of staff during Israel's brutal military reoccupation of the West Bank in 2002 and thus responsible for targeted assassinations and other violations of international law. Human-rights lawyers accused the government of a 'creative legal interpretation' to protect Mofaz from an investigation by Scotland Yard; the basis of their argument was that, since he was a serving government minister, he was immune from investigation.[31]

London has provided extraordinary de facto support to Israel concerning its building of the wall along the West Bank. Although the British government repeatedly says that it believes the construction of the wall to be illegal, its actions point in a different direction. In October 2003, Britain abstained on the UN Security Council vote declaring the construction of the wall to be illegal. Asked in parliament why it had so voted, Foreign Office minister Bill Rammell said that the declaration 'did not condemn suicide bombings and therefore did not acknowledge Israel's real security concerns'. What Britain wanted was 'a more balanced text'.[32]

Then in late 2003 the government also abstained on a UN General Assembly resolution proposal to seek the opinion of the International Court of Justice (ICJ) on the legality of the wall. Asked in parliament why, Foreign Office minister Baroness Symons said that 'we believe it inappropriate to take such action without the consent of both parties' – an extraordinary example of deference to Israel. This was followed in early 2004 by the Foreign Office lodging an objection at the ICJ which was scheduled to review the barrier's legality, citing technical reasons about the role of the court.[33]

This period has also seen Israel bomb Syria, in October 2003, in an action directed at 'a training camp used by terrorist organisations' allegedly including Islamic Jihad, which had claimed responsibility for an horrific suicide attack on a Haifa restaurant. Israel's obviously illegal action was condemned by France and Germany; yet the Foreign Office simply called on 'all sides to exercise restraint' and said that any Israeli actions to 'protect itself from terrorist attack . . . should be within international law'.[34]

Then in April 2004, Israeli Prime Minister Ariel Sharon announced a unilateral plan to annex six major West Bank settlement blocs and reject the universally recognised Palestinian right of return, as well as a pledge to withdraw from the settlements in Gaza (but with Israel retaining control of the borders). This would make permanent the Israeli occupation of the West Bank, renounce previous UN resolutions requiring Israeli withdrawal and scupper the two-state solution and the possibility of achieving a lasting solution to the conflict. As US analyst Stephen Zunes has pointed out, the plan is a direct challenge to the UN charter which forbids any country from expanding its territory through military force, 'effectively recognising the right of conquest'.

The plan has been warmly welcomed by both the US and Britain. Tony Blair delivered an amazing apologia for the plan in a joint press conference with President Bush, imploring the Palestinians to 'seize this opportunity' in Gaza and 'those parts of the West Bank that will be under their control'. No hint of criticism of Israeli intentions was mentioned, even though the plan undermines just about every public position that Britain has adopted on the need for a comprehensive peace plan. Press reports later suggested that the British government was to make clear to President Bush 'in private' that Britain could not sign up to Sharon's unilateral plan. Any evidence of such a policy has yet to emerge at the time of writing.[35]

The issue of trade sanctions against Israel – reserved for official enemies – is completely off the agenda. Rather, Israel continues to receive preferential trade treatment by the British government and the EU. Britain has designated Israel one of 14 favoured 'target markets'; when asked in parliament what plans the government had to change this status, a DTI official replied: 'None'.[36] Britain has consistently resisted calls for the EU's special trade and aid agreement with Israel to be cut off, despite the urging of the all-party Development Select Committee.

Worth £8.4 billion in EU exports to Israel and £5.3 billion in EU imports, trade could provide a significant lever. The EU, however, has moved in the opposite direction: in December 2003 EU ministers agreed further to liberalise EU markets to Israeli exports. By contrast, Britain has been very active in securing agreement in the EU to ban the political wing of Hamas and place its leaders on a terrorist blacklist. London has reportedly taken the lead in calling for strict European curbs on charities raising funds for Hamas.[37]

In 2003 a group of 30 Israeli Black Hawk helicopter and F-16 fighter pilots said they would no longer bomb Palestinian cities. They were promptly thrown out of the Israeli Air Force. 'This is us being terrorists', one captain, a pilot for 15 years, said.[38] Britain's refusal to take on Israel over settlements, the wall or anything else, and preference for 'constructive engagement' with an Israeli government (under Sharon) that has made plain its commitment to violence, constitute a programme of support for Israel.

What explains British policy? Many of the answers can be found in the secret files of more than 30 years ago. Consider, for example, a Foreign Office report from 1970 called 'Future British policy toward the Arab/Israel Dispute'. This report considers British options for its stance on the Arab-Israeli conflict and especially its effect on the alliance with the US. This report considers adopting first an overt pro-Israel policy, and then a pro-Arab policy. It rejects both, saying that: 'a pro-Israeli policy would destroy all hopes of preserving British economic and political interests in the Arab Middle East'; while a pro-Arab policy:

> would be hard or impossible to adopt: (a) because of British public and political commitment to Israel as an ideal and the political force of support for Israel in the country; (b) because of the pressure which the United States government undoubtedly exert on HMG to keep us in line in any public pronouncements or negotiations on the dispute.

It then considers the middle options, the first of which is 'active pursuit of a settlement without disassociation from the US'. The problem with this is that 'as long as we are associated with the US government in active policies toward the dispute, we shall confirm the Arab belief that we are pro-Israel'. It then considers another option of 'active neutrality', which would mean 'we should have to say and do things the US government did not like and to be more pro-Arab (or at least less pro-Israeli) than the Americans'. However, the disadvantages of this are the damage 'to our world-wide relationship with the US', that it would be criticised by some public opinion in Britain and that 'there is no prospect of a European political entity' playing a 'third force' role.

Therefore, the paper argues for 'the low risk policy', described as 'the less continuously active variant' of the last option above. 'This policy should mean, in practical terms, that our efforts should first and foremost take the form of private pressure upon the US to do all in their power to bring about a settlement'. This would mean Britain would have a 'strictly limited role' while 'modest contributions and not peace plans should be our aim'; that is, to continue doing business with the Arab world, including arms sales, and to maintain commercial links with Israel. In conclusion, it notes that:

> In terms of the national interest, there would be much to be gained by adopting a thoroughgoing pro-Arab policy . . . It would, however, be difficult to defend such a policy on grounds of principle and it would be extremely unpopular in this country. The US government would dislike it intensely and oppose it strongly if it entailed (as logically it should) showing sympathy for the Arab point of view in the international effort to help bring about a settlement. It would be incompatible with support for, or even acquiescence in, the US position in the quest for a settlement.[39]

The policy adopted then differs slightly from the New Labour approach. The evidence suggests that the Blair government is trying publicly to position itself in alignment with the 1970 stance, but in reality has tilted strongly towards Israel. The motives, however, may be the same: these documents openly recognise that it is the fear of upsetting the US which prevents Britain adopting a pro-Arab position.

Moreover, it was argued in files from 1969 that, even given Britain's massive stake in oil in the Middle East and the subsequent need to keep friendly relations with Arab despots, Britain's economic interests in Israel were also a factor. The Joint Intelligence Committee reported in 1969 that:

> rapid industrialisation [in Israel] is taking place in fields where British industry can readily supply the necessary capital goods . . . Israel is already a valuable trading partner with a considerable future potential in the industrial areas where we want to develop Britain as a major world-wide manufacturer and supplier.

Britain's ambassador to Israel added that:

> Israel is already a valuable trading partner for Britain, and . . . there is a high future potential for our economic relations with her . . . On the other hand, it seems hard to avoid the conclusion . . . that our prospects for profitable economic dealings with the Arab states are at best static, and may indeed over the long term inevitably decline.[40]

If this was the case then, it is even more so now, as Britain steps up its trade with Israel, especially in new technologies. It is this priority, together with maintaining special relations with Washington, that defines Whitehall's stance on the plight of the Palestinians.

And others

There are several other cases where Britain is backing state terror. In Nepal, Britain continues to supply military aid and training for security forces guilty of worse abuses and killings than the Maoist rebels they are fighting. In early 2004, Human Rights Watch reported violence on both sides but claimed that 'the Nepalese army has allegedly carried out extra-judicial executions of Maoists and villagers, arbitrary arrests, "disappearances", harassed and intimidated press and NGOs, and interfered in the work of the judiciary'.[41] This is in a conflict that has cost around 4,000 lives. Support for Nepal appears to be another coordinated strategy with the US, which is providing $27 million in military aid along with advisers.

After requests from Nepal for help, Blair 'assured every possible support to Nepal's fight against terrorism'. British military aid, amounting to around £3 million, was agreed in 2002 and involves helicopters and communications equipment. In early 2004 Britain gave the Nepalese army two used vertical-take-off aircraft to search out Maoist guerrillas – funding came from the government's Global Conflict Prevention Pool and was disclosed not in parliament but by British officials in Kathmandu to a Nepalese newspaper.[42]

Britain's 'special representative for Nepal', Jeffrey James, has said that 'Britain is committed to training and other non-lethal assistance to enable the security forces to counter any resumption of hostilities'. Dozens of Nepalese army officers are also being trained at establishments in Britain.[43]

This aid is to a regime in Kathmandu under a king who dismissed the elected government and appointed his own, postponing elections indefinitely. The regime is conducting a crackdown on all political opponents, essentially under the cover of a 'war against terrorism'. It is the most recent in a succession of Nepalese governments that have never seriously addressed the plight of the majority poor in the country or implemented serious land reforms, which explains the popularity of the Maoists in some rural areas.

The Major and Blair governments also provided substantial support to Turkey as it conducted horrific military operations against Kurds in the south-east of the country in the mid- to late 1990s. Three and a half thousand Kurdish villages were destroyed, making at least 1.5 million homeless and killing untold thousands in a war ostensibly against guerrillas of the Kurdish PKK but essentially an attempt to pacify the whole Kurdish region. Britain continued arms exports throughout this period, the Major government having increased them during the period of the worst atrocities in 1994–1996. Normal trade and diplomatic relations have also continued under New Labour which, as with Russian atrocities against Chechens, publicly backed the line that Ankara was fighting terrorism rather than – as was the reality – practising it.

As well as continuing trade and military relations, London has acted as Turkey's most effective advocate in Brussels for Turkey's bid to join the EU – a process which has hitherto led to some human-rights reforms in Turkey, but with torture and other domestic repression remaining widespread. By 2003–2004 hundreds of thousands of Kurds were still unable to return to their villages; many were actively prevented by Turkish security forces, others feared reprisals. Most Kurds continue to live in poverty in already overcrowded Turkish cities.

There is one more aspect of Turkey's horrific strategy for dealing with the Kurds that should give cause for concern for those engaged in a war against terrorism – the fact that for more than two decades the Turkish government funded and armed Islamic radicals in the south-east of the country to help crush the PKK rebels. Once the region was pacified and the PKK declared a unilateral ceasefire, the Turkish security forces tried to clamp down on the group that it had previously funded – the Hezbollah – and members began to look to other radical Islamic groups for support. Those other groups had also been tolerated by the Turks as they grew and sent many militant warriors to Afghanistan and Bosnia to fight in the jihad. It was individuals from these groups who drove the suicide bombs into the British consulate and HSBC bank in Istanbul in November 2003.[44]

This is yet another example of the cyclical nature of British and US foreign policy. Western priorities contribute to the growth of radical groups; these groups become enemies and commit gruesome acts; the Western response is to commit further gruesome acts, provoking the rise of more radical groups – all of which policies are justified at every step as a means of upholding the noblest virtues.

The list of British support for terrorism could go on. Some instances reveal more direct involvement, including the various past assassination attempts against foreign leaders conducted by Britain; the bomb attack on Libyan leader Colonel Qadafi in 1996 by a group funded, according to former MI5 officer David Shayler, by MI6; and British collusion with paramilitary groups in Northern Ireland. Such collusion led to at least 30 murders, according to the Stevens report released in April 2003, and may also have led to the bomb attacks in Dublin in 1974 that killed 26 people.[45]

The following chapters focus on two countries in particular where Britain has given its backing to campaigns of state terror: Nigeria and Indonesia.

10

NIGERIANS: WAR FOR OIL

Nigerians have long been victims of their own governments, a succession of which – mainly military – have abused the country since independence. Most leading political figures have apparently seen high office as an opportunity to plunder the country's revenues for their own personal gain; consequently, Nigeria has become one of the most corrupt countries in the world. A major reason for this is Nigeria's oil resources, which have enriched a tiny elite while at best hardly benefiting, and at worst actually impoverishing, the majority of Nigeria's population. After decades of oil production have produced almost $300 billion in revenues, per capita income is less than $300 a year.

Less well known is that Britain has played an important role in this state of affairs. The declassified files concerning the Nigerian civil war in the late 1960s clearly show British complicity in the Nigerian government's aggression against the region of Biafra, where an independence movement was struggling to secede from Nigeria. This brutal civil war resulted in between one and three million deaths; it also significantly helped to shape modern Nigeria, and not least the current division of oil revenues between the central government and the regions and people.

The struggle for an equitable sharing of resources is ongoing and the poverty-stricken people of Nigeria's oil-producing regions are among the most exploited in the world. They face a combination of the power of the Nigerian state and its 'security' forces, the oil companies and their Western backers. Current British policy provides an instructive example of the level of humanitarian concern in international relations.

Obasanjo versus Mugabe

One of Britain's key allies in Africa is Nigerian President Olusegun Obasanjo. The public could be forgiven for thinking that Zimbabwe has the most repressive African government of the day; in reality, Obasanjo's rule has been far more violent and bloody. In contrast to the media's portayal of Mugabe, there has been virtual silence on Nigeria's current regime, and even less said about British backing for it.

The Obasanjo government came to power in 1999 and was widely welcomed since it represented a return to civilian rule in Nigeria. Since then, however, around 10,000 people have been killed in inter-communal violence. The military has often openly fanned the tensions and indulged in atrocities of its own.[1]

In November 1999, the military massacred up to 2,000 people in Odi, Bayelsa state, after an armed gang killed 12 policemen. In October 2001 the military killed more than 200 unarmed civilians in towns across Benue state after the murder of 19 soldiers. No action has been taken against those soldiers responsible in either case. In 2003, mainly during the elections in April and May, hundreds of people were killed in Delta state in ethnic and political fighting. Nigerian security forces killed dozens of people in indiscriminate attacks against Ijaw villages.[2]

Meanwhile, throughout Nigeria as a whole, 'extrajudicial executions by the police remain a chronic problem' and 'the approach to law and order still appears to be primarily one of confrontation and violence rather than prevention and respect for the rights of suspects', according to Human Rights Watch.[3]

The oil-rich Delta state is the scene of routine human-rights violations by the military and ongoing protests by local communities about oil company operations, especially Shell, the leading Western oil company in the country. It is a militarised area; the army, navy and paramilitary mobile police are deployed at oil facilities across the Delta. Reports from fleeing refugees indicate that the Nigerian military is engaged in scorched-earth violence designed, like the Odi massacre, 'to teach the Ijaws a lesson'. Human Rights Watch notes that 'the military has responded to community protests (which are sometimes peaceful, but other times take on a violent or criminal nature) with indiscriminate reprisal attacks against entire towns and villages'.[4]

A variety of ethnic groups live in Nigeria's oil-producing areas, with Ijaws comprising the largest of the groups, numbering around 8 million, together with the Ogonis and others. They have failed to benefit from oil production while oil companies have been allowed to confiscate their land, collude with corrupt politicians in the capital and pollute their environment. When they protest, the oil companies call in the military to repress them further. The oil companies have thus remained complicit in many human-rights abuses, even after worldwide attention was focused on them following the execution of Ogoniland human-rights leader Ken Saro-Wiwa and nine others in 1995.

Britain's enduring policy is to back the Nigerian government by remaining silent on human-rights abuses by the military and oil companies, while offering training to dozens of Nigerian army officers at establishments in Britain. Before Tony Blair visited Nigeria in February 2002, Human Rights Watch called on him to raise the subject of human-rights abuses with Nigeria 'given the close ties between your government and that of President Obasanjo'. It noted in particular the massacres in October 2001 which 'President Obasanjo appeared to defend'.[5]

During this visit, however, Blair did not publicly raise human-rights issues either in the Delta or elsewhere in the country. Instead, he delivered a speech to the Nigerian parliament mentioning Britain's 'special bond with Nigeria' and saying that British companies were 'major investors' and that 'trade is growing'. He also managed to wish Nigeria good luck in the African Nations Cup. The only things he didn't mention in a long-ish speech were human rights and oil. A section in the speech on 'conflict' failed to mention anything about the conflict in the country he happened to be in. A section on 'governance' failed to say anything about governance in Nigeria or about how oil revenues were failing to reach virtually anyone outside the audience he was speaking to. This speech was delivered just four months after Blair had told the Labour party conference of the need to 'heal the scar on the conscience of the world', meaning Africa.[6]

In April 2003 Human Rights Watch again wrote to the British government. This time it was:

> to express our concern at the failure of the United Kingdom government to denounce publicly incidents of violence and intimidation which occurred in several areas of Nigeria during the National Assembly elections.

Referring to the Foreign Office statement which described the 'relative calm in which the elections took place', Human Rights Watch commented that 'in a situation where we have seen serious violence, with deaths and injuries, it is extraordinary for the government to talk of "calm"'. Rather, Britain was choosing instead to put a positive gloss on the elections – in which our man won again, thanks partly to massive election rigging – a contrast to the stream of criticism delivered over Zimbabwe's rigged elections in 2000.[7]

In February 2004, the British government made a formal intervention in the US justice process in an attempt to stop British companies being sued in the US for human-rights violations committed in other countries. This followed a decision by the US courts in February 2002 not to dismiss two lawsuits brought against Shell for human-rights violations against executed Nigerian human-rights leader Ken Saro-Wiwa.

This move, the *Independent* reported, followed months of lobbying by British businesses, notably Shell. The government argued that the US law:

> interferes with the sovereignty of the governments of other sovereign nations by subjecting their nationals and enterprises to risk of conflicting legal commands and proceedings and the costs of defending themselves against private law suits.[8]

– the same sovereignty and law, that is, which Blair condemns for curbing his plans for 'humanitarian' intervention in Iraq and elsewhere.

The current British priorities in Nigeria – strong backing for the Nigerian government and protection of the oil companies – are long-standing, and have many of their roots in policies of 30 years ago. The conflict then was essentially over the same issue as in the oil-rich regions today – how Nigeria's resources should be divided between the central government and the regions. Then, as now, the central government had a simple solution: it would exploit and control these resources for its own benefit; then, as now, Britain backed it. The price of this civil war, which then affected millions of lives, is still being paid today.

Background to civil war

For those in Britain old enough to remember the war in Nigeria in the late 1960s, the word 'Biafra' probably conjures up images of starving children – the result of the blockade imposed by the Nigerian government in Lagos to defeat the secession of the eastern region. For Biafrans themselves, the period was one of immense suffering. It is still not known how many died as a direct result of the war and the blockade, but it is believed to be between one million and three million.

For those seeking to understand Britain's role in the world, there is an important side of the Biafran story to add – British complicity in the slaughter. The declassified files show that the then Wilson government backed the Nigerian government all the way, arming its aggression and apologising for its actions.

The immediate background to the war was a complex one of tensions and violence between Nigeria's regions and ethnic groups, especially between those from the east and the north. In January 1966 army officers had attempted to seize power. The conspirators, most of whom were Ibos (from the east) assassinated several leading political figures as well as officers of northern origin. Army commander Major General Ironsi, also an Ibo, intervened to restore discipline in the army, suspended the constitution, banned political parties, formed a Federal Military Government and appointed military governors to each of Nigeria's regions.

Ironsi's decree in March 1966, which abolished the Nigerian federation and unified the federal and regional civil services, was perceived by many not as an effort to establish a unitary government but as a plot by the Ibos to dominate Nigeria. Troops of northern origin, who dominated the Nigerian infantry, became increasingly restive and fighting broke out between them and Ibo soldiers in garrisons in the south. In June, mobs in northern cities, aided by local officials, carried out a pogrom against resident Ibos, massacring several hundred people and destroying Ibo-owned property.

In July 1966 northern officers staged a counter-coup, during which Ironsi and other Ibo officers were killed. Lieutenant Colonel (later General) Yakubu 'Jack' Gowon emerged as leader. The aim of the coup was both to take revenge on the Ibos for the coup in January and to promote the secession of the north, although Gowon soon pulled back from calling explicitly for this. Gowon named himself the Supreme Commander of the Armed Forces and head of the military government. This was rejected by the military governor in the eastern region, Lieutenant Colonel Ojukwu, who claimed, with some justification, that the Gowon regime was illegitimate.

Throughout late 1966 and 1967 the violence escalated. In September 1966 attacks on Ibos in the north were renewed with unprecedented ferocity – stirred up, eastern region officials believed, by northern political leaders. Reports circulated that troops from the northern region had participated in the massacres. The estimated number of deaths ranged from 10,000 to as high as 30,000. More than one million Ibos returned to the eastern region in fear.

In January 1967 the military leaders met in Aburi, Ghana. By this time the eastern region under Ojukwu was threatening secession. Many of Ojukwu's eastern colleagues were now arguing that the massacres the previous September showed that the country could not be reunited amicably. In a last-minute effort at Aburi to hold Nigeria together, an accord was agreed that provided for a loose confederation of regions. Gowon issued a decree implementing the Aburi agreement and even the northern region now favoured the formation of a multistate federation. The federal civil service, however, vigorously opposed the Aburi agreement and sought to scupper it.

Ojukwu and Gowon then disputed what exactly had been agreed at Aburi, especially after the Federal Military Government (FMG) issued a further decree in March which was seen by Ojukwu as reneging on the FMG's commitment at Aburi to give the eastern region greater autonomy. The new decree gave the federal government the right to declare a state of emergency in any region and to ensure that any regional government could not undermine the executive authority of the federal government. Ojukwu then gave an ultimatum to Gowon that the eastern region would begin implementing its understanding of the Aburi agreement, providing for greater regional autonomy, by 31 March.

While Biafra was threatening to secede and declare an

independent state, the FMG imposed sanctions against it to bring it into line. On 26 May the eastern-region consultative assembly voted to secede from Nigeria and the following day Gowon declared a state of emergency throughout the country, banned political activity and announced a decree restoring full powers to the FMG. Also announced was a decree dividing the country into twelve states, including six in the north and three in the east.

On 30 May 1967 Biafra declared independence and on 7 July the FMG began operations to defeat it. It lasted until January 1970, when an extremely well-equipped Nigerian federal army of more than 85,000 men supplied by Britain, the Soviet Union and few others, took on a volunteer Biafran army, much of whose equipment came from captured Nigerian supplies.

It remains far from clear as to where the blame lay for the failure of peaceful negotiations. It does appear, however, that the FMG did go back on its agreement at Aburi as to the extent of regional autonomy it was prepared to offer the easterners. Before they began to back the FMG unequivocally when war commenced, British officials had previously recognised the legitimacy of some of Ojukwu's claims. The British High Commissioner in Lagos, Sir Francis Cumming-Bruce, had told Gowon in November 1966, for example, that the September 1966 massacres of the Ibos in the north 'changed the relationship between the regions and made it impossible for eastern Nigerians to associate with northerners on the same basis as in the past'. The issue was one of basic 'law and order and physical safety throughout the federation'. He told Gowon that the FMG had to go 'a considerable distance to meet the views of Colonel Ojukwu'.[9]

British officials also recognised that the Aburi agreements were 'extremely woolly on many important points and lend themselves to infinite arguments over interpretation'. By the end of January 1967, Cumming-Bruce was saying that both Gowon and Ojuwku were 'seriously at fault and they share responsibility for poisoning of atmosphere [sic]'.[10]

Then there was the wider question of whether Biafra should have been allowed to establish its independence. British officials feared that if Biafra were to secede many other regions in Africa would too, threatening 'stability' across the whole of the continent. Most of the great powers, including the US and the Soviet Union, shared this view.

Yet there appears to be no reason why Biafra, with its 15 million people, could not have established a viable, independent state. Biafrans argued that they were a people with a distinctive language and culture, that they were Christian as opposed to the Muslim communities lumped into the Nigeria federal state, which had, after all, been a colonial creation. In fact, Biafra was also one of the most developed regions in Africa with a high density of roads, schools, hospitals and factories. The struggle for an independent state certainly appeared to have the support of the majority of Biafrans, whose sense of nationhood deepened as enormous sacrifices were made to contribute to the war effort.

What is clear is that the wishes of the Biafrans were never a major concern of British planners; what they wanted, or what Nigerians elsewhere in the federation wanted, was simply not an issue for Whitehall. The priorities for London were maintaining the unity of Nigeria for geopolitical interests and protecting British oil interests. This meant that Gowon's FMG was backed right from the start.

Nigerian aggression, British support

'Our direct interests are trade and investment, including an important stake by Shell/BP in the eastern Region. There are nearly 20,000 British nationals in Nigeria, for whose welfare we are of course specially [sic] concerned', the Foreign Office noted a few days before the outbreak of the war.[11] Shell/BP's investments amounted to around £200 million, with other British investment in Nigeria accounting for a further £90 million. It was then partly owned by the British government, and was the largest producer of oil in Nigeria, providing most of the country's export earnings. Most of this oil was in the eastern region.

Commonwealth minister George Thomas wrote in August 1967 that:

> The sole immediate British interest in Nigeria is that the Nigerian economy should be brought back to a condition in which our substantial trade and investment in the country can be further developed, and particularly so we can regain access to important oil installations.

Thomas further outlined the primary reason why Britain was so keen to preserve Nigerian unity, noting that 'our only direct interest in the maintenance of the federation is that Nigeria has been developed as an economic unit and any disruption of this would have adverse effects on trade and development'. If Nigeria were to break up, he added:

> We cannot expect that economic cooperation between the component parts of what was Nigeria, particularly between the East and the West, will necessarily enable development and trade to proceed at the same level as they would have done in a unified Nigeria; nor can we now count on the Shell/BP oil concession being regained on the same terms as in the past if the East and the mid-West assume full control of their own economies.[12]

Ojukwu initially tried to get Shell/BP to pay royalties to the Biafran government rather than the FMG. The oil companies, after giving the Biafrans a small token payment, eventually refused and Ojukwu responded by sequestering Shell's property and installations, forbidding Shell to do any further business and ordering all its staff out. They 'have much to lose if the FMG do not achieve the expected victory', George Thomas noted in August 1967.[13] A key British aim throughout the war was to secure the lifting of the blockade which Gowon imposed on the east and which stopped oil exports.

In the run-up to Gowon's declaration of war, Britain had made it clear to the FMG that it completely supported Nigerian unity. George Thomas had told the Nigerian High Commissioner in London at the end of April 1967, for example, that 'the Federal government had our sympathy and our full support' but said that he hoped the use of force against the east could be avoided. On 28 May Gowon, having just declared a state of emergency, explicitly told Britain's defence attaché that the FMG was likely to 'mount an invasion from the north'. Gowon asked whether Britain would provide fighter cover for the attack and naval support to reinforce the blockade of eastern ports; the defence attaché replied that both were out of the question.[14]

By the time Gowon ordered military action in early July, therefore, Britain had refused Nigerian requests to be militarily involved and had urged Gowon to seek a 'peaceful' solution. However, the Wilson government had also assured Gowon of British support for Nigerian unity at a time when military preparations were taking place. And Britain had also made no signs that it might cut off, or reduce, arms supplies if a military campaign were launched.

The new High Commissioner in Lagos, Sir David Hunt, wrote in a memo to London on 12 June that the 'only way . . . of preserving unity [sic] of Nigeria is to remove Ojukwu by force'. He said that Ojukwu was committed to remaining the ruler of an independent state and that British interests lay in firmly supporting the FMG.[15]

Before going to war, Gowon began what was to become a two-and-a-half-year shopping list of arms that the FMG wanted from Britain. On 1 July he asked Britain for jet fighter/bomber aircraft, six fast boats and 24 anti-aircraft guns. 'We want to help the Federal Government in any way we can', British officials wrote.[16] However, Britain rejected the request for aircraft and boats, fearing that they would publicly demonstrate direct British intervention in the war. London did, however, agree to supply the anti-aircraft guns and to provide training courses in how to use them.

The Deputy High Commissioner in Enugu, Biafra's main city, noted that the supply of these anti-aircraft guns and their ammunition would be seen as British backing for the FMG and also that they were not entirely defensive weapons anyway since 'they could also take on an offensive role if mounted in an invasion fleet'. Nevertheless, the government's news department was instructed to stress the 'defensive nature of these weapons' when pressed but generally to avoid publicity on their export from Britain. High Commissioner Hunt said that 'it would be better to use civil aircraft' to deliver these guns and secured agreement from the Nigerians that 'there would be no publicity' in supplying them.[17]

Faced with Gowon's complaints about Britain not supplying more arms, Wilson also agreed in mid-July to supply the FMG with the fast patrol boats. This was done in the knowledge that they would help the FMG maintain the blockade against Biafra. Wilson wrote to Gowon saying that 'we have demonstrated in many ways our support for your government as the legal government of Nigeria and our refusal to recognise the secessionists'. He also told him that Britain does 'not intend to put any obstacle in the way' of orders for 'reasonable quantities of military material of types similar to those you have obtained here in the past'. Gowon replied saying that 'I have taken note of your concurrence for the usual purchases of arms supplies to continue and will take advantage of what is available now and others when necessary'.[18]

By early August Biafran forces had made major gains against the FMG and had invaded the mid-west region. Commonwealth minister George Thomas noted that 'the chances of a clear-cut military decision being achieved by either side now look rather distant'. Rather, 'we are now faced with the probability of an escalating and increasingly disorderly war, with both sides shopping around for arms'. In this situation, he raised the option of Britain launching a peace offensive and halting all arms supplies. But this was rejected by David Hunt in Lagos and others since it would cause 'great resentment' on the part of the FMG against the British government and be regarded as a 'hostile act'. Instead, the government decided to continue the flow of arms and ammunition of types previously supplied by Britain but to continue to refuse supplies of 'sophisticated equipment' like aircraft and tanks.[19]

The decision to continue arms exports was taken after it had become clear in the behaviour of the Nigerian forces that any weapons supplied would be likely to be used against civilians.[20] It was also at a time when Commonwealth Secretary General Arnold Smith was making renewed attempts to push for peace negotiations after having been rebuffed by Gowon in a visit to Lagos in early July.

By early November 1967 the FMG had pushed back the Biafrans and captured Enugu; British officials were now reporting that the FMG had 'a clear military advantage'. Now that Britain's client seemed like winning, talk of reducing arms to it disappeared; George Thomas now said that 'it seems to me that British interests would now be served by a quick FMG victory'. He recommended that the arms export policy be 'relaxed' and that Lagos be supplied with items that 'have importance in increasing their ability to achieve a quicker victory'. This meant 'reasonable quantities' of equipment such as mortars and 'infantry weapons generally', though not aircraft or other 'sophisticated' equipment.[21]

On 23 November 1967 the Cabinet agreed that 'a quick Federal military victory' provided the best hope for 'an early end to the fighting'. By early December, Commonwealth Secretary George Thomson noted that the 'lack of supplies and ammunition is one of the things that are holding operations up'. He said that Britain should agree to the FMG's recent shopping list since 'a favourable response to this request ought to give us every chance of establishing ourselves again as the main supplier of the Nigerian forces after the war'. If the war ended soon, the Nigerian economy would start to expand and 'there should be valuable business to be done'. Also:

> Anything that we now do to assist the FMG should help our oil companies to re-establish and expand their activities in Nigeria after the war, and, more generally should help our commercial and political relationship with post-war Nigeria.

He ended by saying he hoped Britain could supply armoured cars since they 'have proved of especial value in the type of fighting that is going on in Nigeria and the FMG are most impressed with the Saladins and Ferrets' previously supplied by Britain.[22]

As a result Britain supplied six Saladin armoured personnel carriers (APCs), 30 Saracen APCs along with 2,000 machine guns for them, anti-tank guns and 9 million rounds of ammunition. Denis Healey, the Defence Secretary, wrote that he hoped these supplies would encourage the Nigerians 'to look to the United Kingdom for their future purchases of defence equipment'. By the end of the year Britain had also approved the export of 1,050 bayonets, 700 grenades, 1,950 rifles with grenade launchers, 15,000 pounds of explosives and two helicopters.[23]

In the first half of the following year, 1968, Britain approved the export of 15 million rounds of ammunition, 21,000 mortar bombs, 42,500 Howitzer rounds, 12 Oerlikon guns, 3 Bofors guns, 500 submachine guns, 12 Saladins with guns and spare parts, 30 Saracens and spare parts, 800 bayonets, 4,000 rifles and two other helicopters. At the same time Wilson was constantly reassuring Gowon of British support for a united Nigeria, saying in April 1968 that 'I think we can fairly claim that we have not wavered in this support throughout the civil war'.[24]

These massive arms exports were being secretly supplied – indeed, stepped up – at a time when one could read about atrocities committed by the recipients in the newspapers. After the Biafran withdrawal from the mid-west in September 1967 a series of massacres started against Ibo residents. The *New York*

Times reported that more than 5,000 had been killed in various towns of the mid-west. About 1,000 Ibos were killed in Benin city by local people with the acquiescence of the federal forces, the *New York Review* noted in December 1967. Around 700 Ibo males were lined up and shot in the town of Asaba, according to the *Observer* in January 1968. Eyewitnesses claimed that the Nigerian commander ordered the execution of every Ibo male over the age of ten.[25]

Nigerian officials informed the British government that the arms were 'important to them, but not vital'. More important than the actual arms 'was the policy of the British government in supporting the FMG'.[26]

This support was now taking place amid public and parliamentary pressure for a halt to British arms to Lagos, with 70 Labour MPs, for example, filing a motion for an embargo in May 1968. Yet the real extent of arms supplied by Britain was concealed from the public.

Throughout 1967 and 1968, ministers had been telling parliament that Britain was essentially neutral in the conflict: it was not interfering in the internal affairs of Nigeria but simply continuing to supply arms to Nigeria on the same basis as before the war. As the declassified files show, this was a lie. For example, Wilson told the House on 16 May 1968 that:

> We have continued the supply . . . of arms by private
> manufacturers in this country exactly on the basis that
> it has been in the past, but there has been no special
> provision for the needs of the war.[27]

One British file at this time – mid-1968 – refers to deaths of 70,000–100,000 as 'realistic'. The Red Cross estimated that there were around 600,000 refugees in Biafra alone and was trying to arrange desperately needed supplies to meet needs, around 30 tons a day.[28]

Humanitarian suffering, especially starvation, was severe as a result of the FMG's blockade of Biafra. Pictures of starving and malnourished children went around the world. The FMG was widely seen as indulging in atrocities and attacks against civilians, including apparently indiscriminate air strikes.

The files show that Wilson told Gowon on several occasions in private letters that he had successfully fended off public and parliamentary criticism in Britain, in order to continue to support the FMG.[29] As in Vietnam at the same time (see Chapter 12), Wilson was not going to be deflected by mere public opposition, whatever the level of atrocities and casualties.

By mid-year, with federal forces in control of Port Harcourt, the most important southern coastal city, British officials noted that 'having gone this far in supporting the FMG, it would be a pity to throw away the credit we have built up with them just when they seem to have the upper hand'. Britain could not halt the supply of arms since 'apart from other considerations, such an outcome would seriously put at risk about £200m of British investments in non-Biafra Nigeria', George Thomson explained to Harold Wilson.[30]

It was at this point that British officials sought to counter widespread opposition to the Nigerian government by conniving with it to improve the 'presentation' of FMG policies. Britain urged the FMG to convince the outside world that it was not engaged in genocide or a policy of massacre and to make public statements on the need for a ceasefire and humanitarian access to Biafra.

High Commissioner Hunt suggested to Gowon that the federal air force be used for 'psychological warfare' and to drop leaflets over the Ibo towns which would help the FMG score a 'propaganda point'. Officials noted that their support for the FMG was under attack and that 'our ability to sustain it . . . depends very much on implementing enlightened and humane federal policies and securing public recognition for them'. What was needed was 'good and well-presented Nigerian policies which permit that support to continue'. Wilson therefore urged a senior Nigerian government official, Chief Enahoro, 'to make a greater effort to ensure that their case did not go by default'.[31]

The files indicate that these 'presentational' issues were much more important to British officials than the suffering of the Biafrans. British officials ruled out threatening to cut off, or reduce, arms exports to force the FMG to change policies. The issue that most concerned the government at the time was that it would be forced to withdraw or reduce its support for Gowon in the face of public pressure.

By mid-1968 British officials had still had no talks with Ojukwu and other Biafran leaders; offers from the latter had been refused. So supportive was Wilson of the FMG that he even asked the Nigerians in advance whether they would have 'any difficulties' if a British official met a Biafran representative. Chief Enahoro replied that this would be acceptable provided the contacts were 'strictly private and had no formal character'.[32]

In early August FMG forces had retaken the whole of the south-eastern and Rivers states and the easterners were now confined to a small enclave, blockaded from the outside world. Commonwealth minister Lord Shepherd minuted Harold Wilson saying, that 14 months since Biafran secession:

> Our support for the FMG finds us in the position in which we are on comparatively good terms with the side which is in an overwhelmingly advantageous position . . . It is important, therefore, that we should not be manoeuvred by pressure of opinion inspired by Ojukwu's publicity, into abandoning at this late stage all the advantages which our policy so far seemed likely to bring us.[33]

The same month, the Red Cross estimated 2–3 million people 'in dire need' and a similar number were facing shortages of food and medical aid.[34]

Wilson did not succumb to public pressure. The following month he told Gowon that:

> The British government for their part have steadfastly maintained their policy of support for Federal Nigeria

and have resisted all suggestions in parliament and in the press for a change in that policy, particularly in regard to arms supplies.[35]

The Foreign Office argued that 'the whole of our investments in Nigeria and particularly our oil interests in the south east and the mid-west will be at risk if we change our policy of support for the federal government'.[36]

In November, Lord Brockway and his committee for peace in Nigeria met Wilson and urged him to halt arms sales and to press for a ceasefire, estimating that there could be 2 million deaths from starvation and disease by the end of the year.[37] Wilson not only rebuffed this plea; the files reveal that two days later he agreed to supply Nigeria with aircraft for the first time in a covert deal.

The Nigerians had been pressing Britain to supply several jet aircraft, specifically to attack the runways used by Biafran forces (which also needed to be used to deliver humanitarian aid). Wilson said that Britain could not supply these directly but there were such aircraft in South Yemen and Sudan previously supplied by Britain. The Nigerians, he said, should procure the aircraft from them which 'would not directly involve the British government'. The company to deal with in those two countries was Airwork Limited, which was later to be used by the British government to conceal its involvement in its dirty war in Yemen. The British government also agreed to put the Nigerians in touch with 'suitable pilots'.[38]

British arms supplies were stepped up again in November. Foreign Secretary Michael Stewart said the Nigerians could have 5 million more rounds of ammunition, 40,000 more mortar bombs and 2,000 rifles. 'You may tell Gowon', Stewart instructed High Commissioner Hunt in Lagos, 'that we are certainly ready to consider a further application' to supply similar arms in the future as well. He concluded: 'if there is anything else for ground warfare which you ... think they need and which would help speed up the end of the fighting, please let us know and we will consider urgently whether we can supply it'.[39]

Other supplies agreed in November following meetings with the Nigerians included six Saladins and 20,000 rounds of ammunition for them, and additional monthly supplies of ammunition, amounting to a total of 15 million rounds on top of those already agreed. It was recognised by the Defence minister that 'the scale of the UK supply of small arms ammunition to Nigeria in recent months has been and will continue to be on a vast scale'. The recent deal meant that Britain was supplying 36 million rounds of ammunition in the last few months alone. Britain's 'willingness to supply very large quantities of ammunition', Lord Shepherd noted, 'meant drawing on the British army's own supplies'.[40]

At the same time the Foreign Office was instructing its missions around the world to lie about the extent of this arms supply. It sent a 'guidance' memo to various diplomatic posts on 22 November saying that 'we wish to discourage suggestions' that the Nigerians, in their recent meetings with British officials, were seeking 'to negotiate a massive arms deal'. Rather, 'our policy of supplying in reasonable quantities arms of the kind traditionally supplied' to Nigeria 'will be maintained but no change in the recent pattern of supplies is to be expected'.[41] So deep is the culture of lying at the Foreign Office, it appears that policy is to keep its own officials in the dark.

By the end of 1968 Britain had sold Nigeria £9 million worth of arms, £6 million of which was spent on small arms.[42] A quarter of Nigeria's supplies (by value) had come from the Soviet Union, also taking advantage of the war for its own benefit and trying no doubt to secure an opening into Nigeria provided by this opportunity. British officials consistently justified their arms supply by saying that if they stopped, the Russians would fill the gap. It was Britain's oil interests, however, that was the dominating factor in Whitehall planners' reasoning.

By the last two months of 1968, with hundreds of thousands now dead, the fighting had reached a stalemate. The FMG had taken all Biafran territory apart from a small enclave consisting of 3 million people in an area the size of Kent. Biafrans were now dependent on two airstrips for outside supplies which were limited by both Gowon's and Ojukwu's refusals to allow sufficient numbers of aircraft to land. Humanitarian agencies were continuing calls for a ceasefire as suffering, especially starvation, had reached crisis proportions.

'We shall continue to maintain our present policy, despite these heavy pressures on us', Wilson told Gowon in November. Foreign Secretary Stewart instructed Lord Shepherd, on a visit to Lagos, to tell Gowon of the extraordinary steps Britain was taking to support him. Gowon should realise, Stewart said, that opposition to British policy 'cuts right across the normal political or party divisions in the country and is especially strong in the various churches'. He added that 'similar feeling is also expressed within the Cabinet itself'[43] – such was the thin base on which British support for the FMG was being provided. (One wonders about similar memos being written by Tony Blair to George Bush in 2003.)

The Wilson government was keen to present itself as engaged in the search for peace – the files show that officials knew they would not otherwise have been able to justify their support for the FMG. British government activity in peace negotiations invariably sought to avoid the involvement of the United Nations. The intention was to maintain a united Nigeria and to achieve a solution on FMG terms only.

In public, British statements consistently blamed only the Biafrans, not the FMG, for obstructing peace negotiations and the delivery of humanitarian aid. There were numerous proposals and counter-proposals made by both sides on the issue of night or day flights, and river or land routes into Biafra. The FMG feared that the Biafrans would use the cover of humanitarian aid supplies to slip in arms deliveries; while the Biafrans believed the FMG would poison the supplies.

Meanwhile, millions of people suffered without aid. There is no doubt that Ojukwu and the Biafran leadership were partly responsible for this failure, yet so were the FMG. Starvation of the Biafrans was no mere byproduct of the war; it was a deliberate part of the FMG's war policy.[44]

Several memos by British officials that reached Wilson and other ministers painted a more accurate picture than the one pushed in public. These said that it was as least as much the FMG that were to blame as the Biafrans.[45] Yet this never upset British policy to side unequivocally with Gowon's FMG.

In March 1969 Wilson gave a public interview and lied that 'we continue to supply on a limited scale arms – not bombs, not aircraft – to the government of Nigeria because we have always been their suppliers'. Not only did this conceal the agreements made late the previous year; on the very same day as this interview, the government approved the export of 19 million rounds of ammunition, 10,000 grenades and 39,000 mortar bombs – bombs, that is, that Wilson had said Britain was not supplying at all, still less on a vast scale.[46]

A day before the Wilson interview, a Foreign Office official had written that 'we have over the last few months agreed to supply large quantities of arms and ammunition' to Nigeria 'to assist them in finishing the war in the absence of any further [peace] negotiations'. He also noted that 'we have flown small arms ammunition to Nigeria . . . using Manston airport in Kent without attracting unfavourable press comment'.[47]

It was therefore perhaps no surprise that Gowon could write to Wilson in April saying that 'of all the governments in the Western world, yours has remained the only one that has openly maintained its policy of arms supplies to my government'.[48] France, Belgium and the Netherlands, among others, had all announced a halt; the US continued its policy of not supplying arms to either side.

Two senior British RAF officers secretly visited Nigeria in August 1969 to advise the Nigerians on 'how they could better prosecute the air war'. The main British interest, the files make clear, was to provide better protection of the oil installations, but the brief for the two officers stated that this impression should not be given to the Nigerians. The officers subsequently advised the Nigerians on a variety of tactics on 'neutralisation of the rebel airstrips'. It was understood that destruction of the airstrips would put them out of use for daylight humanitarian-relief flights. It is not clear whether such advice was put into action.[49]

In December 1969, just before the final push that crushed the Biafrans, Foreign Secretary Michael Stewart was calling for stepping up military assistance, including the supply of more armoured cars – which, he wrote, 'have undoubtedly been the most effective weapons in the ground war and have spear-headed all the major federal advances'.[50]

Biafran resistance ended by mid-January 1970. Wilson then sent another message to Gowon saying that 'your army has won a decisive victory' and has achieved 'your great aim of preserving the unity and integrity of Nigeria':

> As you know I and my colleagues have believed all along that you were right and we have never wavered in our support for you, your government and your policy, despite the violent attacks which have been made on us at times in parliament and in the press as well as overseas.[51]

The Deputy High Commissioner in Lagos added:

> There is genuine gratitude (as indeed there should be) for what Britain has done and is still doing for this country, and in particular for Her Majesty's Government's courage in literally sticking to their guns over Biafra.[52]

The toll of the war was counted in a report for the British High Commission at the end of the month. It referred to a relief agency report estimating 1.5–2 million people were being fed with food relief supplies, around 700,000 of whom were refugees in camps dependent entirely on food aid.[53] Three million refugees were crowded into a 2,500 square kilometre enclave in which not only food but medicine, housing and clothing were in short supply. The Biafran economy was shattered, cities were in ruins and schools, hospitals and transport facilities destroyed.

INDONESIANS: TOOLS OF COVERT ACTION

Few people have suffered as much from Britain's backing for repressive regimes as those living in the islands of Indonesia. From the 1940s until today, these Unpeople have been killed in their hundreds of thousands by governments in Jakarta which have been given support from London.

This chapter looks at two episodes, one current, one from the late 1950s. The current episode concerns Britain's strong backing for Jakarta's attempts to crush separatists; the past episode concerns British covert support for separatists against Jakarta. London may have switched sides, but its strategy has been remarkably consistent: forces are supported according to their ability to do Whitehall's bidding; the Indonesian people affected are an irrelevance.

The war in Aceh

The most recent episode in London's long backing for Indonesian aggression began in 2003. While British ministers were expounding the importance of upholding the highest moral values when it came to dealing with the Saddam regime, their allies in Jakarta were indulging in atrocities in Aceh province.

The 4 million people in Aceh, on the northern tip of the island of Sumatra, have a long history of resistance to rule from Jakarta. For 30 years they thwarted Dutch military efforts to 'pacify' and colonise the region. After Indonesian independence in 1949, Aceh was granted special region status that was meant to give the Acehnese control over education, religion and some local laws; this autonomy, however, failed to be implemented.

Long-held resentment against rule from distant Jakarta exploded in the mid-1970s after huge natural-gas reserves were discovered. Jakarta allowed these resources to be extracted with few revenues returning to benefit the Acehnese themselves. In 1976 the Free Aceh Movement (GAM) was founded to fight for independence and open resistance to Jakarta's rule broke out.

The response by the Indonesian regime under General Suharto, fresh from engaging in aggression in East Timor, was to designate Aceh a 'military operations zone' and indulge in a campaign of brutality and repression. This reached a peak in the years from 1989 until the fall of Suharto in 1998. During that time thousands of Acehnese were killed, tortured and 'disappeared'. The military announced the ending of the 'military operations zone' in 1998 but in 1999 and 2000 a series of further military and police operations were launched, involving several massacres in which scores of people were killed.

In 2000 there was a 'humanitarian pause' loosely supervised by a Geneva-based human-rights centre but violence was stepped up again in May 2001 when Indonesia launched new military operations. Around 2,000 more people, the vast majority civilians, were killed. The next year saw a further 1,300 killings. Since 1976, the conflict has cost around 15,000 lives in total. GAM has gained in strength and popularity under Indonesian brutality, has operated in all parts of Aceh and has been in effective control of village and local administrations, at least until the latest Indonesian offensive which sought to crush it.[1]

On 19 May 2003 Indonesian President Megawati Sukarnoputri

launched full-scale military operations in Aceh against GAM. This decision unilaterally broke a six-month ceasefire and a process of dialogue between the Indonesian government and GAM. The ceasefire period had resulted in a marked decrease in civilian deaths, a return to normality in many parts of the province, and was welcomed by the Acehnese. Following the May intervention, involving over 30,000 Indonesian troops, Human Rights Watch documented an upsurge in killings by the Indonesian forces, crackdowns on NGOs and the media and destruction of 425 schools in the province. It also noted that there were plans forcibly to relocate up to 200,000 people from their homes and put them in special camps under military guard.[2]

By June 2003 the Indonesian human-rights organisation Kontras reported that 40,000 people had become refugees. By August the press was reporting that well over 1,000 civilians had been killed, rising to around 3,000 by early 2004.[3]

In November 2003 the Indonesian government extended the operation in Aceh for a further six months. 'The operation is proceeding at a level which is causing widespread civilian loss of life, gross violations of human rights and the destruction of Aceh's public infrastructure', the human-rights organisation Tapol noted. 'In case after case, soldiers have gone into Acehnese villages and publicly executed or beat people seemingly at random', said Human Rights Watch. 'If the aim is to instil fear in the populace, sadly it's working'.[4] Thousands of refugees were reported to be fleeing their homes while those who remained were subject to shortages of food, water, sanitation and breakdowns in basic services such as health care. The Indonesian offensive nominally ended in May 2004 with the lifting of martial law. Yet in the latter part of the year fighting was continuing and 'the majority of the population continues to live in fear, with widespread reports of killings, torture and disappearances', according to Human Rights Watch.[5]

British arms have been used by Indonesia in its offensive; London has refused to cut off supplies. The Blair government ignored evidence that the Indonesians were preparing to use British-supplied Scorpion tanks in Aceh by failing to deliver any advance warning to Jakarta; 36 of these tanks were subsequently deployed and used in Aceh from June. By the end of 2003 Saracen armoured vehicles supplied by Britain were also being used.

On the first day of the military campaign Hawk aircraft supplied by Britain were also deployed in Aceh. The *Guardian*'s John Aglionby reported that 'they were used primarily to scare and intimidate people on the ground by flying low over targets already attacked with rockets by other aircraft and then over terrain in advance of parachute drops by 600 paratroopers'. Reports from GAM further into the campaign said that Hawks were used to attack villages in north Aceh while other sources said they also took part in bombing raids in other parts of the province. Air-force chief of staff, Marshall Chappy Hakim, was reported by Indonesian newspapers to have said that he discussed the possibility of using Hawks with the British ambassador two months previously and no objection had been raised.[6]

Foreign Office minister Mike O'Brien claimed that the British government had received assurances from Jakarta in 2002 that it would not use British equipment offensively or in violation of human rights. Indonesia, however, disputed that any such agreement existed, said that Hawks were not being used offensively anyway and pledged to continue to use them. 'I am going to use what I have', military commander General Sutarto said. 'After all, I have paid already'.[7]

Faced with obvious embarrassment and public pressure, the Blair government was reported in June 2003 to be threatening to refuse export licences for spare parts for Hawk aircraft because of their use in Aceh.[8] Foreign Office minister Mike O'Brien reportedly flew to Jakarta to urge President Sukarnoputri not to use British arms offensively in human-rights violations – an interesting position to adopt, given the lack of any other conceivable use to which Indonesia can put this equipment.

An Indonesian military spokesman said in June 2003 that the Scorpion tanks being used in Aceh 'will become a key part of our campaign to finish off the separatists'. They 'are not to kill the people but to kill those who are controlled by [GAM leader] Hasan de Tiro to kill people'. He said that Indonesia would continue to use them and that 'there's no need for permission'.[9]

In January 2004, the Indonesians announced that they were withdrawing the Scorpion tanks from Aceh and replacing them with a locally produced model. It was not clear whether this came as a result of pressure from Britain, where the Foreign Office said it had issued 'reminders' to Indonesia that it should not use them for internal repression. It was reported that local television in Aceh had shown heavy machine guns mounted on Scorpions firing on GAM positions on several occasions.[10]

In February 2004 the *Guardian* reported that Britain had relaxed its arms-exports policy towards Indonesia. Previously, the British government had requested advance notice from the Indonesians before they used British equipment. But in 2003 the Foreign Office removed this request since, it claimed, Jakarta had given a fresh 'assurance' that no British equipment would be used to violate human rights or in offensive operations.[11]

The concept of 'assurances' is a public-relations exercise on Whitehall's part to try to convince the public of its humanitarian concerns. That 'assurances' from the Indonesians are worthless has been shown time and again; the Indonesians have used British equipment, including Hawks, for repression on at least eight different occasions from 1996 until the 2003 intervention in Aceh. In this light, it is difficult not to believe that the equipment is being supplied by Britain to provide Jakarta with the necessary armoury to crush separatism, which the Indonesian military sees as its primary purpose. The only complication for Whitehall is that it is hard to conceal from the public, which in my view explains Mike O'Brien's protests.

After the launch of Indonesia's campaign in Aceh, Britain, together with Australia, delivered a stark message of support to Jakarta. In a joint statement Foreign Secretary Jack Straw and his

Australian counterpart, Alexander Downer, said that 'the UK, Australia and the international community as a whole support Indonesia's territorial integrity'. They said that they urged a 'peaceful' solution to the conflict and urged both the Indonesian government and the GAM 'to return to the negotiating table'.[12]

The basic reason for supporting Indonesia's 'territorial integrity' is to ensure that its vast economic resources are available to British and Western corporations. Aceh, and other provinces with which Jakarta is at war, such as West Papua, is rich in liquid gas and petroleum, and provides around 15 per cent of Indonesia's oil and natural-gas exports. Britain is the largest foreign investor in Indonesia after Japan and has invested $38 billion in the country since 1967, amounting to over 15 per cent of foreign investment.[13]

It appears to have been the Indonesian military that pushed the civilian government to break the ceasefire and launch the campaign in Aceh, defying some government ministers. The military never agreed in the first place to entering into dialogue with GAM; they feared Aceh's secession from Indonesia and the loss of prestige and resources this would entail.[14]

The Indonesian military is also more generally on the offensive politically, increasingly dictating government policy and reversing some aspects of the civilian supremacy that had been established since the fall of Suharto. The rise of the military is therefore, if anything, being strengthened by importing British arms.

British arms sales to Indonesia have increased from £2 million in 2000 to £15.5 million in 2001 and to £41 million in 2002. The number of licences approved rose from 54 in 2001 to 182 in 2002, reaching the highest number of licence issues in the last ten years. The range of equipment being exported includes aircraft cannons, armoured vehicles and components for air missile-launching equipment, combat aircraft and tanks. As Tapol has pointed out, these increases in military exports appear connected to the Indonesian military's wish to upgrade its offensive capabilities in areas of conflict such as Aceh and

West Papua. Under New Labour Britain has sold £375 million worth of arms to Indonesia.[15]

The intentions of the recipients have been made clear. General Sutarto, Indonesia's military commander, has told his forces that 'you must chase and wipe out GAM...you are trained to kill, so wipe them out'. As troops were being parachuted into the province, Sutarto was urging them to 'hunt down and exterminate' the separatists, 'chase them, destroy GAM . . . Don't talk about it, just finish them off'.[16]

The Aceh operation was planned and implemented by many of the same men who directed the violence in East Timor in 1999. Indeed, one general charged with extensive human-rights crimes in East Timor failed to appear before a special tribunal in Jakarta in May 2003 because he was too busy on the Aceh campaign.[17]

Indonesian aggression is taking place not only under the cover of the 'war against terrorism'. Recent media reports have cited Indonesian generals' references to the US war on Iraq as justification for the operation. US tactics have also been imitated, with Indonesia 'embedding' journalists with military units.[18]

Andrew Tan, an expert on regional insurgencies at Singapore's Institute for Defence and Strategic Studies, has commented that 'this is the right time to go back to war. In the context of the war against terrorism, there are few, if any, diplomatic costs to seeking a military solution'. Similarly, Lesley McCulloch, a research fellow at the Monash Asia Institute, comments that the precedent set by the invasion of Iraq and the ousting of an 'undesirable' regime has encouraged the Indonesian generals to take advantage of the current international political climate which 'provides the perfect arena for a massacre'.[19]

Anglo-American covert action

The story was somewhat different in the late 1950s. Britain and the US had long wanted to remove then President Sukarno. Sukarno's nationalist domestic policies and a foreign policy of non-alignment were a direct threat to Washington and London. The latter were especially concerned about the growing popularity and influence of the Communist party (PKI) on the Sukarno government. The Foreign Office, for example, viewed with 'anxiety' the 'trend of events in Indonesia' especially the recent 'electoral results' showing that the PKI 'has grown in strength to a disquieting degree'.[20]

British planners were also mindful of the government's recent takeover of Dutch commercial interests. The Foreign Office wrote that 'clearly a serious blow has been struk [sic] at the confidence of all foreign concerns trading in and with Indonesia'. The latter 'is a country with a vast population and great potential wealth, and one in which United Kingdom interests are by no means negligible'.[21]

In late 1957 dissident colonels in the Indonesian army were leading a challenge to Jakarta's rule in the outlying provinces. By the end of the year Jakarta's authority did not spread much beyond the island of Java and the north-eastern area of Sumatra; elsewhere, local commanders were in practice operating their provinces independently. In January 1958 a rebellion against the central government broke out in Sumatra and Celebes. The causes were described by the British ambassador in Indonesia as the desire to end the Indonesian government's inefficient economic policy and a demand for more self-government for the richer provinces. He also noted that 'anti-communism' has been included in the aims of the rebels and 'in order to attract Western support, it has been made to appear one of the main purposes of the rebellion'.[22]

On 15 February, the rebels proclaimed a Republic of Indonesia in the city of Padang; following which the Jakarta government began military operations to crush the rebellion. By June the government had almost succeeded: Padang had been recaptured and the dissidents, although still in control of large areas of Sumatra, were forced to resort to guerrilla warfare. Their rebellion finally petered out and they surrendered in 1961.

The US and Britain covertly supported this rebellion in its early phase, perhaps hoping to see Sukarno overthrown, or at least for what Foreign Secretary Selwyn Lloyd understood as the rebels' 'nuisance value'. This meant using the rebellion to press the Jakarta government to adopt policies of London's and Washington's pleasing.[23] When their clients outlived their usefulness – which the rebels did as soon as Jakarta had won the main war – London and Washington dropped them and re-engaged with Jakarta.

The covert programme was US-led, with Britain lending some important aid. The British files of this period are heavily censored but still shed some light on the British role; an excellent book by Audrey Kahin and George Kahin serves as a guide to US activities.[24]

A prime mover in the British operation was Sir Robert Scott, Britain's Commissioner General in Singapore. In December 1957, Scott lamented 'the effects of the developing crisis in Indonesia in terms of dislocation of economic interests' and that Indonesia 'may pass under communist control'. Referring to the 'anti-communist elements in Sumatra and the other outlying provinces', he told the Foreign Office:

> I think the time has come to plan secretly with the Australians and Americans how best to give these elements the aid they need. This is a bold policy, carrying considerable risks . . . The action I am recommending will no doubt have little influence with President Sukarno. They are not designed to; I believe it should be one of our aims to bring about his downfall.

Scott's aims included 'to limit the mischief the communists can do in Java, to save Sumatra' and 'to win complete American cooperation both public and private'. Maintaining the unity of Indonesia, however, was imperative.[25]

There was some opposition in the Foreign Office to these proposals. One official, O. C. Morland, wrote that Scott was 'on the wrong track' and that: 'the result of secret help to the outer provinces would be to arouse keen resentment in Java and to increase the risk of armed conflict between the outer provinces and Java'.[26]

Foreign Office opposition was overruled and the British covert role initiated. In February 1958, top-secret discussions in Washington between British, US and Australian officials 'revealed substantial agreement on the main lines of Western policy' in Indonesia, the Foreign Office reported. They should '(a) discreetly support and attempt to unite anti-communist elements in Java', so as to counter the increasing influence of the PKI. They should also '(b) respond where practicable to requests for help from the dissident provincial administrations'. But '(c) do nothing to further the break-up of Indonesia'.[27]

Recently declassified Australian documents show that on 11 March Australian Prime Minister Robert Menzies was informed that Prime Minister Harold Macmillan and Foreign Secretary Selwyn Lloyd believed 'that it is essential in the interests of the UK government and the West that the dissidents in Sumatra should at the worst be able to make a draw of it'. This meant 'considerable support for the dissidents from the West'. According to these files, Lloyd had advised Macmillan:

> As to the implementation that you and I discussed on Saturday night of covert action and what we called the 'overt but disavowable' aspect, I feel we have got to take considerable risks to see our policy succeed.

The following day, 12 March, it was agreed between Britain and the US 'that all help that is possible to provide should be given to the dissidents although every possible care should be given to conceal the origins'. Sir Robert Scott even suggested as a 'longer term proposition' that Britain, the US and Australia 'should look into the possibility of encouraging rebellion on Amboina and the Moluccas [in eastern Indonesia], to widen the basis of any international attitude that the Indonesian government was not in control of the country'.[28]

Serious US covert operations had already begun in the autumn of 1957. The US then authorised $10 million to be spent in support of the dissident colonels and arms were soon provided from US submarines and aircraft from the Philippines, Taiwan and Thailand. According to the Kahins, the US supplied enough arms for 8,000 men. The CIA recruited around 350 Americans, Filipinos and nationalist Chinese to service and fly a small fleet of transport aircraft and 15 B-26 bombers. This rebel air force conducted numerous bombing raids on cities and civilian shipping, even destroying one British tanker. In April 1958 the British files reported that 12 of the crew of 26 on a 1,200-ton Panamanian steamer were killed, and a 5,000-ton Italian ship was sunk with 12 of her crew missing.[29]

According to the Kahins, Britain also provided a small quantity of arms to the rebels and British warplanes flew reconnaissance missions over Sumatra and eastern Indonesia. Aside from that, the major British role was to provide the use of British military bases in Malaya and more importantly Singapore, then still colonies, for covert operations. This included the US use of Singapore to drop arms to the rebels.

'Americans agreed they would take action from United Kingdom territories only with our consent', the Colonial Secretary told the British Governors of Singapore, North Borneo and Sarawak (the latter in Malaya) in a top-secret message of February 1958. He also noted that 'Governor Singapore has reported that his ministers are privately inclined towards helping dissidents' but that since London formally recognises the Jakarta government 'Singapore cannot overtly take sides' – meaning this role would need to be kept secret.[30]

A US brief prepared for US Secretary of State Dulles after meetings with the British in December 1957 states:

> We were promised [by the British] the maximum use of Singapore for operations, keeping in mind no arms shipments to dissidents would come thru [sic] that

port, that knowledge of British consent to our operations be tightly held, and neither it nor our operations become subject to pol [sic – i.e., political] comment in Singapore.[31]

These criteria, however, were soon ignored, the Kahins note, and by early 1958 British facilities in Singapore were welcoming the US navy. A British submarine was also seen apparently rescuing US paramilitary advisers as the rebels' positions collapsed; it was attacked by the Indonesians off Celebes.[32]

Britain's ambassador to Indonesia, MacDermot, also told the Foreign Office that 'secret assurances of support by Malaya and Philippines would be most useful together with increased news cover acquired in our information broadcast [sic] to Asia about Indonesia'.[33]

In June 1958 the Foreign Office was noting that 'for more than six months now' Britain had been 'principally motivated by our hopes that the activities of rebel groups in Indonesia would be of advantage to the Western cause'.[34] But policy had changed in alliance with the Americans. Western support for the rebels was now explicitly to be used as a tool to press Sukarno.

In May, with the Indonesian army having pushed back the rebels, the US ambassador in Indonesia was instructed by the State Department to tell Sukarno that if he removed 'the communist threat' to the government then the US would stop aiding the rebels. The files make clear that Britain supported this strategy.[35] The ambassador instead met Indonesian Prime Minister Djuanda, who essentially rejected the US proposal saying that the rebels would be crushed first.

Nevertheless, the US and British calculation was now that they should abandon the rebels and revert to encouraging 'pro-Western' tendencies in the Indonesian government. This meant pressing Sukarno to remove or undermine senior figures in the government who were sympathetic to or members of the PKI. That said, it appears that the British allowed the dissidents to continue some activities from

Singapore; these finally ended only after Indonesian pressure
on Singapore's first government after independence in 1959.[36]

It was understood that with the Indonesian army having
disposed of the rebels they were 'free to deal with the
communists', the British Ambassador in Jakarta wrote.[37] The
other main US and British policy was to resume arms exports
to the Indonesian military. This enabled them to develop closer
relations with key political figures in Indonesia who would act
as a counter to Sukarno supporters and Communists. The
strategy paid off, with horrendous results. In 1965–1966, these
same generals conducted a campaign of slaughter against the
PKI, leaving up to a million dead, and finally dislodging
Sukarno from power.

A February 1959 policy statement by the National Security
Council, stated that the US should:

> maintain and strengthen . . . ties with the Indonesian
> police and military establishments; and increase their
> capability to maintain internal security and combat
> communist activity in Indonesia by providing appro-
> priate arms, equipment and training, on a limited but
> continuing basis . . . [The US should] give priority
> treatment to requests for assistance in programs and
> projects which offer opportunities to isolate the PKI,
> drive it into positions of open opposition to the
> Indonesian government, thereby creating grounds for
> repressive measures politically justifiable in terms of
> Indonesian self-interest.[38]

In conducting the covert operation, Britain and the US
actually strengthened the forces they were opposing. The war
was a gift to Sukarno, the nationalists and the Communists,
who consolidated their positions as a result. The US role had
ceased to be covert when a US pilot was captured and his papers
displayed to the world's press, which enabled Indonesian
government ministers to claim with some justification that they
were being attacked by the US.

A secret British memo said that the war had made 'Indonesia increasingly vulnerable to economic penetration by the Sino-Soviet bloc'. Ambassador MacDermot, meanwhile, noted in July 1958 that 'the United States has lost much ground as a result of the rebellion' and that the Indonesian Cabinet has 'been quick to seize upon Russian offers for help'. Soviet military aircraft, cargo ships, tankers and other equipment 'have already arrived and Russian progress here during the last year has been astonishing'.[39]

London's backing of separatists to destabilise Jakarta did not end in the late 1950s. In 1963 and 1964, Britain reactivated the policy it had promoted in 1957–1958, supplying weapons and support to rebels in Kalimantan, Sumatra and elsewhere. But again this was only temporary and by January 1965 planners were stating that 'in the long term, effective support for dissident movements in Indonesia may be counter-productive in that it might impair the capacity of the army to resist the PKI'.[40] By 1966, Suharto was firmly in control – since then, the good guys have been in power in Jakarta and our enemies have therefore become those who challenge them.

12

VIETNAMESE: SECRET SUPPORT FOR US AGGRESSION

What was the British role in the most sustained use of firepower against a country in history? British academics have been silent on this (as far as I am aware) even though the files have been declassified for some years. I know of only one detailed study, which covers the period 1961–1963 only, by a German journalist.

As one generation of people is being politicised by the invasion of Iraq, a previous generation was politicised by the defining issue of those times, the unprecedented US onslaught on Vietnam. What the protesters of the 1960s could not have known, however, is what British officials and ministers were doing behind closed doors to support the US aggression.

The declassified British files on the Vietnam war are little short of a revelation. They show that Britain backed the US at virtually every stage of military escalation, and also played its own important secret role in the war. These documents show that Britain is complicit in US aggression and shares some responsibility for it.

During the war the US used 15 million tons of munitions, twice as much as in the Second World War. Between 2 million and 3 million people, perhaps even more, are estimated to have died.[1] The wholesale destruction of villages and killing of innocent people was a feature of the war from the outset, as was widespread indiscriminate bombing. The actions and objectives of the US and its local allies have been well documented by Noam Chomsky and others, while the political and social background to the war has been analysed notably by historian Gabriel Kolko.[2] These analyses undermine the false framing that still appears to dominate much of modern discussion: that the US was engaged in a noble cause that went badly wrong.

Background to the war

After France had been defeated in 1954 in its brutal eight-year attempt to reconquer Vietnam, the Geneva Accords temporarily divided Vietnam between North and South at the 17th parallel and envisaged elections in 1956 that were meant to lead to unification. The northern half of the country was under the control of the Communist party. What the US subsequently confronted in South Vietnam was a liberation movement – the Viet Minh, designated 'Viet Cong' by the US – calling for reunification with the North, a foreign policy of neutrality, major land reform to benefit the rural poor, the overthrow of the US-backed regime of Ngo Dinh Diem and abolition of the US economic monopoly and bases in the South.

According to Gabriel Kolko, author of perhaps the most comprehensive analysis of the Vietnam war, the history of Vietnam after 1954 'was only incidentally that of a civil war'. Rather, 'it was essentially a struggle between a radicalised Vietnamese patriotism, embodied in the Communist party, and the United States and its wholly dependent local allies'.[3]

Land reform lay at the root of the war. By the time of the Geneva Accords, the Communists in the South controlled at least 60 per cent of the territory and had begun a major transformation of the land system affecting most of the population in one way or another. This revolution by the Viet Minh movement had redistributed huge areas of land to previously landless peasants and those who had supported the resistance to the French, much of it transferred at the expense of the French and the largest Vietnamese landowners. In the North, land reform, which had mobilised the poorer peasants in opposition to the French, had enabled the landless and poor peasants to improve their position radically. The transformed land system was 'essentially equitable' in the North, Kolko comments.[4]

The land measures begun by the Diem regime in South Vietnam in 1955 were essentially a counter-revolution aimed at abolishing the Viet Minh reforms and returning to the traditional peasant-landlord structure to disenfranchise the poor. At the root of the war in South Vietnam lay both this land-reform programme and the sheer repression and terror of the Diem regime, which killed thousands of people in the late 1950s.

By 1961 hundreds of thousands of hectares of land had been taken back by the Diem regime. The Communist party in the North backed the creation of the National Liberation Front (NLF) in South Vietnam for achieving unification and for promoting its political programme through the whole country. By the early 1960s large-scale upheavals in the rural areas of the South increased as Communist party members began to take over many villages, mobilising people and calling for land for the peasants. The NLF's land-reform programme was immensely successful in engaging a large percentage of the peasantry to participate directly in the process of land redistribution and giving them a stake in the success of the revolution. This helps explain the widespread popularity of the NLF.

The US's major fear was that the revolution in Vietnam would spread, threatening US security and business interests elsewhere in the region. 'The fall of Indochina would undoubtedly lead to the fall of the other mainland states of Southeast Asia', the US Joint Chiefs of Staff had argued in 1950. 'Major sources of certain strategic materials' as well as communications routes were at stake. If Vietnam 'fell', the 'principal world source of natural rubber and tin, and a producer of petroleum and other strategically important commodities' would also be lost in Malaya and Indonesia.[5]

That the US and South Vietnam had violated the Geneva Accords – which required nationwide elections to be held in 1956 – was recognised by British officials. The Foreign Office noted in private that:

> The United States government . . . supported and encouraged the efforts of the South Vietnamese government to ignore the political provisions of the Geneva Agreements and to consolidate an anti-communist regime in the South.[6]

The British recognised in private the 'historical distortion' that the US was putting on the Geneva agreements in public. British policy, like that of the US, was to back a divided Vietnam and to oppose what it recognised as Ho Chi Minh's call for 'free general elections throughout the country'.[7]

It was also recognised by British planners that the liberation movement in the South was popular, certainly much more so than the Diem regime. The British ambassador, Harry Hohler, said that the greatest rival to President Diem was the President of North Vietnam, Ho Chi Minh: 'more than any other, he commands the following and respect which could give him power in South Vietnam'. Foreign Office official Edward Peck confirmed the British opposition to democracy in the country by writing that 'the most sinister alternative [to rule by Diem] is of course the probably still popular appeal of Ho Chi Minh'.[8]

The British military attaché wrote in a report in February 1963 of the contrast between security arrangements between Ho Chi Minh in Hanoi and Diem in Saigon. 'When Ho Chi Minh travels no extra precautions are observed and he mingles freely with crowds as he wishes. A strange contrast to Saigon, with several armed police always on each corner'.[9]

In May 1961 a British embassy official was told by the US ambassador that one problem with the introduction of full democracy in the South was that 'fully elected village councils if introduced now might merely facilitate the transfer of control to the Communists'. It was understood by early 1962 that the Viet Cong were in control of the 'majority of villages in South Vietnam' and that they were winning 'the battle for minds of the peasantry'.[10]

Another crucial issue was the extent to which the Southern liberation movement was controlled from the North. In public, British (and of course US) leaders continually said that Hanoi was simply directing the 'communist insurgency' in the South, refusing to concede that this was primarily an indigenous liberation movement. But what planners understood in private provides a more accurate picture. In June 1961, for example, Edward Peck noted that 'our current assessment is that most of the insurgents come from inside South Vietnam itself and that there are only relatively few contacts with the North'. Another official said that Britain lacked 'any real proof that the trouble in S. Vietnam is directed from N. Vietnam'. However, 'on the other hand, US intervention in S. Vietnam is open for all the world to see'.[11]

By November 1961, Peck was noting that 'undoubtedly, some supplies, propaganda and cadres come down through the country [from North Vietnam] but the idea of a thickly populated line of communication is nonsense'.[12]

This date is important since it coincides with the US intervention in South Vietnam. It shows that at this time, British officials did not view the 'insurgency' as directed from outside, but more logically as an indigenous rebellion. In public, however, this was never conceded throughout the long years of the Vietnam war. British officials consistently backed the line that the US was fighting externally backed 'aggression', which was itself an important source of diplomatic support to Washington and helped the US to misrepresent the conflict.

As for whether it was really the Soviet Union and China which was behind the uprising in South Vietnam, the Foreign Office stated in June 1962 that 'the Russians do not welcome a war in Indo China and we do not believe that the Chinese would

intervene unless they felt that the security of North Vietnam
was directly threatened'.[13]

South Vietnamese President Diem was recognised as being
dictatorial and unpopular and received the strong backing of
the British as well as US governments. 'The Diem regime lacks
popular support', the Foreign Office said in July 1961. It was 'a
clumsy and heavy-handed dictatorship which is conspicuously
lacking in popular appeal'. Numerous files refer to Diem's
'rigid and autocratic rule', 'authoritarian and uncompromising
nature' and his 'extreme over-centralisation' of power.[14]

Even more extreme was Diem's brother and right-hand man,
Nhu, who 'attaches every bit as much importance to the
apparatus of a police state as the most enthusiastic advocate of
the social order of "1984"', as the British ambassador put it. It
was Nhu who, according to a Foreign Office briefing paper, was
'primarily responsible for the authoritarian and quasi-fascist
tendencies of the Vietnamese government'.[15]

The April 1961 elections won by Diem were recognised as
being 'certainly rigged' while by 1962 there was 'growing
corruption at every level, the inevitable result of prolonged
foreign subsidy' – from Britain's key ally, that is. Overall,
British planners knew that 'the regime here is absolutely
dependent upon the Americans for survival'.[16]

In fact, the Diem regime was responsible for inflicting sheer
terror on the population. A 1972 study prepared for the
Pentagon states that:

> There can be no doubt that innumerable crimes and
> absolutely senseless acts of suppression against both
> real and suspected communists and sympathising
> villagers were committed. Efficiency took the form of
> brutality and a total disregard for the difference
> between determined foes and potential friends.

It is estimated that more than 10,000 had been killed by the
Diem regime by 1957 and about 66,000 killed between 1957
and 1961.[17]

'We are committed to backing Diem to the end', the British embassy noted in July 1961, reflecting British public statements which did not mention the frank admission in the files as to Diem's dictatorial and repressive features.[18] The reason was that the British, and the Americans, apparently believed that Diem was the only counter to 'communist intervention'.

In December 1961 Ambassador Hohler sent an extraordinary letter to Foreign Secretary Alec Douglas-Home, saying that:

> We should not be too greatly moved by complaints that the Vietnamese authorities are holding large numbers of individuals in detention camps. At the worst period in Malaya we had over 10,000 people in detention without trial.

He recommended that the Diem regime should improve its 'information services' and that Britain should help. One Foreign Office official noted that Hohler's despatch was 'largely an apology for President Diem' who has surrounded himself with 'evil and powerful advisers'. At this time British officials were aware that there were around 30,000 political prisoners in South Vietnam.[19]

British and US support for Diem lessened only after it became clear that Diem was refusing to accept US (and British) advice on how to win the war. He thus became a liability, and eventually had to be overthrown.

Support for US intervention

British interest in backing the US was not only to support its ally; the fear was also that the 'fall' of South Vietnam 'would be disastrous to British interests and investments in South East Asia and seriously damaging to the prospects of the Free World containing the Communist threat'. Britain's commercial interests in Vietnam itself were very modest, with exports averaging only around £2 million a year in the early 1960s.[20]

Britain welcomed the US 'counter-insurgency' plan submitted

to Diem in February 1961, partly since it was based on proposals by Britons, Robert Thompson and Field Marshall Gerald Templar, both 'counter-insurgency' experts who had plied their trade to ferocious effect in the war in Malaya. This plan called for an increase in the South Vietnamese army of 20,000 troops to deal with the insurgency.

But the first major escalation was the US intervention of November 1961 when the Kennedy administration sent helicopters, light aircraft, intelligence equipment and additional advisers for the South Vietnamese army. Soon after this the US air force began combat missions.

'The administration can count on our general support in the measures they are taking', Foreign Secretary Douglas-Home said. It was clearly understood in various memos by British ministers and officials that this intervention was a complete violation of the 1954 Geneva Accords which put limits on the number of US military forces acceptable in Vietnam and which was now being superceded.[21]

Britain had a particular responsibility to uphold this international agreement since it was a co-chair of the Geneva Accords, with the Soviet Union. But the British connived with the US and promised not to raise the issue. 'As co-chairman, Her Majesty's Government are prepared to turn a blind eye to American activities', the Foreign Office secretly stated. Douglas-Home wrote to Secretary of State Dean Rusk to tell him 'to avoid any publicity for what is being done', i.e., in the November intervention. He 'assured Mr Rusk that he will turn a blind eye to what goes on'.[22]

British planners had hoped that the US would not openly commit combat troops to South Vietnam for fear of the international repercussion of Vietnamese being killed by Americans, and that the reaction in Vietnam itself would be 'unfavourable'.[23] But they immediately acquiesced. 'The United States government is determined to prevent the fall of South Vietnam to the Communists and this policy is supported by HMG', the Foreign Office noted in March 1962.

In February, Ambassador Hohler said that 'we must clearly give the sorely tried Americans all the support that we can for the courageous action they have taken here' and counsel patience for the US 'clamour for results'. He said that he thought the British role should be to urge the US 'to avoid unnecessary provocation in an increasingly dangerous situation' while 'we should do our best to make it clear to them that we are on their side'.[24]

By mid-1962, Hohler was saying that as regards military intelligence, 'this embassy now enjoys closer relations with the Americans than ever before'. The military attaché was receiving weekly US military reports and he enjoyed 'excellent working relations' with US military officials. 'Though there are, inevitably, differences of emphasis', Hohler added, 'I would not say that there are any basic disagreements between us'. A Foreign Office brief similarly noted that 'there are no major differences of view [between Britain and the US] about the measures needed to defeat the Viet Cong'.[25]

It is plausible to argue that if the British had acted at this stage in their role as guarantor of the Geneva Accords, they just might have been able to prevent the US intervention, or undermine it in some way. They could have at least made it more difficult for the US by stressing the stipulations in the accords for elections and limits on military involvement. But there was no question of Britain acting in this way. Indeed, it is important to realise that Britain backed the military not the diplomatic option.

'Surely we should aim to divert and not to focus international attention on our actions in Vietnam while we get on with the task of defeating the Viet Cong', Foreign Secretary Douglas-Home wrote in November 1961.[26] (The use of 'we' here suggests the extent to which British ministers regarded the war as their struggle also.)

Thus the Foreign Office made clear, in private, its opposition to a UN or other international conference on Vietnam, saying that 'until the insurgency is mastered and the South Vietnamese are in a position to negotiate on an equal footing with the North, a conference could achieve nothing useful'. Translated from diplo-speak: the war must continue since the South Vietnamese regime lacks any popular support and is bound to lose out in any deal. The fear, indeed, was that 'the West would be faced with . . . proposals for the reunification and neutralisation of Vietnam'.[27]

In May 1962 Prime Minister Harold Macmillan sent a personal letter to President Diem saying that 'we have viewed with admiration the way in which your government and people have resisted' North Vietnamese attempts to 'overthrow the freely established regime in South Vietnam', adding 'we wish you every success in your struggle'.[28]

Other files show the British fear of a North Vietnamese peace offensive and the danger that 'if a Communist campaign for international discussions gets under way it will receive a great deal of support'. The 'neutral countries' were bound to support such a campaign and 'in many countries of the West it might also be thought quite reasonable that we should try for a peaceful negotiation over Vietnam'. But not in British government circles. Instead, since the US 'have overall relative military superiority and are ready for a real trial of strength', then 'this must not be bargained away'.[29]

Hohler also said in November 1961 that he agreed with the US ambassador, Nolting, that 'this was not the time for the political reform' of the Diem regime. Foreign Office official Fred Warner agreed, saying that 'this is not the time to talk about liberalisation [of the Diem regime, meaning to push for democratic reform]. Military measures must be given priority'.[30]

Throughout 1962 and 1963 the US poured money and military equipment into South Vietnam while US 'advisers' 'daily accompanied the Vietnamese forces into battle', Ambassador Hohler commented. Seventeen months into the war – in April 1963 – the Foreign Office stated that 'it would be a mistake to abandon present policies of going all out for a military victory'. It noted that 'the communists' might soon press for a negotiated settlement based on neutrality for South Vietnam. 'We remain strongly against giving this any encouragement'.[31]

This continuing British support for war rather than diplomacy is easily explained: throughout the first half of the 1960s, Britain thought the US could win. Hohler's recognition that 'people are horribly tired of a war' did not shake his preference, or that of his bosses in London, for the military option.[32]

My research for this chapter involved looking at most of the British planning files for over a decade between 1961 and 1972, which consisted of hundreds of documents. As in the other episodes described in this book, there are no concerns expressed in any of these files for the people on the receiving end of Anglo-American policy. British officials were perfectly aware of what was happening to ordinary Vietnamese. In December 1962, for example, Ambassador Hohler noted the South Vietnamese forces' 'indiscriminate air activity' and the killing of innocent villagers. The only reservation expressed was that this would have an adverse 'psychological impact' and is 'grist to the mill of local communist propaganda'.[33]

By December 1962 US State Department intelligence was reporting that 'indiscriminate bombing in the countryside is forcing innocent or wavering peasants towards the Viet Cong' and that over 100,000 Montagnards have fled Viet Cong-controlled areas due in part to 'the extensive use of artillery and aerial bombardment and other apparently excessive and indiscriminate measures by GVN [i.e., South Vietnamese] military and security forces'. This had 'undoubtedly killed many innocent peasants and made many others more willing than before to cooperate with the Viet Cong'.[34]

January 1962 is the first mention in the British files that I have seen of a 'chemical substance used for clearing strips of jungle vegetation'. In March the following year, Foreign Office official Fred Warner wrote that 'there is no doubt the Americans have used toxic chemicals' and that 'we believe that these chemicals are a legitimate weapon' to destroy the insurgents' cover. He noted that the Soviet government had made an official request to the International Control Commission (ICC) of the Geneva Accords, which Britain co-chaired, to mount an investigation. But Warner said this was simply a matter for the ICC, not Britain. Again, British officials protected the US, and the consequences were horrific.[35]

Over a nine-year period beginning in late 1961, 20 per cent of Vietnam's jungles and 36 per cent of its mangrove swamps were sprayed by the US, with 42 per cent of the spraying allocated to food crops. In 1963 the US began to study the dioxin in the major defoliant being used – Agent Orange – suspecting it might cause cancer, birth defects and other grave problems. The fears were confirmed by 1967 but never affected policy in any way.[36]

At the same time, British officials also knew that napalm was being used. Ambassador Hohler rejected the idea of a complaint, saying that the war in Vietnam 'is a very ruthless one and there is little to choose between the two sides when it comes to cruelty'. An appeal against the use of napalm might 'satisfy some tender consciences', Hohler noted, but 'the net result would probably be to draw attention to a practice that has hitherto been largely overlooked'.[37]

When the subsequent Wilson government raised its concerns to the US about the latter's use of gas and napalm in Vietnam it was always in the context of 'difficulties' that this caused with the presentation of policy to the public. There is no evidence that British officials were motivated by anything else – that they might have been opposed to the use of such weapons because of the effect they had on people.

Britain's support for Diem

Britain provided considerable direct support to the Diem regime and US military in support of the US war. British aid to Diem was formally provided in the British Advisory Administrative Mission (BRIAM). BRIAM was agreed in July 1961 and began work in Saigon two months later with a small team of experts in 'counter-subversion', intelligence and 'information', its activities intended to complement those of US advisers. The head of BRIAM, Robert Thompson, quickly became one of, if not the most, important of Diem's foreign advisers.[38]

The British government's claim that BRIAM had a purely civilian (and not military) role, maintained in various parliamentary answers and debates, was a complete lie. The memo proposing the establishment of BRIAM says that training was to be provided 'over the whole counter-insurgency field'. Ambassador Hohler said in June 1962 that Diem had ratified 'proposals for the conduct of the war put forward by the highly-experienced Advisory Mission (BRIAM)'. Around 300 Vietnamese soldiers were trained in 'counter-insurgency' in Malaya in 1962–1963 alone. By August 1963 the Diem regime was described as 'most appreciative of the type of training and of the assistance' provided by the British.[39]

I found other examples of British military cooperation with the Diem regime and the US during this time:

• In late 1962 a team of 20 British technicians, all given American Service identity cards, installed and began to operate a navigation system for US warplanes. This was described as 'invaluable for pin-pointing targets for straffing [sic], bombing, supply dropping and dropping parachutists'.
• In November 1962 the British government agreed to loan the US two Ferret armoured cars to be tested in Vietnam. This followed a US military official's inspection of Ferrets in action with the British army in Malaya, with which he 'was most impressed'.
• In late 1962 a British Lieutenant-General was allowed to accept a US invitation to take part in the work of the US's Advanced Research Projects Agency in Bangkok, in the course of which he was required to operate 'in the forward areas of South Vietnam'. He was described as a Combat Research Officer.[40]

The major British contribution to the war, however, was Robert Thompson's counter-insurgency programmes, based on (extremely brutal) measures in Malaya, which led to the 'Delta Plan' and the 'strategic hamlets' programmes in Vietnam. US military officials, it was reported, were much impressed by Thompson and 'were most anxious' that the 'valuable experience we had gained in Malaya [be] put to the best possible use in South Vietnam'.[41]

At the Diem regime's invitation, Thompson, then a senior official in the colonial Malayan government, visited South Vietnam in April 1960 and produced a report on 'anti-terrorist operations'. This report 'impressed the Vietnamese government', the Foreign Office later noted, and provided the basis for the US counter-insurgency plan of February 1961.

In late 1961, Thompson produced a draft of 'a campaign on Malayan lines' that was to be known as the Delta Plan. The aim, according to the Foreign Office, was 'to dominate, control and win over the population, particularly in the rural areas, beginning in the delta' region. The proposal involved establishing curfews and prohibited areas to control movement on all roads and waterways to 'hamper the Communist courier system', along with 'limited food control' in some areas.

'If the system works successfully', the Ambassador wrote, 'this provides the main opportunity for killing terrorists'. As and when the areas are declared 'white', i.e. free of 'terrorists', social improvement would follow along with the relaxing of controls. According to the Foreign Office, 'Thompson considers that the struggle will last some five years and that the campaign must be conducted on methodical lines with the country being cleared area by area'.[42]

In February 1962 the Diem regime asked Thompson to put the Delta Plan into practice, but implementation by Vietnamese forces was 'ineffective', partly due to the poor application of the strategic hamlets programme, according to the Foreign Office.[43] Largely based on the Delta Plan, the US produced a further 'counter-insurgency' programme for operations in the Delta.

Thompson's Delta Plan was also the basis for the US
'strategic hamlets' programme, devised by Roger Hilsman at
the US State Department. 'Hilsman's basic concept owes a
great deal to Thompson', one British official in the Washington
Embassy commented. According to the State Department:

> The strategic hamlet is essentially a fortified hamlet . . .
> A fence of bamboo and barbed wire is built around the
> entire hamlet, and a ditch or moat is dug around the
> fence; the ditch or moat, in turn, is encircled by an
> earthen mound. The area immediately around the
> village is cleared to permit fields of fire and to avoid
> giving guerrillas and terrorists hiding places close to the
> hamlet.[44]

The programme began in late 1961 and became national policy
in April 1962, with such 'strategic hamlets' soon established all
over the country.

In February 1963, Ambassador Hohler told the Foreign
Secretary that with the building of 'strategic hamlets' and
'resettlement' 'there are new burdens to be borne' by the
Vietnamese peasants. 'The benefits of the hamlets programme
have, for the most part, yet to be seen', he added. Strange, then,
that Edward Heath, then Lord Privy Seal, should say in answer
to a parliamentary question just two months later that:

> The 'strategic hamlet' programme is giving improved
> security to villagers and a chance to build up again the
> traditional system of Vietnamese village councils and
> communal activity. We hope this improvement can be
> maintained.[45]

In reality, the 'strategic hamlets' programme was extremely
brutal and the fortifications were often little different from
concentration camps. Peasants were ordered to abandon their
homes and land for new sites in often quite distant locations,
while the cash and building materials they were allocated were
inadequate. They were also compelled to give much of their

labour to building stockades. The South Vietnamese officials governing this process were there 'to loot, collect back taxes, reinstall landlords and conduct reprisals against the people', according to one US marine 'pacification' expert quoted by Gabriel Kolko. Above all, the programme failed to address land redistribution, which fuelled the popularity of the National Liberation Front.[46]

By the end of 1963 Thompson had become critical at the ineffectiveness of the Vietnamese and US in implementing 'strategic hamlets', saying that they had been created in a haphazard way and that military operations were not designed to support the programme. To 'save' the programme he said 'the government must be absolutely determined and, if necessary, ruthless'. He advised that when the 'strategic hamlets' were being constructed no house should be left outside the perimeter and all should be persuaded 'and forced if necessary' to move their houses inside. 'In constructing the hamlets, peasants should be required to give their labour, preferably during off-seasons, free', Thompson urged. 'Dusk to dawn curfews outside the hamlet should be imposed and enforced'.

Reiterating that the government must be prepared to be ruthless, Thompson adds:

> Just as an example of a ruthless measure, I quote the case of a village in Malaya (Jenderam) of about three thousand inhabitants. This was a very bad area and the village itself was a centre of support and supply for a large unit of communist terrorists when most of the other areas around it had been cleared. Having given the inhabitants a choice between the Government and the communists and having failed to make any headway by appealing to or persuading them to cooperate we moved in several battalions at dawn one morning and moved the whole village out. Everyone in it, men, women and children, went into detention for two years.

> All the houses were razed to the ground. Surprisingly,
> this did not cause a public outcry and the effectiveness
> of the result, by leading to the elimination of the
> communist terrorist unit concerned, silenced all
> criticism. When the area was finally cleared of terrorists
> the people were allowed to return and the restoration of
> the village was then heavily subsidised by the govern-
> ment. It is now peaceful and prosperous . . . There is no
> easy way if victory is to be achieved. A price has to be
> paid now by the population to prevent a much heavier
> price being paid later.[47]

The Foreign Office stated in January 1964 that Thompson's
'main contribution' to BRIAM's operations had been 'to
convince the Vietnamese authorities of the usefulness of
strategic hamlets'. At the same time, Britain's new ambassador
in Saigon, Gordon Etherington-Smith, was recognising the
reality of the programme as implemented. He said that it was
'widely unpopular' and that the new government – which had
just overthrown Diem – 'have no intention of incurring the
same unpopularity by forcing the peasants into hamlets against
their will'. The programme had become 'discredited' and was
no longer being carried out as it had been envisaged by Diem.
It had also been pushed forward 'too fast' and not enough had
been done, he said, to ensure that 'communist influence was
effectively removed' from the hamlets.[48]

The British government has never admitted that British
forces fought in Vietnam. Yet the files confirm that they did,
even though several remain censored.

In August 1962, the military attaché in Saigon, Colonel Lee,
wrote to the War Office in London attaching a report by
someone whose name is censored but who is described as an
adviser to the colonial Malayan government. This adviser
proposed that an SAS team be sent to Vietnam, which Lee said
was unacceptable owing to Britain's position as co-chair of the
Geneva Accords. Then Lee writes:

However, this recommendation might be possible to implement if the personnel are detached and given temporary civilian status, or are attached to the American Special Forces in such a manner that their British military identity is lost in the US Unit. However the Americans are crying out for expert assistance in this field and are extremely enthusiastic that [one inch censored] should join them. He really is an expert, full of enthusiasm, drive and initiative in dealing with these primitive peoples and I hope that he will be given full support and assistance in this task.

'These primitive peoples' is a reference to the Montagnards in the highlands of the central provinces of Vietnam. Lee continues:

It is . . . clear that there is enormous scope for assistance of a practical nature on the lines of that already being undertaken by the Americans. Thus it is strongly recommended that such British contribution [sic] as may be feasible be grafted on to the American effort in the field, particularly in view of their shortage of certain types of personnel. The ideal solution might be to contribute a number of teams to operate in a particular area fully integrated into the overall American and Vietnamese plan. The civil side could be composed of carefully selected Europeans and Malayans with suitable experience, and the military element could be drawn from the SAS regiment which operated for many years amongst the Aborigines in Malaya. Suitable steps could doubtless be taken to give them temporary civilian status. Although we should have to rely on the Americans to a great degree for logistic support, it might still be possible to provide a positive contribution in this field such as specialised equipment. A less satisfactory solution might be to integrate certain specialists into existing or projected American Special

Forces Teams, although the main disadvantage here, particularly on the Aborigine side would lie in the fact that many of the experienced Malayan personnel would not speak English and would have to rely on the British element as interpreters when dealing with the Americans.[49]

This team was sent, and was known as the 'Noone mission' under Richard Noone (the figure whose name is censored in these files) and which acted under the cover of BRIAM. The covert operation began in summer 1962 but there are only a few further references to it in the available files. One shows that it was still in operation in late 1963; by which time Noone was still providing reports back to the Foreign Office.[50]

Other covert aid provided by Britain included secret flights from Hong Kong to deliver arms, especially napalm and 500-pound bombs. Aid on the intelligence front took various forms, including forwarding reports to the Americans from MI6 station heads in Hanoi. The British monitoring station at Little Sai Wan in Hong Kong provided the US with intelligence until 1975. The US National Security Agency coordinated all signals intelligence in South-east Asia, and Little Sai Wan was linked to this operation. Its intercepts of North Vietnamese military traffic were used by the US military command to target bombing strikes over North Vietnam.[51]

The end of this first period of the war is marked by the overthrow of the Diem regime in November 1963. The run-up to his removal was marked by the emergence of a 'determined popular movement' led by the Buddhists which directly challenged Diem's authority and which was put down with brute, bloody force.

The British mildly protested to Diem about these repressive measures, largely since they feared that Britain, and the US, would be 'tarred with his brush', as the Foreign Office put it, and that such repression would endanger the stability of the regime and the prosecution of the war. By September 1963, however, the ambassador was explicitly telling the Foreign Office that the war could not be won with Diem in power and that he should be overthrown.[52]

The military coup of 1 November was actively backed by the US and strongly welcomed by Britain, and General van Minh emerged as the new leader. The main British priority was to ensure that 'the war effort and the conduct of public business should be as little upset as possible'. Ambassador Etherington-Smith noted that the new regime stood a chance of success in the war 'provided they are prepared to wage the war in the countryside with sufficient firmness and resolution'.[53]

Dissident in the Foreign Office

As well as the change of regime, there had been another important development towards the end of this period, at least in the internal British planning record. This was a memo from Kenneth Blackwell, Britain's Consul-General in Hanoi (i.e., its top diplomat in North Vietnam) to the Foreign Office in May 1963. In this memo, Blackwell, who had just completed a year in Hanoi, blows apart all of Whitehall's public positions and reveals its fake analysis. It is worth considering at length.

Blackwell began by noting that the conflict is 'basically a political and not a military problem – a struggle for the hearts and minds of the people of South Vietnam'. 'To occupy the country indefinitely as the Americans seem prepared to do is, I am sure, no answer'. The 'only alternative is a political settlement' which is possible only if the South Vietnamese government can satisfy the needs of its 13 million people. What is needed, he said, was 'modern social welfare – in particular free education and free medical treatment for all', 'land reform, i.e., the abolition of landlordism', 'democracy' through free elections and 'independence and neutrality – the withdrawal of all foreign armies and military bases from its territory [sic]'.

Also needed, Blackwell wrote, were 'a greater equality – a narrowing of the excessively wide gap between the upper and lower classes, the ruling classes and the mass of the people'. Also, 'a certain degree of socialism in the form of the nationalisation of the bigger monopolies, especially when held by foreigners'. Then the crucial admission: 'Communist propaganda . . . claims·that most of these requirements are part of their program [sic] and they do in fact carry out some of the more spectacular and popular ones.'

Blackwell does say that his programme differs from that of the 'communists' in that it provides for genuine democratic government and it gives peasants individual control of their land. He adds that 'there is certainly a case for getting rid of the excessively wealthy, largely parasitic and superficially Euro-peanised landlord class which is the curse of most Asian countries'. And he adds that 'one of the major faults of American policy (at least in the past) seems to me to have placed too great a reliance on this class . . . because they are (naturally) violently anti-Communist.'

On North Vietnam, Blackwell says:

> I think we are making a mistake if we assume that North Vietnamese interference (which in any case when compared with American aid to the South Vietnamese government is chicken feed) is the cause of the trouble and that without it all South Vietnamese (or even a majority) would flock to the support of Diem. I am convinced that the political question which I have described above, would still exist even if the opposition was suppressed to a greater degree than is at present possible.

Then Blackwell says that North Vietnam:

> has expressed its support for a program [sic] almost identical with the one I have described. They have said in fact that they would accept a neutral and independent government in the South (although of course they hope that the two governments will eventually agree to the

peaceful unification of the country) . . . Whereas in Germany and Korea and virtually everywhere else in the world we favour the determination of the future of nations (especially the joining together of the two halves of one artificially divided nation) by the free choice of the people – namely by free elections, in South Vietnam we have allowed ourselves to be jockeyed into the position of refusing to allow elections which should under the Geneva Agreement have been carried out in 1956, and thereby laying ourselves open to the accusation of being opposed to the principle of national self-determination.

He concludes by saying that:

I fully recognise the difficulties of taking any action on the above lines and that on balance HMG would probably prefer the devil they know (the Diem government and American military support for South Vietnam) to the devil they do not know (the holding of an international conference and the neutralisation of South Vietnam).[54]

There is no evidence that British policy changed whatsoever after these pronouncements by our man in Hanoi, which effectively undermined the entire British (and US) framing of the war. Much of Blackwell's analysis here is accurate, and confirms the immorality of the British position throughout the US war of aggression.

Military escalation, British backing

After the overthrow of Diem, Vietnam was ruled by a succession of military-controlled governments, under the dominant figures of General Nguyen van Thieu and Nguyen Cao Ky. These governments continued the basic repression of the Diem regime and in doing so received the backing of the US and also Britain.

In its annual review for 1964, the British embassy in Saigon noted the continuing rise of 'popular pressures' in South Vietnam led by the Buddhists and other groups 'with their emphasis on freedom from any sort of regimentation or discipline'. Just as problematic, from the embassy's point of view, was the 'neutralist trend' championed by these groups and that they were calling for 'the possibility of ending the war by negotiation'. The British ambassador noted that 'any hope of political stability from now on will depend on whether the popular forces . . . can somehow be contained'.[55]

The favoured method of establishing control over the South Vietnamese countryside shifted away from 'strategic hamlets' to 'pacification'. This was 'the most important aspect of the anti-communist struggle', according to Ambassador Etherington-Smith, who gave 'pacification' strong support and was keen to offer the US 'expert advice' in this field.[56]

'Pacification' meant that a substantial proportion of the peasantry was forced off the land against their will. The most conservative estimate is that at least half of the rural population was pushed into refugee camps or urban settings, many repeatedly. South Vietnamese government figures for refugees or war victims during 1965–1972 are around 7 million, about one-third of the population and half the peasantry.[57]

The period 1963–1966 was marked by massive escalation in US aggression. By 1966 US troops in Vietnam had risen to 370,000 and 'American air raids on North Vietnam were carried out nearly every day throughout the year', the British embassy's annual review for 1966 noted.[58]

Fundamental British support for the US continued. Prime Minister Douglas-Home stated in March 1964 that in recent talks with President Johnson, 'I reaffirmed my support for United States policy which . . . is intended to help the Republic of South Vietnam to protect its people and to preserve its independence'.[59]

A May 1965 Foreign Office brief outlines British interests. It stated that Britain's 'direct involvement in Vietnam is insignificant' but 'that our interests as a non-communist power would be impaired if the United States government were defeated in the field, or defaulted on its commitments'. US prestige was therefore in danger and defeat 'would damage America's standing all over the world'. Similarly, 'American abandonment of South Vietnam would cause both friend and foe throughout the world to wonder whether the US might in future be induced to abandon other allies when the going got tough'. Consequently:

> It is in Britain's interests to give support for our major ally. Whenever we declare our determination to seek a peaceful settlement we should accompany this with an expression of general support for the Americans, while avoiding passing judgment on their specific actions. Behind this general public support, we would then have a better opportunity of conveying in private any criticisms we may feel justified.[60]

Another British interest was in securing US backing for its policy in Malaya. A Foreign Office brief of December 1964 noted that 'not least because we need American support over Malaysia, we probably have no option but to give diplomatic support, as long as we can, to whatever policy the US government choose to adopt [in Vietnam]'.[61] The key was to ensure the US continued to support Britain's defiance of Sukarno's Indonesia in the latter's military confrontation with Malaysia, then still a British colony. The reference to British support for 'whatever policy the US government choose to adopt' – a chilling phrase – proved correct.

In the first half of the 1960s, British officials generally believed the US war was winnable and therefore continued to support Washington knowing that it would continue to inflict massive casualties. In December 1963, for example, Robert Thompson noted that 'the fighting will be bitter and the casualties heavy (over 100,000 government and Vietcong)'. He thought that peace would not be restored until the end of the decade.[62]

But by 1965 the situation on the ground had changed, and it had become clear to British officials that the US could not in fact win the war. This did not stop them continuing to support the US, however. In March 1965 Wilson's personal adviser, Joe Wright, noted that 'the Americans are in a hopeless position in South Vietnam' and 'cannot win and cannot yet see any way of getting off the hook which will not damage their prestige internationally and the President's position domestically'.[63]

After Wilson became Prime Minister in October 1964, basic public professions of British support for the US continued. But the declassified files show that Wilson gave President Lyndon Johnson a greater degree of backing in secret, at every stage of escalation. This support was proffered behind the scenes since British public opposition to the war was widespread. It is a good example – as with Iraq more recently – of how elites see the need to contain the public by private understandings on both sides of the Atlantic.

It is interesting to consider the various military escalations of the war, and the British reaction, one by one.

In February 1965, the US took the war into a devastating new phase by beginning the bombing of North Vietnam in its 'Rolling Thunder' campaign. The files show that the British had already promised support for this bombing in discussions in Washington the previous December. Britain had agreed to give 'unequivocable [sic] support to any action which the US government might take which was measured and related strictly to North Vietnamese and Viet Cong activity'. Two days after the attacks began, Foreign Secretary Michael Stewart informed the embassy in Washington of the 'military necessity of the action' and told the Prime Minister that 'I was particularly anxious not to say anything in public that might appear critical of the US government'.[64]

Since Britain was one of the few powers that failed to condemn the US bombing, the Prime Minister's personal adviser noted that 'for presentational reasons, therefore, it was highly desirable that the Prime Minister should be seen to be consulting the Americans'. Wilson wanted to fly to Washington (he was refused by Johnson), about which Wright wrote:

> He [Wilson] was perfectly prepared to back the Americans in what they had to do in South Vietnam. But it would be easier for him to do this if he were seen to be in discussion with the President of the United States.[65]

The British knew that US strikes on North Vietnam were illegal. Indeed, British officials had warned the US, in May 1964, that such strikes would create 'difficulties' for Britain. In discussions with the US then, the British Foreign Secretary had said that:

> Article 51 [of the UN charter, under which nations could act in self-defence] could only be invoked in the case of actual armed attack not merely against infiltration or subversion. He did not see how the UN charter could be invoked to justify an attack on North Vietnam.[66]

It appears from the record that Wilson did try to restrain Johnson from all-out attacks on North Vietnam at this time – i.e., strikes that would go beyond the 'measured' attacks against strictly military targets. But he told him personally that 'whatever measured response you take . . . we shall be backing that too' since 'we have been extremely loyal allies on this matter'.[67]

On 17 February 1965 the US ambassador in London, David Bruce, told Wilson that the US was planning not simply 'tit-for-tat' attacks on North Vietnam but 'continuing air and naval action against North Vietnam whenever and wherever necessary'. The record of this conversation shows that Wilson raised some concerns about this policy going beyond the previous agreement on only 'measured' attacks. He complained that the US was not at the same time putting forward any proposals for a political solution. However, Wilson concluded by saying that Britain 'would, of course, have to support the United States without seeing any light at the end of the tunnel'. By mid-March Michael Stewart was noting that Britain was backing the US in its wider bombing campaign in the North 'however much we dislike it'.[68]

British support was clearly outlined in a Foreign Office brief in March:

> Although from time to time we have expressed cautionary views in response to notifications of US plans for attacks against the North, we have at no stage opposed them. Our comments have been mostly on the timing or public presentation of the attacks . . . HMG . . . have at no stage opposed the policy being followed by the US but rather by suggesting minor changes in timing or presentation from time to time, have acquiesced in it.[69]

In parliamentary debates following the beginning of the US bombing of North Vietnam, Wilson refused to condemn US actions. Rather, he noted that 'we fully support the action of the United States in resisting aggression in Vietnam'. This support continued after Britain had been privately informed by the US in April that attacks would take place against 'economic and industrial targets' as well as military targets, in a bombing campaign that would 'continue without pause' – i.e., would go well beyond what Britain had hitherto promised to support.[70]

After Wilson had fended off MPs' questions on Vietnam and offered no criticism of US policy in parliament on 9 March, Secretary of State Dean Rusk telephoned the British embassy in Washington saying that 'he greatly appreciated the way in which the Prime Minister handled questions on Vietnam in the House today. He was most grateful'. By the time Wilson met Johnson in Washington in April, the US President 'expressed very deep appreciation of the line we [Britain] had taken on Vietnam'. Britain's ambassador in Washington had similarly told President Johnson that the US 'was receiving staunch support from the British government'.[71]

The bombing of North Vietnam was greatly welcomed by the

British embassy in Saigon. Ambassador Etherington-Smith noted that the attacks were 'a logical and inherently justifiable retort' to North Vietnamese 'aggression'. He said that 'since the West had been losing the battle in the political and counter-subversive field, they should concentrate on the military sector in order to gain time' – a further admission, in effect, of the moral bankruptcy of US/British policy and the resort to war to overcome it.[72]

He also noted that the attacks had resulted in 'a distinct feeling of relief and a noticeable, if temporary, relaxation of political tension'. The bombing had created a:

> tonic effect both as a means of retaliation against Northern aggression, as an indication of increased American involvement and as offering hope of an early victory or at least an early end to the war.

It was also a tonic in response to the 'political and popular pressures' that had 'grown alarmingly in the past year'.[73]

Our man in Saigon well understood what the eventual outcome of the US bombing might be. He was told by General Maxwell Taylor, the US ambassador to Vietnam, that if North Vietnam did not yield then 'this would make things very simple, because Hanoi and the North would be destroyed'. Etherington-Smith's support came despite the view of the consul general in Hanoi who said that the attacks 'have, if anything, increased Northern determination to prosecute the war in defiance of the Americans'.[74]

The bombing of North Vietnam continued against bridges, railways and road vehicles, power plants, harbour facilities, military barracks, supply depots, military radio stations and other economic and industrial targets. By mid-year the US was averaging 80–100 sorties a day, with 500 aircraft carrying 3,000–5,000 bomb loads, according to the British files. British officials were also informed by the US that these attacks were 'being very gradually stepped up all the time and that this would continue'.

I found no opposition to this bombing, or any concern about the effect it might be having on people, anywhere in the government files. It has been estimated that 80 per cent of the casualties from the bombing of North Vietnam were civilians.[75]

When the US first used its own aircraft in South Vietnam in March 1965, this was also welcomed by the British ambassador, who said that it had 'beneficial effects' both on the Vietnamese government and the 'morale of the American pilots'. On 8 March the US landed 3,500 marines in South Vietnam which the Foreign Office said in private was 'in contravention of Article 16 and 17 of the 1954 agreement, but we have not yet received any protests on the subject' – therefore, best keep quiet. This illegal act was also welcomed by the British ambassador in Saigon who said it was 'a logical continuation of the policy begun with the air strikes on North Vietnam', a sign of the US 'determination to step up their effort in Vietnam'.[76]

Then, in June 1965, the US announced that US ground forces would now be going into combat on a routine basis – in effect, another significant escalation of US strategy, even though US troops were already regularly involved in combat. One Foreign Office official wrote:

> I feel sure we should try to help the US administration, who have now been landed in some difficulty in handling the president's announcement, by implying that the commitment of ground troops is mostly a matter of degree.

Thus British officials passed to the US State Department a copy of their draft response to the US announcement. 'I think the draft reply would be the best way of meeting the concern we can expect to be expressed in the House of Commons', one official noted.[77]

On 25 July 1965 Johnson wrote to Wilson saying that he was increasing the number of troops, possibly to double the 80,000 already there. Wilson's reply said that 'I can assure you that Her Majesty's Government are determined to persevere in their support for American policies which I believe to be in the interests of peace and stability'. He also boasted to Johnson that:

> Our attitude has been of great benefit to the United States government in terms of international opinion, for our example has helped to restrain a number of European and Commonwealth countries from giving more vocal and forceful expression to their own apprehensions about the course of American policy in Vietnam.[78]

The comparisons with Iraq in 2003 are difficult to avoid.

Etherington-Smith in Saigon was extremely enthused about the new US commitments, noting that Johnson's announcement had created a 'more hopeful atmosphere'. It will provide the US 'with a striking force of supremely well-equipped, highly air-mobile troops available for operations in any part of the country . . . to inflict heavy punishment on the Viet Cong'.[79]

The Foreign Office said in September that 'we are glad that the arrival of large American reinforcements has enabled so much progress to be made towards stabilising the military situation in South Vietnam'. It had 'restored Vietnamese morale and enabled striking military successes to be achieved against the Viet Cong'.[80]

The next major escalation was the direct bombing of North Vietnam's two largest cities, Hanoi and Haiphong.

British officials consistently told the US that they could not be seen to support US attacks against these cities, due to public opposition. They consistently told the US that if it decided to bomb Hanoi and Haiphong they would publicly have to dissociate the British government from the strikes. What the files reveal is that when the US told Britain in June 1966 that it was indeed going to bomb the two cities, Britain connived with the US to continue to back it in private.

The files show that the British were at pains to minimise the effect of the British 'disassociation' from the US. One of Wilson's advisers wrote:

What we might do, when the bombing happens and you put out your statement, is to send a further short message to the President, saying that, as he knew, we could not avoid disassociating ourselves from this action, but that in doing so, we did our best to take account of the points he asked for; and that, as he knew, the statement implied no change in our policy of support for him generally over Vietnam.[81]

Thus the British passed the draft response to the US for approval. Wilson wrote to Johnson saying that:

Dean [Rusk, US Secretary of State] tells me that you understand why we must publicly disassociate ourselves and you know that it will not affect our general support . . . you have my personal sympathy in finding yourself confronted with such a choice.[82]

After Johnson informed Wilson that the US had decided to strike at oil installations in Hanoi and Haiphong, Wilson replied that he was grateful for the advance warning, and that he would have to be seen to disassociate Britain from these actions. He added:

But I wish to assure you that, in this statement, we shall make it equally clear that we remain convinced that the United States government are right to continue to assist the South Vietnamese and that the onus for continuing the fighting and refusing a negotiation [sic] rests with Hanoi.[83]

The actual response made in public by the government came on 29 June, saying that it noted 'with regret' the attacks on targets 'touching on the populated areas of Hanoi and Haiphong' and that 'we have made it clear on many occasions that we could not support an extension of the bombing to such areas, even though we were confident that the United States forces would take every precaution, as always, to avoid civilian casualties'. Then the statement reiterated that the US were right to 'assist' South Vietnam etc., as outlined above.[84]

This statement is so full of qualifications that, together with the promises of ongoing support in private, it was no more than a PR exercise to placate public opinion at home. Indeed, on the same day that Wilson delivered the statement, the US Vice President and Defence Secretary both met the British ambassador in Washington. The latter recorded that 'both said that the Prime Minister's position was well understood and indicated that there would be no hard feelings'.[85]

Then Wilson wrote again to Johnson and in effect apologised for the British public, saying that since they were 'physically remote from the problem' and were 'not suffering the tragedy of the losses which your people are suffering', this 'serves to increase the lack of understanding of my full support for your basic policy'. He then said 'I cannot see that there is any change in your basic position that I could urge on you' and that 'I want you to realise that . . . we have differed in detail . . . but never in basic policy'. Where the British government has 'had to express a different point of view', 'I must be quite frank in saying that this is the price I have to pay for being able to hold the line in our own country'.[86]

While this was going on, Wilson told parliament that 'in regard to bombing policy, we have made it clear that we would totally oppose any bombing involving Hanoi or Haiphong'.[87]

There is no evidence that I found that British 'opposition' to the bombing of Hanoi and Haiphong was due to humanitarian concerns. Rather, the concern was that such a strategy would impede rather than help the US prosecution of the war. As an official in the British embassy in Washington put it, the New China News Agency would 'no doubt flood the world with pictures of mangled babies in the maternity ward of a Hanoi hospital, which could do a great harm to the Americans'. He also argued that it might backfire on the US since the North Vietnamese government might simply retreat to the hills.[88]

Britain continued to avoid engagement in a possible

negotiated settlement to the war until it became clear that the US could not win it. The Foreign Office noted, for example, that in the discussions with the Americans in December 1964:

> We did not then take the opportunity to recommend to the US government a policy of seeking negotiations on Indo-China. On the contrary, we promised qualified support to the American policy . . . of military pressure on North Vietnam aimed at winning the war rather than negotiating a settlement.

The problem was that 'in the present circumstances these [negotiations] could only lead to a settlement gravely adverse to Western interests and deeply humiliating to the United States'.[89]

It was only in early 1965, by which time British ministers and officials realised the war was unwinnable, that they began even half-seriously to promote peace negotiations. They approached the Soviet Union, the Commonwealth and the countries involved in the Geneva Accords and essentially called for a settlement along the lines of the 1954 conference: free elections in South Vietnam, the neutralisation of North and South Vietnam with no foreign troops and no military alliances with others – that is, a settlement along the lines that London had previously rejected in favour of the chance of the US winning the war. North Vietnam had presented a four-point programme by 1965 that called for the evacuation of US forces from South Vietnam, no US alliance with the latter, South Vietnam to accept the domestic programme of the National Liberation Front and an end to US aggression against South Vietnam.

The files make clear that Britain promoted negotiations not only to placate public opinion by wanting to be seen to be a peace-maker while it really backed the war; it also did this specifically in support of US military policy. A Foreign Office brief, for example, states that 'British initiatives of this kind would complement American military pressure and make it much easier to justify to British public opinion our continued support for American policy in Vietnam'.[90]

It was sometimes very frankly put. Thus the Foreign Office's Edward Peck wrote to Etherington-Smith in Saigon that:

> The government are fighting a continuous rearguard action to preserve British diplomatic support for American policy in Vietnam. They can only get away with this by constantly emphasising that our objective, and that of the Americans, is a negotiated settlement.[91]

Promoting negotiations for Britain meant enabling the US 'to withdraw from Vietnam without major damage to American prestige'. The Foreign Office stated that 'our efforts to promote negotiations must . . . proceed hand in hand with continued support for American policy'. The policy was to promote 'a negotiated settlement on terms acceptable to the Americans'.[92]

By February 1965 British officials were being told that US embassy staff in Saigon no longer considered victory 'but an improved negotiating position, to be the objective of military action against North Vietnam'. The British ambassador noted in the same month that 'Johnson regarded action against the North as a prelude to eventual negotiation'.[93]

This use of force to achieve a political goal is terrorism, and was a policy supported by the Wilson government. Foreign Office Minister Lord Walton, for example, noted in late 1964 that the US:

> should step up military activities to the maximum of her powers during the next two to three months: at the same time the United Kingdom, as co-chairman should press for a reconvening of the Geneva conference.[94]

Thus when Wilson told parliament in June 1965 that 'the bombing of North Vietnam is not related to any attempt to try to persuade or force Hanoi to come to the conference table', this is the opposite of what his officials were saying. It is hard to believe this was not simply yet another lie.[95]

Direct British support for the US military and Saigon government continued although US requests in 1965 for Britain openly to send troops were rejected. The request was described by one Foreign Office official in this way: 'what the President wants is for a few British soldiers to get killed in Vietnam alongside the Americans so that their photographs can appear in the American press'.[96]

In the British propaganda system, the customary (and usually only) reference to British policy in the Vietnam war was the Wilson government's refusal to agree to US requests to deploy troops. This certainly infuriated President Johnson and it was a public rebuff to the US. Yet Britain did virtually everything else to back the US war.

BRIAM continued to train Vietnamese army and police officers in Malaya while the fiction was maintained that Britain was providing no military advice. In 1964–1965, 356 South Vietnamese were given 'military training' in Malaysia; it was agreed to increase this military training after requests from the US during the talks in December 1964. Indeed, the files show that the US paid an 'allowance' to BRIAM members who in 1967 came under US military command. The Foreign Office notes that 'in order to maintain a publicly defensible position' that BRIAM was not providing military training – i.e., to lie – 'HMG decided that the additional American payments' were to be paid through the British embassy and not through individual contracts.[97]

Officials from Britain's Jungle Warfare School in Malaya also personally visited South Vietnam to give advice on 'counter-insurgency'. Robert Thompson attended numerous meetings with US military officers and continued to advise the US and Vietnamese. However, in doing so he must, the Foreign Office noted, 'be careful to make it clear that his military advice . . . is given in his personal capacity as an expert on these problems and not on behalf of Her Majesty's Government'.[98]

When Thompson suggested taking US military officers in Vietnam to Borneo to show them British military operations, the Foreign Office told him that any Americans should 'travel in plain clothes and no publicity would be given to their presence in Malaysia'. 'We would regard this as a natural counterpart of the visits paid to Vietnam by various British serving officers' who had been able to 'see something of the conduct of operations in that country'. Observation visits to Vietnam by serving British personnel were 'restricted on political advice to occasional short visits . . . with the minimum risk of publicity'.[99]

British officials were keen to get serving military officers into Vietnam to observe US operations but were fearful of the publicity. Therefore, Defence Secretary Denis Healey suggested that the embassy in Saigon could be used as a cover and two new assistant defence attaché posts were created. They began in January 1966 and were still there two years later. These were seen as 'the only way of introducing extra British military personnel into Vietnam which could stand up to critical public comment in this country', the Foreign Office noted.[100]

When BRIAM was technically wound up, the British advisory mission was formally incorporated into the embassy. One BRIAM official, Dennis Duncanson, continued his work as adviser to the Saigon government on 'information work and psychological warfare, for which he has a real talent', one Foreign Office official noted. One problem was in finding a suitable cover for this role so an official hit on the idea of saying Duncanson was an 'Aid Advisor'. Another official wrote that 'the title of "aid advisor" is an inspiration, which will make it easier to defend this appointment if it is ever challenged in Parliament'.[101]

Britain also provided arms to the US for use in Vietnam. Ministers debated in 1965–1966 whether to impose general conditions on arms exports to the US for use in Vietnam and decided against. This was done in the knowledge that supplying such arms was a breach of the Geneva Accords. In September 1965, for instance, the Foreign Office agreed to export 300 bombs intended for the US air force 'for use in Vietnam', saying that 'there must be no publicity' and that 'delivery should be in the UK'. The previous month the Foreign

Secretary had agreed to provide the US with 200 Saracen armoured personnel carriers for use in Vietnam 'providing that delivery took place in Europe' and that there was 'no unavoidable publicity'.[102]

Indeed, a specific public-deception strategy was pursued. In June 1965, for example, the British government told the Americans that if they requested weapons specifically for use in Vietnam Britain would not be able to provide them, but if they just asked for the arms in a 'general enquiry' without mentioning Vietnam, then Britain would.[103]

Wilson told parliament in June 1967 that: 'we believe that, in our position as co-chairman [of the Geneva Accords] . . . we should not be shipping arms directly for use in Vietnam'.[104] This was the official position decided in early 1967 that allowed 'non-lethal' items to be exported to the US. It also allowed lethal items to be supplied, provided that delivery was not made before the end of 1967, then the British estimate of when the Vietnam war would end.

The non-lethal/lethal distinction – a Whitehall classic – was as fictional then as it is now. In May 1967, for example, Wilson approved the supply of 'forgings and casings for various types of United States bombs and ammunition' after being told that these bombs could be for use in Vietnam. In June 1967 Britain also agreed to repair in Singapore Australian guns for use in Vietnam 'provided we can be sure of no (no) publicity'. In September 1970, the Conservative government relaxed the restrictions further and bombs and helicopter machine-gun turrets were sold to Thailand while the Thais were engaged in air attacks on Cambodia and Laos.[105]

The way out and British interests

The size of the US force in Vietnam rose to half a million by 1967 as the US deepened the war through the late 1960s, with mounting casualties. The size of this force meant that the US could not be militarily defeated but neither, it was openly recognised, could the war be won, largely owing to the lack of popular support for the South Vietnamese government and to Viet Cong success on the ground, notably the 1968 Tet (new year) offensive.

In South Vietnam in 1967, according to the British embassy in Saigon, 'corruption was unchecked, the government showed no capacity to govern and the Viet Cong remained the country's best-organised political force'. Twenty-five thousand political prisoners languished in South Vietnam's jails. By 1970, British officials continued to recognise that the Thieu government, which they continued to back, was 'still short on popular appeal'. After nearly five years in power Thieu had made 'little progress . . . in building for his regime a base of organised political support'. Rather, the regime's basic strategy was to repress popular, political forces – as well known to planners now, at the end of the decade, as it had been under Diem at the beginning.[106]

US brutality increased through a deepening of 'pacification' and 'Phoenix' operations. 'Pacification' programmes such as Operation Speedy Express, to name but one, begun in early 1969, involved the devastating use of US firepower and caused thousands of civilian casualties. The Phoenix programme had began in earnest in mid-1968 and aimed at assassinating NLF cadres. Abuse and torture of prisoners repeatedly occurred and even the Saigon government stated that 40,000 civilians were killed under the programme. The slaughter of villagers at My Lai, which gained worldwide attention, was just one of numerous massacres by US forces and its allies.[107]

With the war unwinnable, US military strategy was to inflict sufficient violence on Vietnam to allow Washington as good an exit as possible to preserve prestige. In June 1969, President Nixon announced the first US troop withdrawal and said that all US combat troops would leave Vietnam by the end of 1972. The war was escalated – US troops invaded Cambodia in April 1970 and in 1972 the US inflicted devastating bombing on Hanoi and Haiphong as well as mining all North Vietnamese ports. In

January 1973 a peace agreement was signed and the last US troops left in March, after which the US continued to provide huge military aid to the South Vietnam government. In April 1975, Communist forces entered Saigon.

As massive public protests took place throughout the US and Europe, British governments did not waver in their fundamental support of US strategy. Vice President Hubert Humphrey told Harold Wilson in April 1967 that 'there were two Prime Ministers on whom he could really rely – those of the United Kingdom and of Australia'. The files show ongoing appreciation by US officials of the support provided by Britain throughout the second half of the decade; these officials frequently contacted their British counterparts to, for example, give praise for performances in parliament that fended off criticism of the US.[108]

Britain's new ambassador in Saigon, John Moreton, wrote in 1971 that due to Britain's economic interests in South-east Asia, especially Malaysia, Singapore and Australia, 'we must do all we can to help our closest ally, the United States, to extricate themselves with honor from their over-commitment'.[109]

The British attitude to the impact on people was starkly put by the Foreign Office's Denis Murray, in February 1967:

> On the political level I must stress that Ministers are anxious to engage as little as possible in the House of Commons in discussions of casualties or damage in North Vietnam caused by American bombing; [sic] since to do so would immediately open the way for a general attack on US policy and on our support for it. This would oblige the Secretary of State, or the Prime Minister, in defending our general support for US policy to risk laying themselves open to charges of defending the results of this policy, eg casualties and damage to civilian property, that they deplore as much as anyone else . . . More generally, there is political danger and embarrassment in trying to define exactly what damage and casualties have occurred; any

> relaxation of the stonewalling would open the way to
> pressure to do so; and in any case I doubt if anyone . . .
> could give an accurate picture . . . For all these reasons,
> Ministers do not wish to reactivate interest, in this
> country, in our estimate of casualties and damage in
> North Vietnam.[110]

The US bombing of North Vietnam continued to elicit
support from ministers and Whitehall officials, the only
reservations being concerns about whether such bombing was
'wise' and likely to 'succeed'. The only protests appeared to
come from an official in the consulate in Hanoi, John Colvin,
who wrote in May 1967 that the bombing was 'unlikely to
succeed' and 'may produce serious epidemics' as well as being
a 'cruel and dishonourable tactic'. By this time, officials
recorded that the US had flown 13,000 sorties in North
Vietnam, an average of 250 a week.[111]

By late 1968 Britain's air attaché in Saigon was noting that
such bombing, which was being carried out over all of North
Vietnam, was aimed at industrial targets, electrical-power-
generating capacity and communications such as rail and
roads. 'On the credit side' of this, he added, 'the destruction of
the North Vietnamese industrial plant and agricultural
production has forced the Russians and to a much lesser extent
the Chinese to make this good, as well as to supply the North
Vietnamese with increasing quantities of weapons, military
supplies and assistance of all kinds'.[112]

A brief for the Prime Minister in October 1967, which was
intended to help Wilson answer parliamentary questions,
suggested a reply saying: 'I do not believe that there has been
any change in the American policy of bombing only military
targets in the North'. This was fiction: an MoD report two
months previously had mentioned the US widening the
number of targets in the North so that bombing was
'increasingly directed toward interdiction or roads and railways
serving Hanoi and Haiphong'. The objective of US bombing

appeared to be 'to provide a position of greater strength in the event of negotiations taking place'.[113]

The British government was so keen not to protest against the US bombing in public that even when Britain's own consulate was damaged in a US raid in November 1967, officials decided to bury the matter and not seek compensation. The Foreign Office noted that 'our aim is to keep the temperature down and we shall therefore not be giving any publicity to American regrets unless the question is raised in either the House or the press'. When proof was provided that it was indeed a US bomb that had damaged the consulate, the Foreign Office stated that 'we shall not make this public'.[114]

When, in late 1971, British officials were expecting the US to renew their bombing of North Vietnam, a Foreign Office official wrote that if such attacks were launched the British government should say that they are consistent with declared US policy and are 'protective reaction strikes' in retaliation for US losses over recent days in Laos. In late December the US launched its heaviest attacks on North Vietnam for a year with a force of 200 fighter bombers. The British government reacted as planned. 'Provided the raids are short and sharp there will be no too emotive reaction' [sic], one Foreign Office official commented.[115]

Of particular interest in this period are the secret files on planners' views on the British interests now at stake.

By the end of the decade British officials were desperate for a US withdrawal, as long as it was on US terms. A draft Foreign Office Planning Committee report of June 1968 concluded that 'it is very much in our interests that the United States should as soon as possible find a means of escape from her present involvement' in Vietnam. The reason was British economic interests. Thus it was believed that US involvement in Vietnam was imposing 'strains on the world monetary system'. This was due to a lack of confidence in the reserve currencies in the monetary system, one of the main reasons for which was the deficit in the US balance of payments caused by spending on the Vietnam war. A US withdrawal 'would have a stimulating confidence effect on the dollar and in [sic] world trade, which should both directly benefit the UK balance of payments'. Since the existing monetary system was dependent largely on the willingness of the European countries to hold an increasing number of dollars in their reserves, a danger was that this would not continue indefinitely. This 'could result in a major monetary crisis which would cause us major damage whatever its outcome'. Therefore, 'on economic grounds alone a continuing United States involvement in South Vietnam would be highly unsatisfactory for British interests'.[116]

However, this did not mean that the best outcome was simply a total withdrawal of US forces. The problem was the massive US operation in Vietnam, not its overall position in South-east Asia, which was welcome. The Foreign Office concluded that the US balance of payments 'can be put right without a total withdrawal'. It was believed that:

> Britain's economic interests would be promoted by a quick settlement in Vietnam only if it was a good settlement. A bad settlement would have as damaging an effect on the world financial situation as the prolongation of the present level of hostilities.[117]

The basic threat was not the one presented to the public – which was of Soviet or Chinese expansion. As a senior Foreign Office official recognised, if the US withdrew from Vietnam, the country 'is unlikely to be Russian or Chinese dominated; but it would certainly be nationalist with a heavy list to the left and strongly opposed to the Anglo-Saxon West'. Rather, a total US withdrawal would encourage other countries in South-east Asia 'to come to terms with the Communists'. In this situation 'our own interests, both trading and political, are likely to suffer'. At worst, 'Western trade in South-east Asia could be snuffed out', while:

the trading advantages which we now enjoy in certain
countries – notably Malaysia and Singapore but
including also in lesser degree Thailand and Indonesia –
might well be wiped out and we would have to start four-
square with our major competitors in Europe and Japan.

Therefore, 'it will be important to try to hold the "danger line"
north of Malaysia and Indonesia which are important as
sources of raw materials as well as markets'. Given the danger
of total US withdrawal, British interests lay in 'protracting these
negotiations as much as possible'.[118]

Eighteen months later, in January 1970, the Foreign Office
produced another brief. It warned again of the danger of a
'precipitate' US withdrawal, which would increase the threat to
'stability' and 'security' 'in influential circles' in South-east
Asian countries. Also, such a withdrawal could have 'a deeply
humiliating effect on American feeling and a traumatic effect
on American foreign policy'. British interests in the war
concerned not only the effects on US foreign policy generally
but 'our substantial trade with and investment in the Southeast
Asian arena'.[119]

The US invasion of Cambodia in April 1970, a further
widening of the war that met with massive public protests in
the US, was firmly supported by British officials. Ambassador
Moreton wrote that 'leaving aside the political risks, I am now
completely convinced of the soundness óf the military arguments in favour of the decision'. He reasoned that this decision
had been taken 'to improve the chances of a negotiated
settlement' and to proceed with troop withdrawals. Britain's
ambassador in Cambodia noted that 'this saves Cambodia from
an immediate communist take-over but increases the long-
term communist threat to the country'. Indeed, within five
years the Khmer Rouge, strengthened as a result of the US
violence inflicted on Cambodia, emerged to enact their 'year
zero', with terrifying consequences for the millions who died in
the killing fields.[120]

Edward Heath is remembered for taking Britain into the European Community; he should also be remembered for providing extreme apologias and support for the US violence in Vietnam. Heath wrote to Nixon in July 1970:

> I do not need to assure you that you have our fullest support in your search for peace in the area. We deeply admire the firmness and persistence which you have shown.

This was in reply to Nixon's letter attaching a report on the US troop withdrawal from Cambodia, which the US had invaded three months previously.[121]

In December 1970, Heath told CBS television in the US that Nixon was carrying out 'an honourable withdrawal. And in the process, if there is difficulty from North Vietnam, then he is bound to take action . . . And this, I think, is quite justifiable'. This was in reference to US bombing of North Vietnam undertaken to strengthen the US negotiating position as US forces withdrew from the region.[122]

In April 1972, Nixon inflicted massive bombing on Hanoi and Haiphong; other cities were also targeted and systematically destroyed. British officials recognised that this bombing was launched 'to attempt to create a position of strength against which to negotiate' by sending a signal to Moscow and Hanoi. It was therefore terrorism.

The government's news department was instructed to say that Nixon had all along 'reserve[d] the right' to bomb North Vietnam. On 17 April Foreign Secretary Douglas-Home defended the US bombing in parliament. This prompted US Secretary of State William Rodgers to phone him 'to thank him very much' and to say 'it was very much appreciated in Washington'. Rodgers informed Douglas-Home 'how pleased the President was'.[123]

The following month, Nixon told Heath that he had ordered the mining of North Vietnamese ports to effect a blockade. Heath replied: 'I fully understand the range of problems caused for you by the flagrant invasion launched by Hanoi', referring to an offensive into South Vietnam. Heath said there would be effects on shipping and 'freedom of navigation' but 'we shall do our best to avoid adding to your difficulties'.[124]

Britain backed the US to the last, throughout the various escalations that inflicted increasing devastation on the Vietnamese people. It provided direct support to repressive and unpopular Vietnamese regimes and the US military, some of whose brutal 'counter-insurgency' programmes were based on British plans. It also engaged in covert action with US special forces and provided important intelligence that aided the US prosecution of the war. From the first days of the US intervention in 1961, planners in Whitehall strongly supported the war and obstructed a diplomatic outcome when it believed the US could win. When by mid-decade it became clear the US could not win, London wanted to be seen to be active in searching for a diplomatic solution, primarily as a way of placating public opinion at home and to secure a negotiated outcome on US terms only. As US violence reached unprecedented heights, Britain secretly reassured the US of its complete backing for the war while issuing the mildest criticism in public of some US actions. Throughout, there was not even the pretence of concern for the victims.

PART IV

COUPS, DICTATORS

13

UGANDANS: THE RISE OF IDI AMIN

In January 2002 the British government declassified some of its planning files on the 1971 coup in Uganda that brought Idi Amin to power.

A search on the BBC website produced 35 mentions of Idi Amin, none of which covered the release of the files. Indeed, at exactly the time BBC correspondents could have been analysing the story of Britain's role in the rise of Idi Amin, they produced a story headlined 'Amin's son runs for mayor'. The only mention on the BBC site I could find of a possible British role was an aside buried in one article. Political commentator Yasmin Alibhai-Brown, a Ugandan Asian expelled by the Amin regime, was quoted saying that Britain was 'implicitly involved in his rise to power'; there was no further comment or explanation from the reporter.[1]

A search on the *Guardian* website produced 208 mentions of Idi Amin; again, the release of the declassified files was not covered. Of the 208, I found two articles that mentioned Britain's acquiescence in the rise of Amin.[2]

Both the BBC and the *Guardian*, and other mainstream media, had ample opportunity to recount Amin's rise to power when he died in exile in Saudi Arabia in August 2003. Yet the only articles I could find on the Internet revealing something of

UNPEOPLE

Britain's role were in the *East African* and in the Ugandan
newspaper the *Monitor*. No one in the British press seems
willing to inform the public of another interventionist strategy
carried out in their name.

The Amin coup

The declassified documents tell us first that British officials
were delighted to see the back of the government of Milton
Obote which Amin overthrew. Eleven days before Amin's coup
on 25 January 1971, Britain's High Commissioner in Kampala,
Richard Slater, ran through the list of problems that Obote was
causing Britain, concluding that Anglo-Ugandan relations were
in a 'deplorable' state.[3] Most prominent of these was Obote's
nationalisation measures and the threat to withdraw from the
Commonwealth if Britain went ahead with resuming arms
exports to apartheid South Africa, as it was then proposing
to do.

On the latter issue, Ugandan Foreign Minister Odaka had
publicly said that to proceed with arming South Africa would
strengthen it militarily, lead to an arms race in Africa, heighten
racial tensions and enable Pretoria to frustrate the prosecution
of sanctions against it. He said that if the sale of arms went
ahead the Heath government would be opposing 'the liberation
of the oppressed majorities in Southern Africa' and strengthening 'the hands of the oppressors'. High Commissioner Slater
said that 'we are in for a difficult time' with Obote if the decision
to resume arms sales go through.[4]

As for nationalisation: in May 1970 Obote announced
legislation whereby the government would take over all foreign
import and export businesses and acquire compulsorily 60 per
cent of the shares of oil companies, manufacturing industries,
banks, insurance companies and other sectors. Compensation
would be paid over periods of up to 15 years out of the profits
received by the Ugandan government.

British officials were aware that this was was entirely legal,

246

but the measures were a direct challenge to British business interests. The threat was recognised by the Foreign Office as having 'serious implications for British business in Uganda and Africa generally'. Crucially, 'there is a danger that other countries will be tempted to try and get away with similar measures with more damaging consequences for British investment and trade'. It noted that three weeks after the Ugandan announcement, the government of Sudan nationalised foreign businesses 'in an even more unacceptable way'.[5]

The fear that Obote's nationalisation would be promoted elsewhere was repeated by a British big business lobby group, the East African and Mauritius Association, which told the Foreign Office that:

> The end result is the loss of British investment overseas and the establishment of precedents which could involve similar action by governments of other territories with adverse repercussions on the British economy.

The danger was of 'the emergence of a pattern' and it urged the British government to make clear to these other governments 'their very grave concern at recent developments in Uganda'.[6]

Fifty British firms operating in Uganda were threatened by nationalisation, the major ones including three banks, Grindlays, Standard and Barclays, and several other large corporations like Shell/BP (then linked rather than discrete companies), BAT, Dunlop, Brooke Bond and Mackenzie Dalgety. By the end of 1970 only one company, Shell/BP, had signed a compensation agreement with the Ugandan government. Foreign Secretary Alec Douglas-Home noted that 'there does not seem at present to be any very hopeful prospect' of these companies negotiating agreements satisfactory to them.[7]

High Commissioner Slater noted eleven days before the coup that 'British interests suffered more than any other' from these nationalisation measures. He also noted that 'to the extent that non-Ugandan interests were liable to be hurt, the measures were popular'. However, 'for the vast majority of what I can only describe as the elite of Uganda, the implications were deeply disturbing'. Under Obote:

> Capitalism has become a dirty word and the well-to-do are wondering whether it might not be wise to turn in the Mercedes Benz for something more modest and sell off a house or two.

As well as nationalisation, there was 'another hazard' for the elite that had appeared 'in the form of stringent anti-corruption legislation' enacted by Obote in June 1970.[8]

Slater is here openly mentioning a clear theme of British foreign policy – that British interests are precisely designed to protect the 'elite' from 'popular measures'.

Another Foreign Office official, Eric le Tocq, conceded that 'we are prepared to believe that the policies which he [Obote] is pushing through may well prove, in time, to be in the best interests of Ugandans'. Also recognised was the 'inequity' of the pre-nationalisation arrangements under the East African Community where many companies remitted their profits to Nairobi 'instead of "reinvesting" them in the country in which they are earned'.[9]

Obote's rule certainly had authoritarian aspects and he had earlier suspended the constitution and assumed control of the state. Yet it was not these negative features of Obote's rule that primarily concerned British planners. At least the Obote regime had promoted several policies beneficial to Ugandans, notably the proclamation of the 'Common Man's Charter' which echoed the call for African socialism by Tanzanian President Julius Nyerere. This provided the backdrop to the nationalisation measures, which, along with the possible Ugandan reaction to British arms sales to South Africa, were the major concerns of British planners.

The coup by then army chief of staff Amin took place while Obote was attending a Commonwealth conference in Singapore and involved the arrest or shooting of officers loyal to Obote, resulting in the deaths of hundreds of people. The coup was immediately welcomed by British officials. Britain was one of the first countries formally to recognise Amin as President, along with the US and Israel; some African states, such as Tanzania and Zambia, refused to acknowledge the legitimacy of the new military regime.

'Our interest in Uganda in terms of citizens, investment, trade and aid programme [sic] are best served in these circumstances by early recognition', the Foreign Office noted. The files show that British officials canvassed other 'moderate' (i.e., pro-British) governments in Africa 'who we judge likely to be sympathetic towards General Amin' to recognise the new regime. 'We are hoping that we can discreetly let General Amin know of these efforts which we are making on his behalf', the Foreign Office noted.[10]

'We have no cause to shed tears on Dr Obote's departure', said the Assistant Under-Secretary of State at the Foreign Office, Harold Smedley. 'At long last we have a chance of placing our relations with Uganda on a friendly footing', High Commissioner Slater wrote to the Foreign Office. Three weeks after the coup, Slater was telling the Foreign Secretary that 'Anglo-Ugandan relations can only benefit from the change' and that Amin was 'deeply grateful (as I am) for the promptness with which Her Majesty's Government recognised his regime'.[11]

Britain thus welcomed the violent overthrow of a government recognised by British officials to be promoting many policies 'in the best interests of Ugandans'. British support also came in full knowledge of why Amin had acted in the first place.

Obote had previously tried to arrest Amin in September 1970 but was prevented by soldiers loyal to Amin. Obote had had to content himself with reducing Amin's powers. He made changes in the structure of the military, entrenching officers loyal to himself. Before leaving for Singapore, he demanded that on his return Amin should provide explanations about the disappearance of arms and corruption in the army. The following week a court case was also due to begin for the murder of Brigadier Okoya, of which Amin was strongly suspected. In the words of British officials 'the coup was probably dictated more by Amin's fear that his own downfall was imminent than by any real desire to save his country from Obote'.[12]

The British welcome also came with no illusions about Amin's bloody past and character. Amin was 'corrupt and unintelligent', Harold Smedley wrote two days after the coup. There was 'something of the villain about him and he may well be quite unscrupulous and indeed ruthless', a Foreign Office official wrote six days after the coup. Richard Slater managed to convince himself, however, that 'despite his limitations, he [Amin] has considerable dignity and more the air of a leader than Obote'.[13]

Amin's recent past allegedly included some gruesome deeds. As an officer in the King's African Rifles in Britain's colony of Kenya in the early 1960s, Amin is believed to have been involved in torture and killing. In one incident, then Lieutenant Amin, responsible for dealing with illegal cattle-rustling, was said to have tortured a whole village before killing eight men. Then Prime Minister Milton Obote was in no position to make him answer for these crimes: he feared the likely reaction of the rest of Africa to the prosecution of a Ugandan soldier just a few months before Uganda's independence.[14]

There was a further hope expressed by British planners – that Amin's military coup might be replicated by other pro-British forces in the continent. Eric le Tocq of the Foreign Office's South-east Asian Department wrote that:

> General Amin has certainly removed from the African scene one of our most implacable enemies in matters affecting Southern Africa . . . Our prospects in Uganda have no doubt been considerably enhanced . . . If Amin's coup is successful, in that he remains firmly entrenched in power, and eventually gains the acceptance . . . of the other black African governments, this will no doubt enhance the temptation to other

African military leaders to follow his example. Events in Uganda will have been noted in Kenya [sic] military circles, though there seems little likelihood of any military move until president Kenyatta leaves the scene. This could conceivably produce a government better disposed to Britain than Kenyatta's political heirs.[15]

When this period is discussed at all in the media (which is rare), the standard line is that given how Amin soon expelled the Ugandan Asians, British planners must have made a 'mistake' in acquiescing in Amin's rise. This is not the case; British policy was far from being a 'mistake'. The fact is that Britain consciously supported and connived in the rise of Idi Amin because of long-standing British interests to get rid of governments like that of Obote who were challenging 'elites' and promoting 'popular measures'. This episode is a microcosm of general British foreign policy and illustrates one of its most fundamental aspects.

Amin effectively reversed Obote's nationalisation plans. 'Many firms were saved from a nasty dose of nationalisation by General Amin's seizure of power', Eric le Tocq later wrote. In May the new regime gave a statement on its economic policy that welcomed private investment. In anticipation of this statement, the Foreign Office wrote that the policy was 'broadly welcome to British companies here and should go a long way towards the restoration of foreign investment confidence in Uganda'. The new regime was showing 'an encouraging attitude in the economic and financial spheres', it noted. 'We expect its policies to be more pragmatic and less ruled by the somewhat rigid doctrines of the Obote regime'.[16]

Terror in Uganda

The subsequent story of Amin's rule is one of repression and terror, a second phase that was in effect also supported by Britain.

By February 1971 Amin had 'concentrated all the powers of parliament and of the former President in his hands', the British High Commission in Kampala noted. He announced that elections would not take place for five years. One Foreign Office official wrote that 'it is now beginning to look as if Uganda may merely have exchanged one form of authoritarian government for another'. In early March a decree banned all political activity for two years and people 'continue to be detained without trial' – the High Commission officials estimated that the number was around 1,000.[17]

The British reaction was instructive. One Foreign Office official wrote that 'I can appreciate that a period of rule free from all politics, if that is in fact a genuine possibility, could be desirable'. The official went on to say, however, that a 'complete cessation' of politics for two years was 'unnecessary', before adding:

> I readily recognise that too much democracy in a country like Uganda at the present stage can be as fatal as too great a degree of authoritarianism. What would seem to be required for the foreseeable future is a realistic balance between firm and, indeed, authoritarian, government and some degree of democratic expression. I believe Uganda needs no necessarily democratic government, but it is important that government should be representative and fair as well as firm.[18]

With power being concentrated into Amin's hands and officials recommending 'authoritarian' government, the Ugandan regime approached Britain for arms. 'Armoured cars can go ahead. Strikemaster aircraft OK. Perhaps Harriers', wrote the Foreign Office's Eric le Tocq. British policy, he said, should be to show a willingness to supply arms to prevent the Ugandans going elsewhere, but also to discourage them from purchases which are 'overambitious, militarily, technically or financially'.[19]

On 21 April a British 'Defence adviser' in Kampala met the Ugandan Defence Minister and subsequently reported that 'the prospects for defence sales to Uganda are both clearer and brighter'. Under discussion were Saladin, Saracen and Ferret armoured cars, Jaguar aircraft, helicopters, radar and light guns. A deal to supply one million rounds of ammunition was approved. A Foreign Office official wrote:

> We consider it important . . . both in order to keep his [Amin's] goodwill and also to assist in maintaining the stability of his regime that we should facilitate as far as we can the meeting of requests for equipment from this country.

Another official wrote of the 'political desirability of supporting General Amin'.[20]

By mid-May, the High Commission recorded continued arrests with up to 1,000 inmates in one prison in Kampala. A further decree issued that month ordered that people could be detained with no time limit if ministers believed that they were engaged in subversive activities. The High Commission was also getting 'several reports' of incidents in which British subjects 'have fallen foul of the army'. In one, a senior expatriate civil servant was severely beaten and his Ugandan deputy beaten to death 'because it was thought that men working under him had been recruited for Obote'.[21]

In early July Amin announced that he wanted to visit Britain in the middle of the month to discuss British training of the Ugandan army and joint military exercises. The British government quickly arranged what was in effect a state visit. After it was decided to host a lunch for Amin, Prime Minister Edward Heath's personal adviser, Peter Moon, wrote that 'the Prime Minister would like the guests to be of high level so that President Amin feels that he is being honoured'. There should be 'senior military representation and British businessmen with interests in Uganda'. It was understood that 'the primary purpose of General Amin's visit is to discuss military matters'; Amin met the Queen, the Prime Minister and the Defence Secretary, among others.[22]

The brief from the Foreign Office read: 'General Amin has abandoned Obote's radical pan-African policies for a more moderate and pro-Western policy'. The new government, a High Commision official wrote, was 'not ideal, but by African standards as good as could be hoped for'.[23]

At these meetings Foreign Secretary Douglas-Home told Amin that 'we would help as best we could' on military and economic aid and with the training of troops, although the supply of Harrier jets would be too costly for Uganda. A £2 million contract to supply 26 Saladin and 6 Saracen armoured personnel carriers was signed. The *Daily Telegraph* wrote in an editorial that General Amin was:

> a staunch friend of Britain . . . His request now for the purchase of equipment for the rebuilding of Uganda's defences deserves the most sympathetic consideration from every point of view.[24]

These July agreements with the Ugandan military were signed while hundreds of soldiers were being massacred by Amin's forces in Uganda. 'The killings took place at a large number of army camps across Uganda', a Foreign Office official wrote the following month. 'A large number of officers and men, in particular from the Acholi and Langi tribes (those associated with Dr Obote) were killed'.[25]

Three days after this note, on 16 August, another Foreign Office official wrote:

> From the point of view of British interests, General Amin's regime has so far served us well. He is extremely well-disposed to Britain . . . and his coup removed one of our more bitter African critics. We have already done much to assist in the establishment and recognition of his regime and we are doing what we can to help him overcome his present difficulties.[26]

By August Amin had announced the establishment of a military junta. In the same month, Britain offered a £10 million loan for three years. High Commissioner Slater was saying that 'despite some obvious deficiencies, he remains a net asset from Britain's point of view'. Slater recognised that the Acholi and the Langi 'have fled or been killed or imprisoned', saying that 'this is the rather sombre background to a bright chapter in Anglo-Ugandan relations'. 'I am sure that he [Amin] is sincerely grateful for what we have done and offered to do', such as early recognition, military and police training and the financial loan. Slater added that:

> So long as he stays in power, Ugandan reactions to controversial British policies in Africa will be containable and the influence of the moderates in the OAU [Organisation of African Unity] will be strengthened. It remains therefore a British interest to see his regime consolidated.[27]

This basic support was being offered despite officials' 'misgivings . . . about the course Uganda is taking'. This included 'the continuing financial mess, with talk of expensive military equipment', the 'dangerous lack of civil law and order' and 'the internecine strife in the army that threatens the whole basis of his rule'.[28] These were the beginnings of the eventual recognition that the Amin regime was so incompetent and corrupt that it was a liability. But this point had not yet been reached.

In November, the Foreign Office noted that 'power remains firmly in Amin's hands' and that 'he is probably ruthless enough to brook no opposition'. It envisaged further 'repressive measures' to 'add to the unspecified numbers of those who have disappeared or are held in prison without trial'. It also stated that 'the prospect is of a continuing slow drift towards bankruptcy and the gradual emergence of the less savoury aspects of a military dictatorship'.[29]

Officials were also becoming increasingly wary of Britain being publicly identified with Amin. Britain's 'public and visible involvement with the regime' such as the military and police training teams and the visiting aid mission, meant that 'we might well be saddled with some of the criticism belonging to the Amin regime'.[30]

One year into the regime's grip on power, in January 1972, Ugandan Defence Minister Oboth-Ofumbi visited Britain to buy arms and was shown 'a wide range of military equipment' and given reassurances of 'our willingness to help'. 'The main obstacle as far as we could see concerned the provision of funds', British officials told him; any lingering human-rights problems appear never to have been raised. Projected sales at this point included an air-defence radar system, fast patrol boats and anti-tank missiles worth £10–20 million. The following month the commander of the British army training team for Uganda visited the country.[31]

By February 1972, High Commissioner Slater could say to the Foreign Office that he 'had no immediate bilateral problems to discuss' with Amin – a few hundred murders, the banning of all political activity and beatings of expat civil servants apparently unworthy of discussion. 'If anything special occurs to you, please let me know', he added.[32]

One thing that did occur to Edward Heath was to send an emissary to Amin hoping that it would 'lead to agreement between us as to how your government can best surmount the difficulties with which it is presently faced'. The emissary, Lord Aldington, sought to advise Amin on economic matters and on arms procurement 'and to secure those orders for the United Kingdom'. In his meetings in March, Aldington proposed sending an MoD team to discuss British arms exports, for which Amin 'expressed complete approval', he noted. Aldington also recommended that Britain send the military training team already agreed to.[33]

Aldington met Amin on 24 March. Four days before, the Foreign Office noted that Richard Slater:

> confirms that during January anything up to 400 detainees at Mutukula were put to death in cold blood

after appearing before some sort of kangaroo court. Mr Slater thinks that Amin must have known what was going on but acquiesced ... An unknown number of people appear to have been killed on 27 February at Soroti as a result ... of army and police brutality.

The same note said that Britain should continue to help the country 'get out of the mess it is in' by economic aid and training missions.[34]

Referring to the 400 deaths, another Foreign Office official noted that Amin may 'have to resort to more unpleasant manifestations of his power in order to retain authority, ie, more disappearances and deaths'. 'He may increasingly become an unsavoury friend to have'. This official also wrote:

It is a nasty business and seems bound to excite international attention. We may well get some awkward parliamentary questions ... We are close to Amin and are known to be close to Amin and some of the odium may well rub off on us. If there are any more reports and if we get a spate of awkward questions, particularly if they refer to the help we are giving Amin, we may find it necessary to ask the High Commissioner to seek from Amin some explanation.[35]

Thus after mass killings and clearly announced decrees of repression, Whitehall might simply seek 'some explanation' from Amin, which might be necessary only because of 'awkward parliamentary questions'.

The files show that by the early months of 1972 there were constant stories of killings by the army. This was when the first eight of the Saladin armoured cars – ideal for domestic repression – were delivered. In May, ministers approved the export of 20 Ferret armoured cars.

Also in May an ex-MP and prominent lawyer, Anil Clerk, was taken from his Ugandan home by the police and was not heard of for weeks. The Clerk case received some press coverage in

Britain, by which time the brutality of the Amin regime was public knowledge. At this point, Foreign Secretary Douglas-Home recommended sending 'a strong message' to the Ugandan government that the Clerk case could lead to a deterioration in relations.[36]

But Clerk's disappearance promoted a rather extraordinary despatch by High Commissioner Slater:

> So now we know who we are dealing with. On the one hand, a man of considerable charm, endowed with tremendous energy, concerned for the welfare of his people, well-disposed towards Britain. On the other hand, a tyrant, vindictive, ruthless, moody and stubborn as a child, often quite unamenable [sic] to reason, pathologically suspicious, a liar and hypocrite. On balance more Hyde than Jekyll, and not the man one would choose to do business with.

But Slater continued; 'we do not have a choice'. 'We cannot tell him to stop murdering people' and 'my plea is for business as usual'. Slater argued that Britain could not conceivably influence Amin by withdrawing some measures of support and any move against him 'would be fraught with consequences for our community [i.e., the thousands of British-passport holders in Uganda] for which we are at present ill-prepared'.[37]

Foreign Office official Simon Dawbarn noted later that there were reports that 'Amin was personally responsible' for Clerk's death but that 'we must go on doing business with Amin' since 'we have too many hostages in Uganda', referring again to the British-passport holders.[38]

The break

It was not until June 1972, according to the files, that British officials began to consider cutting off support to the Amin regime. The Foreign Office recommended to the Prime Minister's personal adviser, Lord Bridges, that the despatch of the military training team should be held up. The reason was that Amin had recently delivered several 'wild and irresponsible' public statements such as calling for 'military action against the "imperialists"' and joint naval exercises between African and Soviet vessels. His hold on the country seemed 'increasingly insecure' and the discipline of the army had deteriorated. 'The army is now feared by the civilian population', the Foreign Office noted. The military training team should be delayed since 'there would be a risk of criticism in the press and parliament which would not be easy to refute'. Heath agreed to delay the despatch of the team in early June.[39]

On 5 August Amin told the British High Commissioner of his intention to expel 80,000 Asian British-passport holders from Uganda, giving them three months to leave, and accusing them of excluding Africans from business and being responsible for illegally exporting capital. Heath wrote to Amin urging him to reverse this announcement saying that:

> The British government have gone out of their way to try to be friendly and cooperate with Uganda ever since your administration took over. We were and are very anxious to help you in all the economic and security problems which face your country. I have hoped that our personal relations could be close.[40]

Right up until the last, British ministers were obsequiously trying to deal with this dictator. Even then, the files show that officials wanted to retain the British army training team in Uganda – 'we thought that it was doing useful work and we did not want the current differences between our two governments to broaden', the Foreign Office explained.[41] It was Amin who expelled the team in September, at the same time as British officials spoke of a break in diplomatic relations. Export licences for 28 armoured cars approved for sale to Uganda were revoked, the other eight having already been delivered.

There is one final aspect to this period of Anglo-Ugandan relations worthy of description. Immediately after his overthrow, Obote made clear his intent to come back and reinstate his government. In early February 1971 British officials were receiving reports of movements by the Tanzanian military close to the Ugandan border which pointed to the possibility of an invasion to reinstate Obote. These military movements were called off abruptly on the evening of 4 February.

The High Commissioner in Tanzania, Sir Horace Phillips, wrote: 'I cannot be sure of the reason' for the halt in these military movements 'but I think it no coincidence that this was just after I had informed' President Nyerere of Tanzania 'of the likelihood of British recognition [of the Amin regime] within a short while'. Britain formally recognised the new government the following day, 5 February. This act meant that what would have been for Nyerere 'action against a rebel regime in support of a legitimate President suddenly assumed the character of an attempted overthrow of an internationally recognised government'. 'It may be', Phillips concluded, 'that this proved an effective deterrent'.[42]

Britain also rejected a second chance to help to reinstate Obote in June 1972. Word had then reached British officials that Obote was in contact with dissident Ugandan army officers who were planning a coup against Amin. A message delivered to British officials said that in future Obote would promise not to adopt the nationalisation measures that he had previously undertaken, and wanted the British reaction as to likely support for this counter-coup. Both Richard Slater in Kampala and the Foreign Office in London agreed not to reply. Slater said that 'Obote in my view has never been and never will be a friend of Britain' and that it was not only nationalisation that was the issue of their dispute. They also mentioned concerns as to whether the coup would succeed and whether the plan was intended to 'compromise us with Amin' – friendly relations then still obviously being of primary concern.[43]

The Amin regime proceeded to expel the Asian community from Uganda, 27,000 of whom were airlifted to Britain. The campaign of terror moved beyond Obote loyalists and the army to the entire country, killing church figures, lawyers, cabinet ministers and anyone else; and between 300,000 and 500,000 people died. The regime's various internal security organisations, notably the State Research Bureau, were responsible for grisly torture and executions.

The regime was stopped only in 1979 when the Tanzanian army, backed by Ugandan exiles, responded to a Ugandan invasion by counter-attacking and eventually overthrowing Amin. Subsequently, Amin escaped to exile in Saudi Arabia where he, his 25 children and 6 wives were provided with income and lavish expenses until his death.

The British government was asked in a parliamentary question in 1998 whether it would call on the Saudi government to expel Amin from its territory. 'We have no plans to make such representations' was the reply by Foreign Office minister Derek Fatchett, Whitehall probably being too busy selling arms to its Saudi clients to worry about bringing a mass murderer to book.[44]

14

CHILEANS: PROTECTING A DICTATOR

In October 1998, former Chilean dictator Augusto Pinochet was arrested on a visit to London. He then began a legal battle to halt his extradition to Spain, where he faced charges of torture during his military dictatorship from 1973 to 1990. The British courts eventually ruled that he was medically unfit to stand trial, and he flew back to Santiago in May 2000.

This case was hailed throughout the mainstream media as an important international precedent: dictators were no longer free to roam the world and could be held accountable under international law. Yet the case just as much demonstrated the opposite – that dictators favoured by the West will continue to escape justice.

Home Secretary at the time, Jack Straw, declared that this was a matter for the courts and not a political decision. Pinochet's supposed medical debilitation was all too easily accepted by the Blair government, which refused to call for fresh medical tests. The extent of Pinochet's illness may have been a fake; he had used a wheelchair for his court appearances in Britain but miraculously stepped out on to the tarmac on returning to Santiago. The press also reported that the British and Chilean governments may have reached an understanding that Pinochet's best chance of release would be on humanitarian grounds.[1]

The British government admitted in October 1998 that Pinochet had visited Britain five times in the previous five years. During the visit in which he was arrested, he had been given VIP status at the airport. The government reportedly came under pressure from the US not to assist his extradition. His chief apologist in Britain, Margaret Thatcher, mounted a campaign in his defence and took tea with the general soon after he was arrested. She told him that 'we are very much aware that it was you who brought democracy to Chile'.[2]

Three years after Pinochet escaped justice, Jack Straw, now Foreign Secretary, refused petitions to ban the entry into Britain of a Chilean navy ship, the *Esmeralda*, that had been used as a torture centre under the Pinochet regime. One of its hundreds of victims, a British priest named Michael Woodward, was tortured to death after his arrest five days after the 1973 coup. Protests from Woodward's sister and human-rights groups were not enough to move Straw. The press also reported that the government was 'busy sealing lucrative arms deals with the Chilean navy' while the 'Esmeralda and its crew of officer cadets is set to get an official Royal Navy welcome'.[3]

This is the most recent instalment in Britain's backing for Pinochet ever since 1973. Much about the US role in the coup has been known for some time. In particular, CIA documents declassified in 2000 confirm the extraordinary breadth of US covert action and dirty operations to topple an unfavoured government and instal a new one.

However, the British documents on the events of 1973 were declassified only on 1 January 2004.[4]

The Pinochet coup

In September 1973, a democratically elected Chilean government under President Salvador Allende was overthrown in a brutal coup organised by the Chilean military with the backing of the CIA. General Pinochet soon emerged as the leader of the military junta, which immediately engaged in gross repression of supporters of the previous government and other suspected opposition figures. All political activity was banned. At least 3,000 people were killed, most executed, died under torture or 'disappeared'.

Allende had been elected with 36 per cent of the vote in September 1970 and appointed President of a Popular Unity government with the consent of the Christian Democratic Party. In his victory speech in November, Allende proclaimed a programme of fundamental economic change, proposing to abolish the monopolies 'which grant control of the economy to a few dozen families', abolish the tax system that favoured the rich, abolish the 'large estates which condemn thousands of peasants to serfdom' and 'put an end to the foreign ownership of our industry'. 'The road to socialism lies through democracy, pluralism and freedom', Allende proclaimed.[5]

The strategy was to restructure society based on three different classes of ownership (state, mixed and private), through the rapid extension of state control over large parts of the economy. This involved the state takeover of both foreign and domestic private interests either by direct nationalisation or by government investment.

These policies improved the position of the poor, especially in the early part of the Allende presidency, through a rise in the minimum wage and special bonuses paid to poorly paid workers. This was matched by growing popularity for the government; in Congressional elections in the year of the coup, 1973, the Popular Unity coalition increased its vote to 44 per cent.

The US government and the CIA had sought to prevent Allende taking office; subsequently their policy was to overthrow him. A declassified CIA report reveals that throughout the 1960s and 1970s the US promoted 'sustained propaganda efforts, including financial support for major news media, against Allende' while 'political action projects supported selected parties before and after the 1964 elections and after Allende's 1970 election'. In the 1960s, actions included financial assistance to the Christian Democratic Party and other parties, the distribution of posters and leaflets, and financial assistance to selected candidates in Congressional elections. By the time of the 1964 election, won by favoured US candidate Eduardo Frei of the Christian Democratic Party, the CIA had provided $3 million to prevent Allende winning.

In the run-up to the 1970 election, the CIA conducted 'spoiling operations' to prevent an Allende victory and President Nixon authorised the CIA 'to seek to instigate a coup to prevent Allende from taking office'. A few days after Allende was elected, the CIA was authorised to establish direct contacts with Chilean military officers 'to evaluate the possibilities of stimulating a military coup if a decision were to be made to do so'. Arms, including machine guns and ammunition, were provided to one of the groups plotting a coup. Ten million dollars was authorised 'to prevent Allende from coming to power or unseat him'.[6]

Once Allende was in office, the CIA funnelled millions of dollars 'to strengthen opposition political parties' and 'also provided assistance to militant right-wing groups to undermine the President and create a tense environment'. CIA money was also used for 'forwarding worldwide propaganda information for placement in local media' and promoting public opposition to Allende among leading Chilean newspapers. Further CIA covert action initiatives were launched in 1971 and 1972 aimed principally at keeping Allende's opponents active by supporting opposition parties.

Also approved were efforts 'to encourage Chilean businesses to carry out a program of economic disruption'. US ambassador Edward Korry explained that the strategy was to:

> do all within our power to condemn Chile and the Chileans to utmost deprivation and poverty, a policy designed for a long time to come to accelerate the hard features of a Communist society in Chile.[7]

After the Pinochet takeover, the CIA notes that it 'continued some ongoing propaganda projects, including support for news media committed to creating a positive image for the military junta'.[8]

Britain's Joint Intelligence Committee recognised that 'the Allende government has been directing its economic efforts primarily at effecting a redistribution of income' in which prices had been held down and salaries allowed to rise. The strategy was recognised as an attempt 'to put right what they regard as economic and social injustices (including foreign domination of certain sectors of the economy)'; Allende was known to be 'committed to proving that socialism can be brought to Chile in a peaceful and democratic fashion'.[9]

Allende's chief heresy was nationalisation. In July 1971 the copper industry – which provided 70 per cent of Chile's export earnings – was fully nationalised and the US-owned copper mines completely taken over by the government, with the unanimous approval of the Congress. The US reacted sharply and cut off all credit and new aid to the government and pressed the World Bank to do the same. The chief US mining corporations, Kennecott and Anaconda, began legal proceedings against the government.

The US ambassador, Davis, told his British counterpart, Reginald Seconde, that the US government were concerned:

> not only about the loss to the copper companies, but also about the precedent that the Chilean action would set for the nationalisation of other big American interests throughout the developing world.[10]

Several banks were also nationalised. In early 1972 the government announced its intention to take over 91 key firms, which accounted for around half of Chile's output. A British Conservative-party briefing paper noted that British companies had been affected by nationalisation 'but it was generally considered at the time that where nationalisation of British assets had taken place the compensation agreed upon had been fair'.[11]

In a despatch just eight days before the coup, British ambassador Seconde admitted that Chile:

has at least caught her social problems by the tail: many people in the poorer and most depressed sections of the community have, as a result of President Allende's administration, attained a new status and at least tasted, during its early days, a better standard of living, though it has been eroded by inflation.

Seconde concluded that 'this is a major achievement and has set Chile apart from most other Latin American states'.[12]

Just three months after Allende assumed office, the Joint Intelligence Committee was concluding that 'Washington is clearly very perturbed by developments in Chile'. As well as nationalisation of US business interests, 'the United States must view the prospect of a moderately successful extreme left-wing regime in Chile with considerable misgiving if only because of the effect this might have elsewhere in Latin America'.

The JIC also expressed the same fear from a British perspective. saying that the course of events in Chile is likely to have 'important repercussions throughout Latin America and perhaps beyond'. 'Allende's victory has been hailed as strengthening the prevailing radical, anti-American trend in Latin America' and may lead to a bloc of 'like-minded states comprising Chile, Bolivia and Peru whose negative attitude towards foreign investment has already been demonstrated'.[13]

Seconde and other British officials also convinced themselves that Allende's policies were leading the country to economic ruin and political chaos. They omitted to mention that this had been aided by the US destabilisation campaign. The main British concern was the threat to Western business interests. Seconde noted that one future option for Chile was a coup: 'If this were to be followed by a military-guided regime', it would likely lead to US aid; 'it is on this that the business community are pinning their hopes'.[14]

The wishes of the business community – along with the US and British governments – were fulfilled. On 11 September, the

Chilean military effected what British officials described as a 'cold-blooded' and 'ruthless' coup. Allende's palace was rocketed by the military and the President apparently committed suicide. Thousands of prisoners were taken, Congress was suspended and all political parties and the trade-union movement were banned.[15]

Summary executions took place throughout the country while the junta, in the words of a British Conservative-party briefing paper two months after the coup, 'is hunting down the former leaders of the Left in order to, in the words of [junta member, Air Force General] General Leigh, "extirpate the Marxist cancer from the country".'[16]

The coup was widely condemned throughout the world as an illegitimate, violent and repressive overthrow of a progressive democratically elected government. It elicited much public outrage, including in Britain, especially as the Heath government did little in public to condemn it. Had the British public known what the government was doing in secret, public outrage would have been even greater.

British interests

The files clearly show that British planners in Santiago and London welcomed the coup and immediately set about conducting good relations with the military rulers, even secretly conniving with the junta to mislead the British public.

British officials were aware of the scale of atrocities. Three days after the coup, Ambassador Seconde reported to the Foreign Office that 'it is likely that casualties run into the thousands, certainly it has been far from a bloodless coup'. Six days later, he noted that 'stories of military excesses and mounting casualties have begun increasingly to circulate. The extent of the bloodshed has shocked people'.[17]

But it did not appear to shock Seconde and his staff in Santiago. He commented that 'we still have enough at stake in economic relations with Chile to require good relations with the government in power'. However, 'it would not be in anyone's interests to identify too closely with those responsible for the coup' – i.e., those good relations should be kept secret.[18]

After cabling London about casualties reaching into the thousands, Seconde told the Foreign Office that 'whatever the excesses of the military during the coup' the Allende government has been leading the country into 'economic ruin'. Britain should welcome the new rulers since 'there is every reason to suppose that they will now . . . try to impose a period of sensible, orderly government'. Indeed, Seconde effectively condoned the political repression, noting that 'the lack of political activity is, for the time being, no loss'.[19]

The ambassador also told the Foreign Office that 'most British businessmen . . . will be overjoyed at the prospect of consolidation which the new military regime offers'. British companies, such as Shell, he added, 'are all breathing deep sighs of relief'. 'Now is the time to get in', he recommended, urging the British government to provide early diplomatic recognition of the new regime.[20]

Foreign Secretary Alec Douglas-Home sent an official 'guidance' memo to various British embassies on 21 September outlining British support for the new junta. It said:

> For British interests . . . there is no doubt that Chile under the junta is a better prospect than Allende's chaotic road to socialism, our investments should do better, our loans may be successfully rescheduled, and export credits later resumed, and the sky-high price of copper (important to us) should fall as Chilean production is restored.[21]

The Foreign Office decided to go to extraordinary lengths to assure the Chilean junta of the British desire for good relations. Eleven days after the coup, Ambassador Seconde met Admiral Huerta, the junta's new Foreign Minister. Seconde's briefing notes for this meeting state:

> I shall put it to him frankly that HMG [Her Majesty's Government] understands the problems which the Chilean armed forces faced before the coup and are now facing: this is a particular reason why they are anxious to enter early into good relations with the new government.

Then Seconde said he would refer to 'our own problems of public opinion at home. It would therefore help us if he [Huerta] could agree that we should be able to say something to reassure public opinion at home'.[22]

Seconde's record of his meeting with Huerta confirms that he said that the British government 'understood the motives of the armed forces, intervention and the problems facing the military government' – diplomatic language for support for the junta. Seconde then gave Huerta a draft form of wording to be used in public by the British government, to which Huerta was asked to agree.[23]

This agreed statement is an apologia for the military junta's actions, undertaken to placate public opinion in Britain that the government should express concern about the situation in Chile. It said that Britain accepted that the internal situation in Chile 'is of course a matter for the Chilean government only' and that the British ambassador had expressed 'the very strong feeling which exists in many quarters in Britain over the deaths of President Allende and others and over the many people arrested'. It added that 'the Chilean government offered assurances that they will deal in a humane manner' with those in detention and in political opposition – an obvious lie, since Seconde and Whitehall were aware of the atrocities being committed.[24]

Foreign Secretary Alec Douglas-Home was delighted with Seconde's success in reaching an agreement with the junta on a form of words. He cabled the ambassador praising him for carrying out a 'difficult brief', adding: 'the statement helped us to defend our relatively early recognition of the new government against domestic criticism'.[25]

A Foreign Office brief noted that 'our major interest in Chile is copper', which accounted for one-third of the UK's copper imports. The disruption in Chile and 'fear for the future' had recently meant large rises in copper prices which were costing the UK an extra £500,000 in foreign exchange. 'We therefore have a major interest in Chile regaining stability, regardless of politics'.[26]

For 'regardless of politics' read: 'regardless of the people of Chile'. That the loss of half a million pounds was deemed more important than the overthrow of a largely successful democratically elected government – recognised even by British officials as improving the condition of the poor – says a lot about the priorities and values of British elites.

According to the government files, there was only one mention in the Cabinet of the coup, when on 13 September:

> the Foreign and Commonwealth Secretary said that following a coup in Chile, President Allende was reported to have committed suicide and a military junta had taken over. It was not yet clear whether the junta was in effective control of the country but he proposed that the question of recognising the new regime should be determined in accordance with the usual criteria.[27]

In a reflective 20-page despatch three weeks after the coup our man in Santiago said that 'the overthrow of constitutional government was not what it may seem in Britain' and that while he recognised that the armed forces were being widely condemned internationally 'this must be put into its proper perspective'. Seconde's analysis referred to the regular defeats that Allende's government suffered in the Congress and the government's retention of power on the basis of a 36 per cent vote, which, he was convinced, would never happen in Britain.

As for the new military junta, Seconde noted that 'circumstances also will push them into directions which British public opinion will deplore' and 'the next few years may be grey ones, in which freedom of expression may suffer'. 'But this regime suits British interests much better than its predecessor . . . The new leaders are unequivocally on our side and want to do business, in the widest sense, with us'.[28]

Political as well as business relations with the new military rulers deepened, despite clear recognition by British planners that 'torture is going on in Chile' and also of the 'allegedly quasi-fascist inclination of the new leaders'. It made little or no difference to British policy that, in the words of one Foreign Office official, 'it seems very hard to foresee a return for many years to anything like democratic government of the kind to which Chile has been accustomed for many years to come'.[29]

Foreign Office minister Leo Amery made clear in private meetings with Judith Hart, Labour's shadow minister for overseas development, that Britain would not suspend its aid programme and credit lines, as some donors had done. In a draft reply to a parliamentary question, the Foreign Office stated:

> Our priorities in Latin America are determined largely by our trading and investment interests . . . On the recent events in Chile, our public policy is to refuse to be drawn into the controversy of the rights or wrongs of President Allende's government or the new military government.[30]

British arms exports to the junta had an instant precedent: aircraft supplied by Britain had been used in the coup to attack President Allende's palace and his residence. The ambassador wrote that during the coup 'Hawker Hunters swept down with their aerial rockets, directed with remarkable accuracy at the Palace, which was severely damaged and set on fire'.[31]

With the junta in power, British officials made clear that arms contracts agreed with Allende would be honoured, involving eight Hawker Hunters and other equipment worth over £50 million. But they went further, saying in the secret files that 'we shall want in due course to make the most of the opportunities which will be presented by the change in government'. Expectations were for new requests for arms from the junta but 'we shall wish to play these as quietly as possible for some time to come' owing to widespread public opposition. The Heath government defied calls from the Labour party to impose an arms embargo on Chile; all the Hawker Hunters had been delivered by the time of the 1974 general election.[32]

A further major task was to counter the British and international opposition to the military regime's atrocities. One extraordinary note from Foreign Office official Hugh Carless to Ambassador Seconde, in December 1973, states that 'unfortunately, there is (as you have pointed out to us) a good deal of fact behind the atrocity stories and that alone makes it impossible for us to counter the propaganda'. 'We can do little about the press', he added 'but you can assure them [the Chilean junta] that we and our Ministers do understand the facts'. Carless also mused that 'Chileans must be wondering why on Earth . . . so much unfair attention is being paid to their change of government'. Another obstacle was the emergence of a worldwide Chile Solidarity Movement, which was likely to remain while the junta remained: 'this means we shall, occasionally, have to adopt a lower profile than we would like' especially when attempting to provide arms, to help the junta with debt relief and to 'rescue them from being pilloried in international meetings'.[33]

The coup may have had important repercussions beyond its impact on ordinary Chileans. As well as showing the world the US willingness to crush a government that had improved the lot of many of its poorer people, it also signalled that the peaceful, democratic path to improving the position of the poor would be met by violence. Ambassador Seconde commented in a despatch after the coup that 'the final seal of failure has now been put on this experiment by the Chilean armed forces'. 'This has some obvious advantages', he wrote, but also disadvantages, one of which was that 'it will be widely concluded that violent revolution is the only effective way to communism'.

Foreign Secretary Douglas-Home similarly suggested that 'the overthrow of Allende has ruined prospects for social change to be achieved democratically in Latin America'.[34]

Pinochet in power

On the first anniversary of the coup, a large advertisement appeared in the conservative Chilean newspaper, *El Mercurio*, congratulating the 'honourable junta' on completing its first year in power. The advert had been placed by the British Chamber of Commerce, whose chair was Reginald Seconde, Britain's ambassador.[35]

Britain's support for the junta was only mildly affected by Labour's election victory in February 1974. The Wilson government announced that no new arms export licences would be granted but, defying parliamentary and public pressure, decided to honour existing contracts to deliver two frigates, two submarines and a consignment of Rolls-Royce engines for the Chileans' Hunter aircraft – thus breaking Labour's pre-election commitment not to supply arms.

When a British doctor, Sheila Cassidy, was arrested and tortured by the Chilean secret police in 1975, a public outcry forced the government to break off ambassadorial relations. However, a diplomatic staff of 13 remained, trade relations were not directly affected and the Chilean ambassador to Britain was not expelled. In 1976, it was also revealed that two years previously the Labour government had allowed 270 Chilean navy personnel to undergo training courses in Britain, followed by 24 in 1975, again as a result of contracts signed under the Heath government.[36]

The Thatcher government backed Pinochet to the hilt. It restored full export credit cover for Chile in June 1979, restored ambassadorial relations in January 1980 and arms exports in July 1980, while claiming that the human-rights situation had improved. The opposite was the case: Britain's decision to resume normal arms sales to Chile in July 1980 coincided with a period in which, according to Amnesty International, 'there has been a steady increase in the abuse of human rights in Chile' with 2,000 people arrested, many of whom were tortured, that year alone. In November 1979, 600 unmarked graves had been discovered in a Santiago cemetery. The extreme right-wing Foreign Office minister Nicholas Ridley argued that 'we don't mix up the two questions of trade and views of the political situation', which was at least honest.[37]

Following the Argentinian invasion of the Falklands in 1982, the Chileans provided a base for the SAS to conduct raids into Argentina; and Chilean naval intelligence passed on intercepts of Argentinian navy radio signals. From the outset of this cooperation, classified telegrams sent from the British embassy in Santiago to the Foreign Office showed that in return for Chilean cooperation, Britain would provide military equipment, cease any lingering criticism of human-rights abuses and help undermine UN investigations into these by opposing the reappointment of the UN's special rapporteur.[38]

Thus Britain abstained on several UN votes criticising Chile's human-rights violations. The Chilean Committee for Human Rights pointed out that in the early 1980s, Britain had been indifferent when it came to concrete action and encouragement for those in Chile defending human rights or intervention in individual cases. Human rights-leaders in Chile complained that, unlike other embassies, the British embassy maintained irregular contact and would not make enquiries when serious human-rights abuses arose.

Britain under Thatcher acted as a major apologist for the Pinochet regime, describing it as 'a moderate and stabilising force' in the region, with which Britain ought to be 'deepening and strengthening political relations', in the words of Trade Minister Peter Rees in 1982.[39]

Military relations remained strong throughout the 1980s. The bulk of Chile's navy was supplied by Britain, which provided around a dozen warships, including frigates, destroyers and submarines. In 1982–1983, Britain sold a dozen Hawker

Hunters, fighter jets and bombers to Chile, held talks in London with the head of Chile's navy and invited the head of the air force to the Farnborough air show (the invitation provoked so much opposition that it was withdrawn). Britain continued to use military facilities in Chile and RAF pilots were secretly sent to provide training to the Chilean air force.[40]

Foreign Office documents leaked in 1985 stated that an arms embargo on Chile would be a 'striking political gesture on our behalf' against human-rights abuses. However, such an embargo would also lead to a scaling down of military cooperation and relations more generally. Little agonising was needed over the ordering of these priorities.[41]

Pinochet's economic strategy closely followed monetarist doctrine, espousing 'free markets' and cuts in public spending and taxes, while providing favourable conditions for foreign investment. Many of Allende's reforms were reversed and a substantial redistribution of income from poor to rich took place. The real incomes of the poorest 20 per cent of Chilean families fell by 30 per cent between 1969 and 1978, while those of the richest 20 per cent increased by 15 per cent. By 1978, the top 20 per cent of households accounted for more than half of all consumption (having risen from 43 per cent in 1969) with the bottom 40 per cent accounting for a mere 14 per cent (down from 20 per cent in 1969).[42]

Political repression and economic strategy went hand in hand: the latter depended on the absence of trade-union pressure and the lack of political opposition. The dictatorship's economic strategy impressed the Thatcher government. Trade Minister Cecil Parkinson noted in 1980 that 'the Chilean economic experience is very similar to what we are developing here'.[43]

By the mid-1980s it was clear that the Chilean experiment had failed in achieving significant economic growth and thus in maintaining a more favourable climate for investors generally. It was at this point that the Reagan and Thatcher governments suddenly discovered the Pinochet regime's human-rights abuses. In December 1984 Britain voted at the UN to condemn Chile for human-rights abuses, and the US later followed by sponsoring a draft UN resolution critical of violations.

The Pinochet dictatorship lasted a long 17 years, until 1990. Currently, some 350 military and police officials implicated in human-rights atrocities in Chile after the military coup of 1973 are facing criminal charges. Among them are 22 generals and 40 colonels. Some might well have had direct dealings with the British governments who armed them. But British ministers continue to evade responsibility for having conferred legitimacy on, and given their backing to, this nasty regime for so long.

15

GUYANANS: A
CONSTITUTIONAL COUP

In 1953 Britain overthrew the democratically elected government in British Guiana, which was then a British colony with an element of self-government. The April 1953 elections had resulted in victory for the People's Progressive Party (PPP) under Cheddi Jagan, a popular, nationalist government committed to a redistributive economic programme intended to reduce poverty. The PPP's plans threatened the British multinational Bookers, which controlled British Guiana's main export, sugar. Britain despatched warships and 700 troops to overthrow the government, under the pretext that they were acting against 'part of the international communist conspiracy' represented by Jagan's policies. With many of the elected PPP leaders jailed, the Colonial Secretary ruled out elections since 'the same party would have been elected again'.[1]

Almost exactly ten years later, British Guiana was faced with the same threat in the eyes of British planners. By 1963, Cheddi Jagan's PPP was again the ruling party in government, having won the 1961 elections. Britain, however, did not want to grant independence to British Guiana if Jagan were to become the first post-independence leader.

There were two differences from 1953. The first was the means: instead of a military intervention, the British effected a 'constitutional coup' to ensure that Jagan would not be re-elected. The second was the context: by 1963, Britain simply wanted to get out of Guiana and hand it over to the US. It was no longer acting primarily to protect its own business interests, but as the lieutenant of the US, which successfully lobbied London to promote a coup on its behalf.

'The sooner we get these people out of our hair the better', Commonwealth Secretary Duncan Sandys told Prime Minister Harold Macmillan in January 1962. Macmillan's adviser, Burke Trend, agreed: 'we are sick of trying to hold the balance between these quarrelsome people and want to wash our hands of them as rapidly as we can'.[2]

US files show that British officials 'assert in private that British Guiana is in the US, not the UK, sphere of interest and they probably consider that its future is not properly their problem but one for the US'. Britain still had substantial commercial interests in the territory – most importantly a $400–500 million investment in the sugar industry – yet it was concern about placating the Americans that was uppermost in British minds.[3]

Background to a coup

British Guiana was a desperately poor country with a population of just over half a million people, half of whom were of Indian origin and around a third of African origin. The economy was dependent on sugar and bauxite with the sugar estates and mining industry 'owned by outside capital', the Joint Intelligence Committee noted. The sugar industry was in the hands of two British companies, Bookers and the Demerara Company, both of which 'have extensive interests in other sections of the economy including importing, general stores and real estate'.[4] These companies made handsome profits while the overwhelming majority of the population endured grinding poverty.

The US files vary between describing Jagan's PPP

programme as 'communist' and 'nationalist'. A US intelligence report from March 1961 notes that it was unlikely that Jagan was seeking to establish a communist regime; but rather 'we consider it more likely that an independent Jagan government would seek to portray itself as an instrument of reformist nationalism which would gradually move in the direction of Castro's Cuba'. It would be 'assertively nationalistic, sympathetic to Cuba, and prepared to enter into economic and diplomatic relations with the [Soviet] bloc, although such a government would probably still be influenced by the desire to obtain economic help from the UK and the US'.[5]

In October 1961, the Director of the Bureau of Intelligence and Research at the State Department, Roger Hilsman – the architect of the brutal 'strategic hamlets' programme in Vietnam – noted that US government thinking at the time was that Jagan was not a 'controlled instrument of Moscow' but 'a radical nationalist who may play both sides of the street but will not lead British Guiana into satellite status'. After independence, Jagan's PPP would 'follow a policy on non-alignment in international affairs, but would probably lean in the Soviet direction', according to another US intelligence report.[6]

The British believed, according to the US files, that 'Jagan is not a communist' but 'a naïve, London School of Economics Marxist filled with charm, personal honesty and juvenile nationalism'. A Whitehall brief of June 1963 noted that under Jagan there was the danger of a 'Castro/communist regime in British Guiana', though this would be a threat 'for political and psychological rather than military reasons'.[7]

Therefore, the threat posed by Jagan's PPP was essentially a radical nationalist one, replicated on numerous occasions throughout the post-war era, but invariably described as purely 'communist' for public relations. This threat was compounded by the recognition in internal State Department files that Jagan 'leads the largest and most cohesive party in the country. He is the ablest leader in British Guiana'.[8]

Before the August 1961 elections, the US feared that, if Jagan won, he would 'make a more determined effort to improve economic conditions' by accepting a loan from Cuba, whose regime was providing a model for others in Latin America, and may threaten 'nationalisation or confiscation of foreign and local businesses'. The PPP drew its support from the Indian community 'including not only poverty-stricken rural and urban workers, but also a considerable number of small businessmen in Georgetown and other centres', a US intelligence report from March 1961 read.[9]

In April 1961, at meetings in Washington, the US had proposed to Britain 'ways and means of ensuring that an independent British Guiana was not dominated by communists'. Foreign Secretary Douglas-Home said that Britain was 'anxious to do everything possible to make sure that British Guiana developed on the right lines'. A group was set up in which US and British officials looked into 'the possibilities of taking action to influence the results of the election' scheduled for August 1961, Douglas-Home noted. But despite US pleas, Britain refused to cooperate in the US plan actively to prevent Jagan winning the election, arguing that it was better to work with him and steer him away from unacceptable policies through financial and economic aid.[10]

The PPP won 20 of the 35 seats in the assembly in the 1961 elections – 45 per cent of the vote – against 11 seats won by the People's National Party, the principal opposition party, under Forbes Burnham.

After the election, the US State Department recommended a programme that combined offering Jagan technical and economic assistance with a covert operation 'to expose and destroy communists in British Guiana' and to find 'a substitute for Jagan himself, who could command East Indian support'. Noting that these two goals were in conflict, President Kennedy's Special Assistant, Arthur Schlesinger, wrote that 'this means that the covert program must be handled with the utmost discretion'. The US policy of assisting Jagan had been agreed with the British, who were still rejecting covert action to oust him. But by October 1961 the files show that US planners were questioning its strategy and wanted to review it with the British. No US aid was, in fact, ever provided.[11]

In February 1962 US Secretary of State Dean Rusk told Foreign Secretary Douglas-Home: 'I have reached the conclusion that it is not possible for us to put up with an independent British Guiana under Jagan'. Jagan had 'grandiose expectations of economic aid', too many 'communist connections' and was professing a stance which 'parallels that of Castro':

> The continuation of Jagan in power is leading us to disaster in terms of the colony itself, strains on Anglo-American relations and difficulties for the Inter-American system . . . I hope we can agree that Jagan should not accede to power again. Cordially yours, Dean Rusk.[12]

This was too much even for the British. Macmillan wrote that he read Rusk's letter with 'amazement', telling Douglas-Home: 'How can the Americans continue to attack us in the United Nations on colonialism and then use expressions like these which are not colonialism but pure Machiavellianism?'

Douglas-Home replied to Rusk and, referring to his view that 'Jagan should not accede to power again', countered: 'How would you suggest that this can be done in a democracy?' Britain, he said, could also not go back on its promise to grant independence.[13]

However, the British government soon acquiesced. At a constitutional conference in March 1960 the principle of independence had been conceded and a new constitution agreed. It was envisaged that independence would take place in August 1963, two years after the introduction of the new constitution.

In March 1962, Colonial Minister Hugh Fraser visited Washington. After meetings with Kennedy and others, Fraser came back talking of an alternative constitution involving proportional representation rather than the present first-past-the-post system. But any proposal on this, he wrote, 'must not flow from us but from the demands of the British Guianese themselves'.

A change in the constitution was necessary since, as a US intelligence report in April recognised, new elections held on the same basis as in August 1961 'would probably return a Jagan government again'.[14]

In May Macmillan told Cabinet Secretary Norman Brook that 'it is surely to our interests [sic] to be as cooperative and forthcoming as we can' towards the US desire for 'a satisfactory solution' in British Guiana. His note to Brook asked him to set up a committee to consider the future of the territory – presumably to work on the fixing of the constitution following Fraser's meetings with the Americans – and also stated that this note was not being copied to any of the ministers concerned.[15]

At this point some of the British files have been censored but it seems that Macmillan wrote to Kennedy informing him of a change of British policy – the beginning, in fact, of a British constitutional coup planning to effect regime change.

Covert action

The US continued covert planning. 'Here is a paper from Dean Rusk which comes out hard for a policy of getting rid of Jagan', one US note from July 1962 reads. 'Should our covert program succeed, we would wish to be in the position of being able to give the successor regime immediate aid', Schlesinger told President Kennedy in September 1962. It is very unlikely that these plans in a British colony could have been conducted without at least a nod and a wink from Whitehall.[16]

The CIA helped to organise and fund anti-Jagan protests in February 1962, which resulted in strikes and riots, and during which the British sent troops to restore order. But the centrepiece of the CIA's covert operation was funding a general strike, which began in April 1963 and lasted for 80 days. CIA agents gave advice to local union leaders on how to organise and sustain the strike; with a budget of $1 million, they provided funds and food to keep the strikers going.[17] This strike was publicly cited by British officials as evidence that Jagan could not run the country.

In March 1963 a note from the US Consul General in Georgetown, Everett Melby, confirms the agreement between the US and Britain:

> that proportional representation (PR) as an electoral system for British Guiana (BG) represents the most practical electoral device for replacing Premier Cheddi Jagan and the People's Progressive Party (PPP) with a more democratic and reliable government.

The use of the term 'more democratic' is the façade maintained even in internal communications for what was in effect a coup. Later in the same memo, Melby noted that 'with the existing electoral districting, he [Jagan] would probably win a majority of seats'.

'An independent Guyana will be within the US sphere', Melby noted, adding:

> It is not in the national interest to have a communist government on the mainland of South America. An independent Guyana with Jagan in office represents such a threat and as such should be removed.

Melby then urged the US government formally to decide on PR for the country. Finally, he noted that he would shortly present 'an outline of several projects which, after the PPP's removal, may be effective in discrediting Jagan with some of his supporters'.[18]

In June, now Prime Minister Douglas-Home met Kennedy in talks in Britain. The brief for Douglas-Home stated:

> If Jagan maintains his hold over the Indians, it is inevitable that in a few years he will lead the government... The normal course would be for us to go ahead

with independence under the present government. Were it not for Jagan's communist leanings we should have no hesitation. But we are willing to consider with the President, the possibility of independence under an alternative (Burnham) government.[19]

During these Anglo-American talks, British officials formally proposed to the Americans to 'establish a Burnham-D'Aguiar [the latter the other opposition party leader] government and then grant British Guiana independence'. Duncan Sandys, now Colonial Secretary, said 'we had to be careful that Jagan should not be put in a position where he would ask for dissolution [of the current government] and new elections, because he would certainly win again'.[20]

On 18 July Macmillan wrote to Kennedy outlining (in the words of the latter's in reply in September) 'your plan for a series of moves in September or October which would result in the removal of the Jagan government'. 'We want to cooperate with you in all ways to help you make your program a success', Kennedy said. He wanted to steer Burnham and D'Aguiar 'on the right path, creating and launching an alternative East Indian party and a real economic development programme'. Kennedy ended by saying that 'this problem is one in which you have shown a most helpful understanding of my special concern'.[21]

Macmillan explained British strategy in his reply to Kennedy. The aim was to summon the three political leaders in British Guiana and 'impose a solution' by establishing 'a new electoral system designed to counteract racialism' (i.e., proportional representation). It was likely, Macmillan wrote, that Jagan would refuse to cooperate, in which case Britain would suspend the constitution. If he did cooperate, 'we shall have to postpone his removal until he shows that he is deliberately obstructing'. Also important was to keep the UN out. A recent proposal for a UN commission needed to be avoided 'since it would be bound to recommend early independence, and would be more than likely to advise the retention of the present electoral system'.[22]

The coup was staged at the end of October 1963 in a constitutional conference. Colonial Secretary Duncan Sandys announced the new electoral system under proportional representation and the holding of fresh elections under the supervision of an official appointed by the British government.

Jagan immediately attacked the British for continuing to refuse to set a date for independence and for rigging the electoral system to bar him from office. He wrote to Douglas-Home pointing out that PR had been rejected in Britain by both the Conservative and Labour parties and that the previous Colonial Secretary, Iain McLeod, had also rejected a call for PR at the 1960 constitutional conference.

A file of 26 November 1963 shows Anglo-American planners gloating at their victory. In a meeting between Douglas-Home and Dean Rusk, 'the Prime Minister said that this had gone off slightly better than had been hoped', the file reads. 'It had even been slightly awkward that Dr Jagan had given so little trouble'.[23]

Jagan may have had (naive) hopes that the incoming Labour government in October 1964 would squash the PR plan. Within days of taking office, however, it had dashed these hopes. 'Bowing to United States wishes', the *New York Times* wrote, the new British government 'ruled out early independence for British Guiana' and was proceeding with elections under proportional representation.

In these elections, held in December 1964, the PPP increased its vote to 46 per cent and won more seats than any other party. But Forbes Burnham was asked to form a government under the new proportional representation system which gave the two opposition parties together a majority of seats. Now that the acceptable leadership had taken office, Guyana could be granted independence, which proceeded in 1966.[24]

The Anglo-American constitutional coup to remove the nationalist threat had successfully countered the democratic voice of the Unpeople of British Guiana. This had been carried out on the understanding that, in the words of then Colonial Secretary Iain MacLeod to Kennedy's special assistant, Arthur Schlesinger in February 1962, 'if I had to make a choice between Jagan and Burnham as head of my country I would choose Jagan any day of the week'.[25]

An earlier brief to the Prime Minister had said that a Burnham-D'Aguiar coalition 'would be inefficient', that 'Burnham himself is unreliable' and that 'any African leader would have great difficulty in governing a country with an overwhelmingly Indian population'.[26] But these were trifling concerns in the pursuit of Anglo-American power.

16

ARABIANS: DIRTY WARS

One of the least known aspects of recent British history is the 'dirty war' conducted by Britain in North Yemen in the 1960s. The episode lasted almost a decade, spanned Conservative and Labour governments, and cost up to 200,000 lives. It also involved lying by the government to the public.

As far as I am aware, the declassified files have been researched by only one British academic, in a book due to appear in late 2004.[1] These files are heavily censored – probably more so than in any other foreign-policy episode I have looked at. Dozens of documents have been retained by the Foreign Office; in the released files, numerous paragraphs or lines are blanked out. The reason given for this secrecy is, inevitably, 'national security'. In my view, the real reason is to protect reputations of the people with blood on their hands: Alec Douglas-Home, Harold Wilson, Denis Healey, Leo Amery, Duncan Sandys, and the unelected officials in Whitehall.

The threat posed by Yemen

In September 1962, the Imam of North Yemen was overthrown in a popular coup. Imam al-Badr had been in power for only a week. He had succeeded his father, who had presided over a feudal kingdom where 80 per cent of the population lived as peasants. The land had been controlled through bribery, an arbitrary and coercive tax system and a policy of divide and rule. The coup was led by Colonel Abdullah al-Sallal and a pro-Nasser, Arab nationalist group within the Yemeni military, which together proclaimed the Yemen Arab Republic. Royalist forces supporting the Imam took to the hills and began an insurgency, supported by Saudi Arabia and Jordan, against the Republican regime. Nasser's Egypt deployed troops in North Yemen to shore up the new government.

Britain soon resorted to covert action to undermine the new Republican regime, in alliance with the Saudis and Jordanis. The declassified files show that many British officials understood that they were supporting the 'wrong' side.

For example, Christopher Gandy, who was Britain's top official in Taiz in North Yemen, noted shortly after the revolution that the rule of the previous Imam 'has made the Imamate unpopular with large elements and those in many ways the best'. The 'monopoly of power' was 'much resented' and was over-turned by the new, Republican government by appointing into office people from 'classes, regions and sects previously neglected in the distribution of power'. Gandy described the Imam's rule as 'an arbitrary autocracy'; the Republicans, on the other hand, were acting collectively through a new government, and were 'much more open to contact and reasoned argument'.[2]

Gandy actually recommended recognition of the new Yemeni regime, saying that it was interested in friendly relations with Britain and that this was 'the best way to prevent an increase' in Egyptian influence. But he was overruled both by his political masters in London and by officials in neighbouring Aden, Britain's then colony. One of Gandy's arguments was that if the Royalists were to restore themselves to power they would have to change their system of rule so as to make themselves popular, which would 'in its turn embarrass us in Aden and the Protectorate' – where Britain was supporting similarly feudal elements against strong popular, nationalist feeling.[3]

After Britain's covert campaign in Yemen was well under way, an official in the Prime Minister's office noted that Egyptian President Nasser had been:

> able to capture most of the dynamic and modern forces in the area while we have been left, by our own choice, backing the forces which are not merely reactionary (that would not matter so much) but shifty, unreliable and treacherous.

Prime Minister Harold Macmillan himself admitted that it was:

> repugnant to political equity and prudence alike that we should so often appear to be supporting out-of-date and despotic regimes and to be opposing the growth of modern and more democratic forms of government.

The Foreign Secretary, Alec Douglas-Home, also conceded that the Republicans' 'attraction for the average Yemeni will be greater' than the Imams', and this would 'cause us a great deal of trouble'.[4]

The military base at Aden was the cornerstone of British military policy in the Gulf region, in which Britain was then the major power, directly controlling the sheikhdoms of the Persian Gulf and with huge oil interests in Kuwait and elsewhere. The coastal city of Aden was surrounded by what Britain had forged into a 'protectorate' of the Federation of South Arabia, a set of feudal fiefdoms presided over by autocratic leaders similar to that just overthrown in Yemen, and kept sweet by British bribes.

It was feared that a progressive, republican, Arab nationalist Yemen would serve as an example to the feudal sheikhdoms throughout the Gulf and the wider Middle East as well as in Aden itself. Foreign Secretary Douglas-Home stated shortly after the Republican coup that Aden could not be secure from 'a firmly established republican regime in Yemen'. A ministerial meeting similarly concluded that if Britain were forced out of Aden it would be 'a devastating blow to our prestige and authority' in the region. Even to recognise the new Yemeni regime might lead to 'a collapse in the morale of the pro-British rulers of the protectorate', putting 'the whole British position in the area . . . in jeopardy'.[5]

The threat, as outlined by Sir Kennedy Trevaskis, the High Commissioner in Aden, was that the Yemeni Republicans 'could expect to win massive support in both' Aden and the federation where 'pro-Republican feeling is strong'. The Republican regime was likely to encourage 'some of our own friends among the rulers' in the protectorate to 'defect and come to terms with the Yemen government'. 'Many would be attracted by' the regime, Trevaskis noted.

These concerns were shared by the arch-medieval kingdom in the region, Saudi Arabia, which feared the spread of the overthrow of monarchies by Arab nationalist forces. It was recognised by British planners that after the Saudis had begun arming the Royalists in Yemen they 'were not greatly concerned about the form of government to be established in the Yemen, provided that it was not under the control of Egypt' – any other government would do.[6]

This threat heightened as Nasser and new Yemeni leader al-Sallal gave diplomatic and material support to anti-British Republican forces in Aden and the federation and conducted a public campaign urging the British to withdraw from their imperial possessions. Trevaskis also commented that if the Yemenis were to secure control of Aden 'it would for the first time provide the Yemen with a large modern town and a port of international consequence'. Most importantly, 'economically, it would offer the greatest advantages to so poor and ill developed a country'.[7]

Britain decided to engage in a covert campaign to promote those forces recognised as 'shifty', 'treacherous' and 'despotic' to undermine those recognised as 'popular' and 'more democratic'. Crucially, they did so in the knowledge that their clients did not stand a chance of winning. The campaign was undertaken simply to cause trouble for the Republicans, and the Egyptians, in Yemen, who held the overwhelming majority of the country and the centres of population.

The files are clear on this point. Harold Macmillan noted in February 1963 that 'in the longer term a republican victory was inevitable'. He told President Kennedy that:

> I quite realise that the Loyalists [sic] will probably not win in Yemen in the end but it would not suit us too badly if the new Yemeni regime were occupied with their own internal affairs during the next few years.

What Britain wanted was 'a weak government in Yemen not able to make trouble'.

A note to the Prime Minister from his foreign-policy adviser Philip de Zulueta similarly states that:

> All departments appear to be agreed that the present stalemate in the Yemen, with the Republicans and Royalists fighting each other and therefore having no time or energy left over to make trouble for us in Aden, suits our own interests very well.

De Zulueta continued: 'our interest is surely to have the maximum confusion in the tribal areas on the Aden frontier' with Yemen.[8]

The covert campaign

Piecing together a brief chronology of British covert action is difficult in light of the wide censorship of the files. But the task is aided by intelligence expert Stephen Dorril's comprehensive book, *MI6*, produced mainly from secondary sources and interviews.

Shortly after the September 1962 coup, Jordan's King Hussein visited London, where he met Air Minister Julian Amery and urged the British government not to recognise the new Yemeni regime. They agreed that MI6 asset Neil 'Billy'

McLean, a serving Conservative MP, should tour the area and report back to the Prime Minister. MI6's former vice chief, George Young, now a banker with Kleinwort Benson, was approached by Mossad to find a Briton acceptable to the Saudis to run a guerrilla war against the Republicans. Young then introduced McLean to Dan Hiram, the Israeli defence attaché who promised to supply arms, money and training, which the Saudis eagerly grasped.[9]

Two days after the coup Prince Hassan, uncle of Imam al-Badr, who had been in New York for the past several years, called on Douglas-Home for help in getting him to the Yemeni frontier where he would make a bid for power. The files indicate that British officials said they could not provide any overt help but by mid-October Hassan was reported to have 'plenty of money and arms'.

In October Britain also considered direct military intervention in Yemen when Prime Minister Macmillan called on the chiefs of staff 'to consider our military resources should we be driven to adopt an overt policy'. Covert operations were preferred, perhaps for the reason later given by Foreign Secretary Rab Butler, who wrote that 'if this had happened a generation ago', we should have used 'North-West frontier' tactics 'which would probably have been effective'. Unfortunately, 'there are severe limitations on the use of such methods in the world as it is today, and we trust that any repetition can be avoided'.[10]

In October McLean visited Saudi Arabia as a personal guest of the King, who called on Britain to provide aid to the Royalists, especially 'air support . . . if possible openly, but if this is not possible, then clandestinely'. McLean also visited Yemen to meet with the Royalists, including Prince Hassan at his headquarters, to assess the situation and delivered a report of his visit to Defence Minister Peter Thorneycroft. By early November, Saudi arms and money were flowing to the Royalists and by mid-November the Foreign Office had produced a policy paper outlining the options open to the government, including covert aid.[11]

In early December, McLean again visited Yemen, where the Imam's forces informed him of the need for arms and ammunition. On returning to London, McLean met the Foreign Secretary, urged British aid and began canvassing the Cabinet for support. McLean was carrying a letter from al-Badr to the Prime Minister asking for support for the Royalists who were disappointed with the lack of aid so far forthcoming from Britain. At the same time, the High Commissioner in Aden said that 'we ought now to be considering definite steps to reinsure ourselves with' the Royalists.[12]

When the British ambassador to Egypt, Sir Harold Beeley, met Egyptian President Nasser's personal adviser, Mohammed Heikal, the latter accused Britain of several aspects of involvement in the fighting in Yemen, notably supplying fighter aircraft to Jordan. Heikal told Beeley that McLean was advising the Royalists, that he had visited the Kings of Saudi Arabia and Jordan, both of whom were now intervening in Yemen. He also said that the Jordanian Air Force Commander who had defected to Egypt 'asserted that his orders, which involved attacking targets in the Yemen, had been given to him personally by King Hussein in the presence of a British Air Advisor'.

Foreign Secretary Douglas-Home was initially against backing the Royalists. On 7 January 1963, McLean's intelligence report was assessed by the Cabinet's Overseas and Defence Committee, which advised the Cabinet not to recognise the new regime, arguing that Britain could not give direct support to the Royalists and that any operation had to be at arm's length.[13]

In late February British positions in the Federation of South Arabia were attacked by Yemeni tribesmen and at the same time Egyptian troops began an offensive into the Royalist-held mountains in Yemen. Colonial Secretary Duncan Sandys and Julian Amery urged retaliation and Macmillan appointed Amery his Minister for Aden with a remit to organise covert British support for the Royalists, working from his office at the Ministry of Aviation.

McLean visited Yemen for a third time on 1 March 1963. Shortly afterwards a Royalist delegation visited Israel, following which unmarked Israeli planes made flights from Djibouti to drop arms over Royalist areas. By early March, the files confirm that Britain was already involved in supplying arms to the Royalists, via Sherif bin Hussein, the tribal leader in Beihan in the federation.[14]

On 1 March the governor in Aden, Sir Charles Johnstone, had proposed withholding arms supplies for two to three weeks since there was now a danger that any arms supplied would fall into Republican hands and could be 'attributed to British support'. He also berated his political masters in London for having refused repeated requests for 'additional supplies to Royalists made by me' in November, December and February. If these supplies had been granted, he added, 'the Royalists would never have got to their present low ebb' in the fighting.

In mid-April 1963, McLean asked the Foreign Secretary for immediate support, and the Saudis stepped in with a small supply of arms and ammunition. According to Dorril, several million pounds' worth of light weapons, including 50,000 rifles, were secretly flown out from an RAF station in Wiltshire. To mask their true origin, they were landed in Jordan for onward transportation via Beihan. By the end of the month, the Royalists had regained some of their lost territory.[15]

At a meeting in late April 1963 – involving MI6 chief Dick White, McLean, SAS founder David Stirling, ex-SAS officer Brian Franks, Douglas-Home and Amery – Stirling and Franks were told there could be no official SAS involvement and were asked to recommend someone who could organise a mercenary operation. According to Dorril, they approached Jim Johnson, recently retired commander of 21 SAS, and Lt. Col. John Woodhouse, commander of 22 SAS. McLean, Johnson and Stirling were introduced by Amery to the Royalist Foreign Minister, Ahmed al-Shami, who wrote out a cheque for £5,000. The SAS men operated through Stirling's Television International Enterprises company, which set up a cover organisation,

Rally Films. The Saudi prince Sultan financed the project with gold bullion. French mercenaries were also recruited, along with SAS volunteers given temporary leave from official duties.

The office of the adjutant of 21 SAS volunteers (TA) in London was used as a clearing ground for the British mercenaries, who, according to the organiser, were paid £150 a month by the Foreign Office and the MoD. In Aden, Tony Boyle, the aide-de-camp to the Aden governor, evolved a system for passing mercenaries through Customs while Sherif Hussein organised a network of safe houses in Beihan from which operations into the Yemen could be launched. As the traffic increased, officers were seconded to the staff of the Federal Regular Army.[16]

The proposed Yemen operation was the subject of fierce debate in Whitehall but the Prime Minister was eventually persuaded to support the operation and instructed MI6 to aid the Royalists. An MI6 task force was set up which then coordinated the supply of weapons and personnel. This was organised by John da Silva, formerly head of MI6's station in Bahrain.

In October Macmillan resigned as Prime Minister and was replaced by Douglas-Home. The new Foreign Secretary, Rab Butler, was opposed to covert support for the Royalists. By December 1963, the new Prime Minister reported that Egypt had so far suffered 10,000–12,000 casualties in Yemen.

British actions continued as SAS officer Jonny Cooper engaged in intelligence activities against Egyptian forces and his team trained the Royalist army. In February 1964 Cooper and his men prepared for their first clandestine air-drop of supplies, codenamed MANGO, with the discreet backing of MI6 and the CIA. Arms and ammunition were parachuted into drop zones manned by Cooper's team, who guided the planes in by radio.[17]

In a memo to the Prime Minister in March 1964, Butler wrote that the Egyptian and Yemeni assertion that supplies for the Royalists are being introduced from the Beihan area [in the federation] has been mentioned in the latest report to the Security Council by U Thant and we have not been able to give an effective reply since we know that this is in fact true.

Butler drew the distinction between aiding the Royalists in Yemen on the one hand – which Britain should not support, in his view – and, on the other hand, aiding activities in the federation and 'across the Yemen border' to prevent subversion. He supported the High Commissioner in Aden's calls for 'a selective system of unattributable retaliation in the Yemeni frontier area for sabotage, mine-laying and so on in the federation'.[18]

Defence Secretary Thorneycroft called for Britain to organise 'tribal revolts' in the frontier areas, 'deniable action . . . to sabotage intelligence centres and kill personnel engaged in anti-British activities', including the Egyptian Intelligence HQ at Taiz, and 'covert anti-Egyptian propaganda activities in the Yemen'. He also argued for 'further assistance' to the Royalists including 'either money, or arms or both'.

By April 1964 the British had already authorised mine-laying (called Operation Eggshell), issuing arms and ammunition to tribesmen in the frontier area (Operation Stirrup) and sabotage in the frontier area (Operation Bangle). A plan 'for the instigation of a revolt in the Beidha area', just inside the Yemen border, had been approved by July at the latest. Three hundred thousand pounds had been released for this purpose, but Egyptian counter-action was preventing the revolt from getting off the ground.

Acts of 'subversion in Yemeni territory against individual targets' were being carried out, however, 'under the control of British officers within the federation', according to an MoD memo. These officers 'can hand out arms and money in installments [sic] according to the local situation and in proportion to the successes achieved'. Operation Rancour was the codeword given to 'current covert operations to exploit [sic] dissident tribes up to 20 miles into Yemen to neutralise Egyptian subversive action against Aden'.[19]

An extraordinary top-secret document in the government files went even further. Entitled 'Yemen: The range of possible courses of action open to us', it considers 'assassination or other action against key personnel' involved in subversion in the federation, 'especially Egyptian Intelligence Service officers'. It also outlines 'action to stimulate a guerrilla campaign' in the frontier area by supplies of arms and money and 'non-retaliatory sabotage' including in Sana'a. It suggests 'closing our eyes' to Saudi arms supplies to the Royalists and undertaking '"black" pamphleteering' in Republican-controlled areas of Yemen and '"black" radio broadcasts' from the federation.[20]

Foreign Secretary Butler gave this paper to the Prime Minister, commenting that 'I should perhaps say' that some of the options 'may involve more political risk' than others:

> For instance, the assassination of Egyptian intelligence officers would no doubt involve a greater chance of discovery and retaliation than supplying the Royalists with money.

As these options were being debated in private, on 14 May 1964 Prime Minister Douglas-Home lied to parliament:

> Our policy towards the Yemen is one of non-intervention in the affairs of that country. It is not therefore our policy to supply arms to the Royalists in the Yemen.[21]

In July Thorneycroft recommended that Britain should, together with Saudi Arabia, be 'sustaining the Royalists during the coming months' by providing arms and money to the 'Royalist tribes'. At the time, the Saudis were asking Britain for £2 million over one year, a quarter of which was for arms. The files also refer to the need for a British decision on whether to agree 'to another proposal to supply rifles' to two tribes for attacks inside Yemen. A detailed plan was submitted to the British in July by Sherif Hussein and Royalists in Yemen calling on Britain to supply 11,000 rifles and £600,000.

At the end of July ministers took the decision to promote 'further measures' to support the Royalists, meaning to 'give all necessary facilities' to the Saudis to secure arms from Britain. Britain's ambassador to Saudi Arabia then met Prince Feisal and told him of Britain's willingness to provide arms to Saudi Arabia for use in Yemen but said London could not provide overt aid directly to the Royalists.[22]

In the summer of 1964, Prime Minister Douglas-Home was faced with opposition from his Foreign Secretary to direct aid to the Royalists, while the Defence Secretary and others argued for precisely that. According to Dorril, Dick White, the head of MI6, won the new Prime Minister over to supporting a 'clandestine mercenary operation'. The go-ahead for full support for the Royalists was sanctioned in the summer of 1964.

In 1964, 48 ex-servicemen were employed as mercenaries, including a dozen former SAS men. MI6 officers provided intelligence and logistical support, while GCHQ pinpointed the location of Republican units. MI6 operatives also coordinated the crossing of tribesmen over the border from the federation into Yemen where they tracked Egyptian army officers. 'In what turned out to be a dirty war, MI6 officers "manipulated" the tribesmen and helped "direct the planting of bombs" at Egyptian military outposts along the frontier, while garrison towns were "shot up" and political figures "murdered"', Dorril notes.[23]

One letter in the government files was written in August 1964 by Colonel Michael Webb, a mercenary who claimed to have recently retired from the army, to Julian Amery. Webb said that he has been fighting with the Imam's forces for the past few weeks and his cover was as a freelance journalist. He had kept the British embassy 'fully informed of my movements and given them all the information I have obtained'.

The following month a note to the Prime Minister recommended the supply of bazookas and ammunition to the Sherif of Beihan 'for use by a dissident group in Taiz' [Yemen]. At the same time, Stirling, Boyle and Royalist Foreign Minister al-Shami met in Aden where they were joined by an MI6 officer and drew up plans for establishing a regular supply of arms and ammunition to the Royalist forces. This would be undertaken either by parachute or overland from Saudi Arabia and Beihan, or via the Yemen coast.[24]

The election of the Labour government of Harold Wilson in October 1964 seems not to have upset the covert operation. Dorril notes secret RAF bombing in retaliation for Egyptian attacks on camel trains supplying weapons to French and British mercenaries. As part of an arms deal with Saudi Arabia, Britain agreed a contract worth £26 million with a private company, Airwork Services, to provide personnel for the training of Saudi pilots and ground crew. Airwork also recruited former RAF pilots as mercenaries to fly operational missions against Egyptian and Republican targets along the Yemeni border. By 1965 MI6 was chartering aircraft with discreet pilots and had obtained the agreement of Israel to use its territory for mounting operations.

Following a ceasefire declared in August 1965, the British-backed mercenaries reverted to supplying medical aid and maintaining communications. By late 1966 the war had restarted and the fighting had reached a stalemate 'but the British were still running an extensive mercenary operation in Yemen with those recruited said to be paid £10,000 per annum' by a mysterious centre in London run by Stirling.

British air operations continued into 1967, according to the files. A Foreign Office note of March 1967 states that the British pilots were recruited by Airwork to fly the five Lightnings and five Hunters already supplied by Britain and that 'we have raised no objection to their being employed in operations, though we made it clear to the Saudis that we could not publicly acquiesce in any such arrangements'.[25]

After Egypt's defeat by Israel in the 1967 war, Nasser decided to pull troops out of Yemen, and in November Britain withdrew from Aden. Yet files of March 1967 refer to ongoing 'covert operations in South Arabia' and to 'Rancour II operations'; most files related to this have been censored. One exception is a June 1967 paper saying that 'Rancour operations in the Yemen have been extremely successful' in driving the Egyptians back from parts of the frontier and tying them down. It then recommends that these operations should continue after the independence of South Arabia (i.e. South Yemen). These could be undertaken 'using as a cover the military mission' for South Arabia, or 'alternatively the new embassy could provide the cover'.[26]

Despite the Egyptian withdrawal the civil war in Yemen continued. In 1969, two mercenaries from the private firm Watchguard were killed while leading a band of Royalist guerrillas in the North. Al-Badr had fled to England where he died, and in March 1969 the Saudis cut off their supplies to the Royalists. A treaty was signed, ending hostilities, the country was reborn as North Yemen. Two hundred thousand people had died.[27]

Aden: The Radfan revolt

The basic British goal in Aden had been outlined in March 1964 by Sir Kennedy Trevaskis, the High Commissioner, in a set of proposals which would grant South Arabia independence but which would also 'ensure that full power passed decisively into friendly hands' and 'which would leave it dependent on ourselves and subject to our influence'.

Much of the population refused to cooperate and Britain soon had to cope with a full-scale revolt, not only among politicised groups in Aden but also in a corner of the federation called Radfan, which broke out in 1964.

The Middle East Commander-in-Chief, Lt. Gen. Sir Charles Harington, recognised that the Radfan tribesmen 'have been eking out a poor and primitive existence for hundreds of years' in a situation where 'there is barely sufficient substance to support the population, families seldom making more than £50 a year profit'. 'Therefore', he wrote, 'the temptation and indeed the necessity to look elsewhere for aid is understandable' – which is what many people did, turning to offers from Egypt and the new Republican government in Yemen. Harington also noted that if Britain 'had given more financial help' to the Radfanis in the past 'the temptation to go elsewhere for the price of subversion might have been avoided'.[28]

Britain resorted to brutal methods against civilians to crush the Radfan rebellion. In April 1964 one minister, Duncan Sandys, called for its 'vigorous suppression' and that the British Commander-in-Chief be authorised 'to use whatever methods are necessary' for success while seeking to 'minimise adverse international criticism'. Action should also include authorisation for the High Commissioner to pay 'personal subsidies' (i.e., bribes) 'to key members of the federal council', i.e., in the Federation of South Arabia.

Air strikes against the rebels were approved in May and Trevaskis suggested sending soldiers to 'put the fear of death into the villages' controlled by the rebels. If this wasn't enough to secure submission, then

> it would be necessary to deliver some gun attacks on livestock or men outside the villages. Since tribesmen have been regularly firing at our aircraft and have hit several of them, we might be able to claim that our aircraft were shooting back of [sic] men who had fired at us from the ground.[29]

The British forces had been authorised by ministers to 'harass the means of livelihood' of villages in order to bring the rebels to submission. There were no restrictions on using 20-pound 'anti personnel bombs' although 'the public relations aspect' of these 'will want very careful handling', the Ministry of Defence noted. Thus the Defence Secretary had asked the Chief of the Air Staff to 'ensure the secrecy of the operation' to use these bombs.[30]

The Chiefs of Staff recognised the importance of public relations generally, concluding in a reflective report on operations in Radfan that 'the greatest need is for an early and clear PR policy for such operations to be established in London'. These brutal campaigns are the precursors of current 'information operations', providing important lessons for Whitehall planners over the decades.

In January 1964, the High Commissioner was given £50,000 to bribe local tribal leaders. He was also provided with £15,000 'to help undermine the position of the People's Socialist Party in Aden', the most important political opposition to continued British rule. Trevaskis also noted that this money would help 'to prevent their winning coming elections'. In July 1964 ministers approved the spending of £500,000 to be used by the High Commissioner 'to distribute to rulers where this would help to prevent tribal revolts'.[31]

Oman: Crushing rebellions

Although many of the circumstances were different, the same basic British interests and policies were evident in British interventions in Oman.

In July 1957 an uprising in central Oman brought about a collapse in the Sultan's authority in the area and threatened control of the country as a whole. Various tribes defecting from the Sultan joined forces with another tribal leader, Talib, who had landed in the country with an unusual combination of arms supplied from Saudi Arabia and backing from Nasser's Egypt. On 18 July Britain decided on air action against the rebels and the following month ground troops were despatched to join the fighting.

Just after Britain had begun its military intervention, Prime Minister Harold Macmillan explained to President Kennedy that 'we believe that the Sultan is a true friend to the West and is doing his best for his people'.[32] As Macmillan would surely have been aware, it would have been hard to discover a more oppressive regime to whose defence Britain leapt than that of the Omani Sultan's at this time. Literally all resources and political power were in the Sultan's hands. He kept hundreds of slaves at his palace, which he rarely left. There was no infrastructure to speak of and the main city did not even have a public electricity supply until 1971. There were hardly any schools or health care, and diseases were rampant.

'There is quite a lot to be said for a reasonably efficient feudalism', Britain's political resident in the Gulf, Sir Bernard Burrows, had commented a few months before the uprising, referring to the Gulf generally where Britain supported similar regimes. Burrows also noted three days after the British decision to intervene that there had been:

> a noticeable swing of general opinion throughout the Sultanate in favour of Talib, who is becoming more and more recognised as the local exponent of Arabism, and against the Sultan, whose popularity is at a very low ebb now.

Burrows was also aware that 'it was fear of the British that kept' the tribes in the Sultanate on the Sultan's side 'and only the thought that we were coming back which kept them from joining the rebels now'. Thus Britain ruled the country with terror and force in the name of the Sultan.[33]

Also instructive are the views of Burrows' replacement, George Middleton. After 18 months of war by the British against the rebels, he told the Foreign Office that 'this is yet another instance of our appearing to back an unpopular, undemocratic and selfish potentate'. He added:

> The condition of the people is miserable, the Sultan is unpopular, there is no central administration . . . and, under the present regime, not a great deal of hope for the future . . . What surprises me, is not that there is still

a rebellion [in the central areas] but that there are not half a dozen similar uprisings in other parts of the country.

However, Middleton's views were countered by his political master Julian Amery, the Colonial Minister. Amery said that the Sultan's record is 'on the whole a good one' since 'he has been loyal to the policy of cooperation with Britain' and has given Britain 'important facilities to the RAF at Masirah and Salalah', towns in Oman. Also, he was an opponent of Arab nationalism and 'the only Arab ruler who gave public support to the Suez expedition' just over two years earlier.[34]

Britain had to intervene since 'successful defiance of the Sultan . . . is likely to have a snowball effect' throughout Oman and other parts of the Gulf, the Foreign Office stated. Bombing would 'prevent the infection spreading' elsewhere in the Gulf 'by showing our friends there that we mean business'.

Defending the regime at all seems morally repugnant in itself; but British actions in the war surpassed even this. Officials in Bahrain, Britain's key diplomatic post in the region, noted that the purpose of British 'air action' in support of the Sultan was 'to show the population the power of weapons at our disposal' and to convince them that 'resistance will be fruitless and lead only to hardship'. The aim was 'to inflict the maximum inconvenience on the population so that out of discomfort and boredom they will turn' against the rebels.[35]

The British bombed water supplies and agricultural gardens – civilian targets and therefore war crimes. In a memo written on 21 July 1957, Charles Gault in Bahrain noted that the Sultan had agreed to air attacks on date gardens which, with attacks from cannon fire, 'would deter dissident villages [sic] from gathering their crops'. He also noted that 'it also appears possible to damage water supply to certain villages by air attack on wells'. This was later described as 'denial of water supply to selected villages by air action'.[36]

The following year Burrows wrote that 'shelling of mountain

villages continues intermittently and is having success in denying the use of the village [sic] and cultivation'. He also noted a recent 'air attack on water supply' of villages in the plains around Saiq and Sharaijah, two Omani towns at the foothills of the Jebel mountain, saying that 'shelling has already rendered cultivation . . . hazardous' in these areas.

Burrows also mentioned that he had advised against similar attacks against the villages of the plains in this area last summer 'on the grounds of adverse political effect' since 'such attacks would have become widely known'. But now 'circumstances have somewhat changed since then'. Villages on top of the mountain of Jebel Akhdar 'are in a somewhat different position' since 'what happens there does not necessarily become widely known throughout the country'. Therefore, Burrows approved of an 'attack on water supply at Said and Sharaijah' and argued for 'rocket attacks on water channel and tanks'.[37]

In April 1958 Macmillan approved British 'attacks by rocket on water supplies', although he failed to approve a proposal from the Defence Minister to bomb 'cultivated areas'. In August 1957 the Foreign Secretary had approved air strikes without needing to give warning. At the same time, the Foreign Office noted that 'we want to avoid the RAF killing Arabs if possible, especially as there will be newspaper correspondents on the spot'.[38]

By October 1957, British and local troops had recaptured the main centres of population while Talib and about 50 rebels then climbed the Jebel Ahkdar mountains and mustered the support of some of the hill tribesmen. At this time the Foreign Office was saying that Burrows, the political resident in Bahrain, 'has recommended that the three villages concerned . . . should be warned that unless they surrender the ringleaders of the revolt, they will be destroyed one by one by bombing'.

Yet the government initially decided against bombing the villages on the mountain since 'world opinion at that time was very flammable'. Instead, an alternative was approved in

February 1958. The British commander in Oman noted in a later report that the British forces lent two 'medium guns' to the Sultan's forces and 'with these, manned by his own men, he could blast the top of the mountain where and when he pleased, without publicity or odium affecting HMG'. However, this strategy failed: the guns did 'insufficient damage', as the 'daily rate of fire' was restricted by the cost and availability of ammunition.

So in March 1958 Britain authorised 'the rocketing and bombing of suspected rebel hideouts' on the mountain and the main routes leading up the mountain. This soon involved air attacks on supply routes, gunning the mountain top and 'air attacks to deny waterways and proscribe cultivation outside inhabited areas', according to the British Commander.[39]

Fighting continued through the summer and the rebels on the Jebel mountain remained undefeated. In November 1958 it was agreed to deploy the SAS to take the mountain. Their actions in this campaign have contributed to the legendary portrayal of the SAS as superhumans. However, it is in part the terrible violence inflicted by the British beforehand, including these unreported war crimes, that explains the success of the SAS.

The assault on the mountain began after British officials had recognised that Talib and another rebel leader wished 'to have peace to live in their villages' and that, even though British officials could not be sure of the leaders' seriousness to negotiate a peace, their conditions 'would at least represent the basis for negotiation'.[40] Not for the last time in the Middle East, Britain instead pushed for the military solution. The SAS were deployed without the agreement of the Sultan; the Sultan was barely consulted on British operations in the war generally, suggesting that it was really a British as much as an Omani war. In January 1959, the rebels were quickly defeated.

The British Commander's report at the end of the war stated that 'great pains were taken throughout the Command to keep all operational actions out of the press' – a strategy aided by the Sultan's complete ban on visas for reporters. 'Throughout the whole campaign', the report noted, 'a game of bluff and deceit was carried out, which at times was far from pleasant'.[41]

The war solved little. As the Foreign Office observed in July 1959, there was no political settlement in the interior and the crushing of the rebellion 'provided no more than a breathing space' for the Sultan. The 'long term problem' lay in the 'continued disaffection of large parts of the interior towards the Sultan', which he was not interested in addressing. The Sultan 'spends nearly all his time inaccessibly' at his palace while 'hardly any of his ministers can be regarded as even moderately competent'.[42]

Five years later, a rebellion broke out in the province of Dhofar. The rebels proclaimed the liberation of Dhofar in 1965; they were later to receive the support of Egypt, Iraq and South Yemen (once the British had been forced out of Aden in 1967), and rename themselves the Popular Front for the Liberation of the Occupied Arabian Gulf (PFLOAG). In response, the British embarked upon another military intervention that lasted until 1974.

The Dhofar uprising was 'an indigenous rebellion against the repression and neglect' of the Sultan, the Foreign Office later said.[43] Even by 1970 it was forbidden to smoke in public, to play football, to wear glasses, shoes or trousers, to eat in public or to talk to anyone for more than fifteen minutes. The poverty and repression that lay at the root of the uprising here, as with those in North Yemen and Aden, were well recognised by British officials. Bill Carden, the British Consul General in Muscat, for example, noted that 'apart from the few who work for the RAF, for the American oil company and for the Sultan, Dhoafris have no means of earning a reasonable livelihood in their country'. Meanwhile, the many who go abroad see 'the unfavourable comparisons between the great amount which is done for the people there and the very little done for them in Dhofar'. Carden noted that 'the Sultan has for too long had too many repressive measures' such as forbidding people to buy bicycles or radios without permission.[44]

By August 1967 Oman was exporting around 10 million barrels of oil a year, with prospects to increase this level massively. The manager of Oman's Petroleum Development Corporation (PDO) was British, and probably the second most powerful man in the country after the Sultan. Shell had an 85 per cent interest in Omani oil. Almost all of Oman's income was generated from oil; the revenues were paid directly to the Sultan, who released a proportion for the exchequer.

'If the Omani rebel movement were to succeed', Britain's political resident in Bahrain commented, and if 'the territory where the oilfields lie were to be separated constitutionally from the coastal area near Muscat where the terminal is situated, the oil company might find itself in great difficulty'.

By 1972 Foreign Office minister Patrick Jenkin was saying that 'success in Dhofar is essential for the Sultan' (i.e., Britain):

> If he fails there and loses his throne as a result, there is little doubt that stability in the Gulf area would be seriously affected, with consequent risk to our substantial commercial interests.[45]

Britain crushed the Dhofar rebellion and also removed the Sultan, who had by then become a liability, in a coup in 1970. The files on this coup remain classified. The beneficiary of the coup, the Sultan's son, Qaboos, remains in power today as Britain's leading ally in the Gulf.

TABLE

BRITAIN AND GLOBAL DEATHS

The following table gives figures on the estimated number of deaths in the post-war period for which Britain bears significant responsibility. I have divided these into four categories of degrees of responsibility:

Direct responsibility British military and/or covert forces have played a direct role.

Indirect responsibility Britain has provided strong support (through trade, arms exports, aid and/or diplomatic support) for allies engaged in aggression or killing.

Active inaction Britain has specifically helped to block international action to halt killings. (This is distinct from 'turning a blind eye', which would include many other cases.)

Others A solitary case, that of the Idi Amin regime's state terror.

Estimates on the number of deaths in any conflict always vary, often very widely. Where there is no footnote, I have used the most commonly cited estimate.

The overall figure is between 8.6 million and 13.5 million – or around 10 million. Of these, Britain bears 'direct responsibility' for between 4 million and 6 million deaths.

This figure is if anything likely to be an underestimate. Not

BRITAIN AND GLOBAL DEATHS

all British interventions have been included: some, such as those in Oman in 1957–1959 and 1964–1974 have been omitted because of lack of data. In the category of 'indirect responsibility', I have excluded many repressive regimes backed by Britain throughout the post-war period; I have tended instead to focus on those cases described in this and previous books. I have also not included the many millions of deaths recorded annually in developing countries from easily preventable diseases and other consequences of poverty. As a major shaper of world order, Britain bears significant responsibility for the global economic system, yet it is impossible to calculate the British share in this blame.

The figures generally refer to the number of 'enemy' deaths rather than total deaths, where it has been possible to disaggregate the estimates.

Finally, I do not pretend this is a fully scientific analysis – the criteria for inclusion, the extent of British responsibility and the estimates on numbers of deaths are of course all open to interpretation. Nevertheless, it gives a reasonably accurate reflection of British responsibility for a very large number of deaths in the post-war world.

DIRECT RESPONSIBILITY

Year	Conflict	Estimated number of deaths	Britain's role
2003	Invasion of Iraq	10,000–55,000[1]	British forces played secondary role to US in military operations
2001	Bombing of Afghanistan	15,000–25,000[2]	Ditto
1999	Bombing of Yugoslavia	1,000[3]	British forces played secondary role to US in military operations as part of wider NATO campaign
1998	Bombing of Iraq	600–1,600[4]	British forces played secondary role to US in military operations
1991	Gulf war	over 100,000[5]	Ditto
1982	Falklands	655	British military fought Argentina
1961–1973	War against South-east Asia	2,00,000–3,000,000[6]	Britain privately backed US strongly, regularly supported it publicly but also played several direct roles: providing military and 'counter-insurgency' advice to South Vietnam; British covert forces took part in the war; intelligence was passed to US military. The British role was therefore more 'direct' than 'indirect'
1962–1970	War in Yemen	100,000–200,000	British secret operation involving covert action and arms supplies
1964–1967	British suppression of Aden revolt	300–900	British 'colonial' government forces responsible

DIRECT RESPONSIBILITY (continued)

Year	Conflict	Estimated number of deaths	Britain's role
1965–1966	Indonesian army slaughters	500,000–1,000,000[7]	Britain provided Indonesian generals with variety of direct, covert support, including 'information' operations[8]
1952–1960	War in Kenya	up to 150,000[9]	British colonial war and 'resettlement' operations[10]
1948–1960	War in Malaya	10,000–13,000	Ditto[11]
1957–1958	Rebellion against Indonesian central government	thousands[12]	Covert operation with US to support the rebellion, including arms supplies
1956	British invasion of Egypt	1,600–3,000[13]	Military intervention with France and Israel
1948–1955	Uprising in Baltic states of the USSR	75,000[14]	British covert operation to fund and support uprisings[15]
1953	Coup in Iran	300	Covert operation with CIA[16]
1950–1953	Korean war	at least 1,000,000[17]	Military played key role technically as part of UN force, in reality led by US
1944–1949	Greek civil war	65,00–80,000[18]	Military/covert operations to support Greek government
1945–1949	War for Indonesian independence	5,000–80,000[19]	Military involvement to suppress independence movement
SUB-TOTAL			4.03–5.71m

INDIRECT RESPONSIBILITY

Year	Conflict	Estimated number of deaths	Britain's role
2000–present	Israeli killings in occupied territories	2,723[20]	Blair government is strong supporter of Israeli policies, in various ways
1999–present	Killings in Nigeria	up to 10,000[21]	Blair government is strong supporter of Nigerian policies, in various ways
1999–present	Second Russian invasion of Chechnya	15,000–25,000[22]	Blair government is strong supporter of Russian policies, in various ways
1996–present	Nepal civil war	3,300[23]	Blair government provides military/diplomatic support to Nepal government
1990–present	Colombia state killings	20,000–40,000[24]	Blair and previous governments are strong supporters of Colombian policies, in various ways
1976–present	Indonesian attacks in Aceh province	15,000	Blair and previous governments are strong supporters of Indonesian policies, in various ways
1969–present	Indonesian attacks in West Papua province	100,000	Ditto
1991–2003	Sanctions against Iraq	500,000–1,000,000[25]	Technically maintained by the UN; in reality supported virtually solely by Britain and US
1999	Indonesian attacks in East Timor	around 5,000	Blair government continued to support, and arm, Indonesia, throughout violence[26]

INDIRECT RESPONSIBILITY (continued)

Year	Conflict	Estimated number of deaths	Britain's role
1984–1999	Turkey's campaign against Kurds	around 30,000[27]	British governments were strong supporters of Turkey's policies, in various ways[28]
1998	US bombing of Sudan	perhaps tens of thousands[29]	Britain strongly supported US attack that destroyed pharmaceutical factory producing most of Sudan's life-saving drugs
1994–1996	Russian invasion of Chechnya	60,000–100,000	Major government provided strong support to Russia, in various ways
1948–1994	Apartheid South Africa state killings	10,000–20,000	British governments consistently backed South African regimes, in various ways[30]
1989	US invasion of Panama	350–3,000[31]	Britain provided strong diplomatic support
1980–1988	Iran–Iraq war	1,000,000	Thatcher government effectively supported Iraq's attack on Iran, supplying it with military equipment and financial aid
1987–1988	Iraq's campaign against Kurds	100,000	Ditto[32]
1984–1985	Ugandan civil war	100,000–300,000	Britain provided strong support to Ugandan government and maintained military training programme
1984–1985	Indonesian state killings	5,000	Thatcher government was strong supporter of Indonesia, in various ways

INDIRECT RESPONSIBILITY (continued)

Year	Conflict	Estimated number of deaths	Britain's role
Early 1980s	El Salvador civil war	75,000–80,000	Thatcher government provided strong diplomatic backing to US strategy supporting Salvadoran regime
1980s	US aggression against Nicaragua	30,000	Thatcher government provided strong diplomatic and other backing, including covert support, to US strategy[33]
1953–1979	Shah's regime in Iran	10,000	British governments provided strong support to Shah's regime, in various ways[34]
1975	Indonesian invasion of East Timor	200,000	Wilson/Callaghan governments provided strong backing to Indonesia, in various ways[35]
1973	Coup in Chile	at least 3,000	Heath government welcomed coup and backed Pinochet regime, as did subsequent British governments
1967–1970	Nigeria/Biafra civil war	1.000,000–3,000,000	Wilson government gave strong backing to Nigeria, in various ways
1963	Iraq killings	5,000	Macmillan government in effect supported massacres and welcomed new military government
1960s	Iraq campaigns against Kurds	12,000–100,000[36]	British governments gave strong backing to Iraq in various ways
SUB-TOTAL			3.32m–6.20m

ACTIVE INACTION

Year	Conflict	Estimated number of deaths	Britain's role
1990s	Yugoslav civil wars	200,000–250,000	Major government played key role to prevent international action against Milosevic regime[37]
1994	Rwanda genocide	800,000–1,000,000	Major government played key role at the UN to prevent international action to prevent or stop genocide[38]
SUB-TOTAL			1m–1.25m

OTHERS

Year	Conflict	Estimated number of deaths	Britain's role
1971–1979	Ugandan state terror (Idi Amin) era	300,000	Heath government welcomed and supported Amin's rule in its first year. Most atrocities were committed after this period but Britain bears significant responsibility in enabling Amin regime to consolidate its rule
SUB-TOTAL			300,000
TOTAL			8.65m–13.47m

CONCLUSION

The world has become a more dangerous place in the past two years, not least due to the actions of British decision-makers. In the context of a so-called 'war against terrorism', there are two sets of fanatics – those prepared to blow up as many innocent people as they can based on commitment to an extreme ideology; and those who, since they believe in controlling the world in the interests of a tiny elite, respond with military interventions likely to recruit more people to the cause. In the middle are caught ordinary people – more accurately, Unpeople ourselves.

In *Web of Deceit* I argued that the root of the problem of British foreign policy is the political system and nature of decision-making itself. Foreign policy is made by a secretive elite protected even from any serious democratic scrutiny, let alone any systematic influence over that policy by the public. There has long been no fundamental difference between the Labour and Conservative parties in foreign policy. As this book tries to show, many of the worst episodes have been presided over by Labour governments. The Blair government is even more militarily interventionist and contemptuous of international law than Thatcher. The invasion of Iraq demonstrated the government's contempt for public opinion – not only that of the personally chosen officials around the Prime Minister, but also of the backbench MPs who protected the government by voting for it. That too much power is invested in a single person and his hand-picked entourage is now perhaps more widely perceived than ever; as is the fact that elected MPs do not generally represent the public interest. Britain will always promote terrible foreign policies until this elitist system is democratised and a fundamental transformation of governance takes place.

Change needs to happen in the context of globalisation, which is concentrating wealth and power into the hands of a small number of private corporations and a transnational political and commercial elite. The global financial institutions need to be reconstituted to promote policies that strengthen communities' and people's abilities to act in their own interests. This means a dismantling of their current strategy of imposing a one-size-fits-all neo-liberal model of market fundamentalism all over the globe, a model being religiously championed by the liberalisation theologists of New Labour – another fanatical devotion to a strategy extremely harmful to ordinary people.

The global justice movement (mislabelled the 'anti-globalisation' movement) offers a counterweight to this transnational elite. By working across borders to press for alternatives, this movement can promote the natural solidarity among ordinary people in an increasingly interdependent world. These tasks are urgent in the light of the ongoing destruction of the environment and deepening poverty and inequality in many parts of the world – including Britain, where child poverty is one of the great scandals of our times.

The government's recent recourse to unprecedented propaganda shows the extent to which the public is feared. A perennial truth which emerges from the declassified files is the public's ability to mount protests and demonstrations that divert the government from its course. The propaganda on Iraq has often been so crude that many, perhaps most, people have been able to see through it. It is far from the case that all, or even most, propaganda works. Much government propaganda is directed towards opinion-formers, such as journalists and academics; these people, in my experience, are usually more deeply indoctrinated than 'ordinary people'. Essentially, it is the function of opinion-formers within the ideological system to convey, often totally uncritically, the policies and proclamations of the state to the public – but the latter are increasingly failing to play their assigned role.

In the talks and meetings to which I have been invited recently, it seems to me that these perceptions are contributing to the emergence of a new radicalism even among previously unpoliticised people. There is an increasing sense that the mainstream parties offer the same and nothing in terms of promoting a foreign policy respectful of human rights and moral values. And there is increasing anger and frustration about people's voices being ignored.

After 11 September there has been a more acute perception that we cannot afford the harmful, unilateralist approach to fellow human beings that either terrorists or indeed in different ways New Labour are promoting. More radical alternatives are needed to the mainstream parties at Westminster and which are based on the fact of global interdependence. In particular, there is widespread recognition that the various activist groups, more radical political elements and social movements need to find a way of coming together behind an alternative political and economic programme. My own view is that an agenda of promoting real democracy – domestically and globally – could provide an umbrella for uniting groups behind a coherent, common programme and appeal to a broad cross-section of people. It is a challenge in which everyone concerned about foreign policy must be involved. I also believe that opposition groups need to engage in harder-hitting campaigning tactics such as non-violent direct action to press for changes in official policies, rather than relying on insider lobbying, rational persuasion or more traditional forms of campaigning.

CONCLUSION

The obstacles to bringing about policies that actually promote human rights and treat people as people rather than Unpeople, remain great. The power of centralised government is growing, with the 'war against terrorism' heralding new laws with which to undermine human rights and clamp down on domestic dissent. State propaganda operations are increasing and the mainstream sources of information remain heavily indoctrinated in their coverage.

Self-education is a vital task. There is a plethora of websites where excellent independent analysis is freely available. The Glasgow University Media Group and Medialens, for example, offer incisive exposure of mainstream media coverage with the latter encouraging supporters directly to challenge instances of misreporting. Other organisations such as Indymedia and Schnews offer alternative media analysis and information on campaigning. A new organisation has recently been set up in the academic world, called the Network of Scholars of International Politics and International Relations (NASPIR), which brings together analysts writing critically on international issues, to share information and to see research as an element in social change.

Then there are organisations working in particular sectors, such as: Justice not Vengeance and Occupation Watch, for Iraq; the website Znet, for international issues and US foreign policy; PR Watch and the Institute for Public Accuracy, for the public-relations industry and disinformation; Corporate Europe Observatory, for the power and lobbying of corporations; Tapol for Indonesia and the Colombian Solidarity Campaign for Colombia; Campaign Against the Arms Trade, for arms exports; Focus on the Global South, Third World Network and the World Development Movement, for development and global economic issues. There are also excellent magazines such as *Frontline, Z Magazine, Third World Resurgence, Lobster*, and *Red Pepper*. And of course there are numerous outstanding journalists and analysts, often collected on the Znet site.

I believe that one of the biggest challenges of all lies in more people making the shift from being 'liberal' to 'radical', to increase the weight of pressure for fundamental change. It still amazes me how many people in NGO circles, where I have often worked, retain essentially liberal outlooks – prepared to accept that reform within the existing system is the only required, or possible, strategy and often barely aware of the ideological role of the mainstream media. Governments are often still viewed in good faith and their public claims accepted, rather than being automatically dismissed or even questioned, as I think should be the default position. This outlook is based partly on lack of knowledge, which is not surprising given the silence of academics and mainstream media reporting. It may be partly due to fears of the consequences at the workplace of adopting a more 'radical' perspective.

But the liberal outlook can also be due to disbelief that fundamental change is possible – a self-fulfilling prophecy. In fact, fundamental change benefiting ordinary people is happening all over the world, at the community, national and global levels. At the community level there are lots of extraordinary initiatives to promote social and environmental improvements. At the global level, the past decade has seen unprecedented radical protest and organisation against global economic liberalisation, from Seattle to Cancun. This global movement has notched up many successes – stopping the Multinational Agreement on Investment, forcing some change at the World Bank and achieving cancellation of some developing-country debts. It needs to go further and translate into influencing policy-making across the board, and ultimately to transform domestic societies generally and global policy-making to become people-centred; no small task.

In my view, many civil society agencies, and especially the charitable NGOs, share the blame for reinforcing the liberal mindset of their supporters by pressing only for mild reform of government policies. Although their work is vital, such organisations also fail to tell their supporters about the systematic responsibility of the British government in, say, poverty or human-rights abuses, and often choose to welcome the mildest of government policy-reform proposals. Most organisations are frightened of criticising government policy beyond certain limits even when the facts warrant it – and these limits are often very narrow.

These organisations play the role of containing wider, radical opposition while appearing to be genuinely independent. It is no surprise that many receive considerable funding from the government, while senior managers often move in ministerial circles and are seduced by the illusion of having serious influence over government policy. Yet, in my experience, their liberal, reformist strategy derives not so much from the restrictions that come with receiving government money, but moreso from seeing their 'supporters' as funders more than campaigners; in other words, the primary aim is to grow and become bigger corporate entities, rather than to prioritise fundamental social change. This also holds them back from forming wider coalitions for radical change.

Few household-name NGOs were formally part of the Stop the War coalition that protested against the invasion of Iraq. Few have played any real role in enhancing the global justice movement. That these well-supported, resource-rich and potentially influential groups are failing to help sow the seeds of fundamental social change is serving to hold such change back.

George Orwell famously wrote of the 'deep, deep sleep of England, from which I sometimes fear that we shall never wake till we are jerked out of it by the roar of bombs'.[1] The process of transforming British foreign policy requires not only bringing together various opposition groups and radicalising many existing organisations, but also a personal transformation, decolonising the mind of accepted truths and received wisdom. This self-education can be a liberating experience in itself, as well as in our own self-interest.

NOTES

1 Occupying Iraq: The attack on democracy

1   House of Commons, Foreign Affairs Committee, *The decision to go to war in Iraq*, Ninth report, Session 2002-03, 7 July 2003, conclusion.

2   Paul Whiteley, 'Baghdad backlash', *Guardian*, 6 May 2003; Evidence to the Defence Committee, 11 June 2003, Q407, www.parliament.the-stationary-office.co.uk/pa/cm200203; 'PM: Authority of the United Nations "is on the line"', 28 February 2003, www.pm.gov.uk

3   See Stephen Shalom, 'The United States in the General Assembly', Znet, 22 April 2003.

4   Medialens, 'Chaining the watchdog, part 2, 3 May 2003, www.medialens.org

5   See *Web of Deceit*, chapters 18 and 19, for the role of the media. See also Justin Lewis and Rod Brookes, 'Reporting the war on television', in David Miller (ed), *Tell me lies: Propaganda and media distortion in the attack on Iraq*, Pluto, London, 2004.

6   'Prime Minister's speech to Congress', 18 July 2003, www.pm.gov.uk

7   Jason Leopold, 'Wolfowitz admits Iraq war was planned two days after 9/11', Znet, 2 June 2003; Mark Hollingsworth, 'Spies like us', *Guardian*, 5 November 2003; Raymond Whitaker, 'Blair told US was targeting Saddam "just days after 9/11"', *Independent* on Sunday, 4 April 2004.

8   There is a variety of evidence as to when Blair took the decision to join the US in the invasion, but all point to 2002: Clare Short said that, while Blair was assuring her of a commitment to secure a second Security Council resolution, Short noted that three 'extremely senior

people in the Whitehall system' said that the Prime Minister had already agreed with President Bush the 'previous summer' to invade Iraq the following February (later extended to March because of Turkey's refusal to accept US troops). 'I think the US wanted to go to war in the Spring and the UK, I now think, had pre-committed to that timetable', Short noted; Evidence to the House of Commons Foreign Affairs Committee (FAC), 17 June 2003, Q64,83,124,129, www.publications.parliament.uk/pa/cm200203; Peter Stothard's book, *30 days*, indicates that Blair believed that by September 2002 the US had already decided to go to war and that Blair had already decided that Britain should be alongside them. Peter Stothard, *30 days: A month at the heart of Blair's war*, Harper Collins, 2003.

9 *Review of intelligence on weapons of mass destruction: Report of a committee of privy counsellors*, HC 898, HMSO, London, 14 July 2004 (hereafter the *Butler* report) paras 429, 427.

10 See evidence to the Defence Committee, 5 February 2004, citing previous evidence given by Air Marshall Burridge, www.publications. parliament.uk/pa/cm200304' and A.Pawson, Ministry of Defence of Defence, evidence on 12 November 2003, www.publications. parliament.uk/pa/cm200304

11 Cited in Glen Rangwala, 'Iraq's weapons of mass destruction: the assessment of the British government – Problems, contradictions, falsehoods', undated, and 'Misled into war', 21 March 2003, www.middleeastreference.org.uk; Hans Blix, Notes for the briefing of the Security Council on the 13th quarterly report of UNMOVIC, UN News Centre, 5 June 2003.

12 Julian Borger, 'Intelligence was wrong, admits general', *Guardian*, 31 May 2003.

13 Jim Lobe, 'Chalabi, Garner provide new clues to war', *Hi Pakistan*, 26 February 2004, www.occupationwatch.org

14 Christine Spolar, '14 "enduring bases" set in Iraq', *Chicago Tribune*, 23 March 2004.

15 'PM statement on Iraq', 25 February 2003, www.pm.gov.uk; Joint press conference with president Bush at Camp David, 27 March 2003, www.pm,.gov.uk.

16 'PM thanks troops in Iraq', 29 May 2003, www.pm.gov.uk

17 Iraq body count, 'Civilian deaths in "noble" Iraq mission pass 10,000', www.iraqbodycount.net; Amnsety International, 'One year after the war the human rights situation remains critical, 18 March 2004, www.amnesty.org; Study by Medact in Shaista Aziz, 'War killed 55,000 Iraq civilians, 11 November 2003, Al Jazeera.

18 House of Commons, *Hansard*, 15 October 2003, Col.244, 1 September, Col.905.

19 House of Commons, *Hansard*, 3 June 2003, Col.293.

20 Human Rights Watch, 'Off target: The conduct of the war and civilian casualties in Iraq', December 2003, www.hrw.org

21 Paul Brown, 'Uranium hazard prompts cancer check on troops', *Guardian*, 25 April 2003; John Pilger, 'A year later', Znet, 23 March 2004.

22 Voices in the Wilderness newsletter, February/March 2004, citing the *Sunday Times* of 25 January, www.viw.uk; Julian Borger, 'Israel trains US assassination squads in Iraq', *Guardian*, 9 December 2003.

23 Rory McCarthy, 'Gunships ram home might of US firepower', *Guardian*, 15 November 2003.

24 Rory McCarthy, 'Uneasy truce in the city of ghosts', *Guardian*, 24 April 2004; Nicolas Pelham, 'No retreat from Falluja, says US', *Financial Times*, 1 May 2004.

25 Rory McCarthy, 'None killed in US convoy as Shia militias fight on', *Guardian*, 10 April 2004; Patrick Wintour, 'Army chiefs resist call for more Iraq troops', *Guardian*, 29 April 2004; Luke Harding, '"It's hell . . . everything will be destroyed', *Guardian*, 30 April 2004.

26 Michael White, 'Leaked memo reveals fear that US tactics are endangering troops', *Guardian*, 24 May 2004.

27 David Teather, 'US begins crackdown as soldiers found dead', *Guardian*, 30 June 2003.

28 Centre for Economic and Social Rights, 'Beyond torture: US violations of occupation law in Iraq', www.cesr.org

29 Human Rights Watch, 'Civilian deaths need US investigation', 21 October 2002; Amnesty, 'One year after the war the human rights situation remains critical', 18 March 2004.

30 Andrew Johnson, 'Did British soldiers lose all control and decency at the notorious Camp Bucca?', *Independent*, 15 February 2004; Richard Norton-Taylor, 'Big rise in civilian death inquiries, *Guardian*, 9 June 2004; Phil Shiner, 'End this lawlessness', *Guardian*, 10 June 2004.

31 'Violations "were tantamount to torture"', *Guardian*, 8 May 2004; David Leigh, 'UK force taught torture methods', *Guardian*, 8 May 2004; cited in Centre for Economic and Social Rights, *Beyond torture: US violations of occupation law in Iraq*, www.cesr.org

32 'British companies must play their part in Iraq, speech, 21 November 2003, www.fco.gov.uk; House of Commons, *Hansard*, 9 December 2003, Col.449 and 20 June 2003, Col.499; 20 June 2003, Col.499; 1 April 2003, Col.624.

33 Joseph Stiglitz, 'Iraq's next shock will be shock therapy', Znet, 17 March 2004.

34 House of Commons, *Hansard*, 20 November 2003, Col.1308; UN Security Council, Resolution 1483, 22 May 2003, paragraph 4.

35 David Teather, 'US set to back state control of Iraqi oil', *Guardian*, 8 January 2004; Glen Rangwala, 'Changing stories on Iraq', 23 January 2004, www.middleeastreference.org.uk

36 House of Commons, *Hansard*, 21 October 2003, Col.163; 11 March 2003, Col.158.

37 Robert Fisk, 'Britain's secret army in Iraq', *Independent*, 28 March 2004; Julian Borger, 'US military in torture scandal', *Guardian*, 30 April 2004; Bill Berkowitz, 'Mercenaries "R" us', Alternet, 24 March 2004, www.occupationwatch.org

38 Rajiv Chandrasekaran, 'How cleric trumped US plan for Iraq', *Washington Post Foreign Service*, 26 November 2003.

39 John Burns and Thom Shanker, 'US officials fashion legal basis to keep force in Iraq, *New York Times*, 26 March 2004; Yochi Dreazen, 'Behind the scenes, US tightens grip on Iraq's future', *Wall Street Journal*, 13 May 2004; Mike O'Brien, 'Iraq stands at the dawn of a new era', 25 June 2004, www.fco.gov.uk

40 Ewen Macaskill, 'US clings to the burdens of power', *Guardian*, 18 May 2004; Timothy Phelps, 'US will control Iraqi forces', *Newsday*, 10 April 2004.

41 Cited in Ed Johnson, 'Blair backpedals on Iraq comments', *Toronto Star*, 26 May 2004; Ewen Macaskill and Sarah Hall, 'US vows to stay in control of Iraqi troops', *Guardian*, 17 May 2005.

42 'PM: Saddam and his regime will be removed', 25 March 2003, www.pm.gov.uk; Wolfowitz, 'We will completely remove Kurdish group from Northern Iraq', *Turkish Daily News*, 1 February 2004; Scheherezade Faramazi, 'Kurds' dream clashes with US plans', *Miami Herald*, 28 January 2004; Steven Weisman, 'Kurdish region in northern Iraq will get to keep special status', *New York Times*, 5 January 2004.

43 'Iraq and weapons of mass destruction: An intelligence assessment', Q&A, www.the-hutton-inquiry.org.uk; Percy Cradock, note, 26 August 1963, FO371/170449/EQ1019/42.

44 Foreign Office, 'The Kurdish problem in Iraq', August 1963, National Archives, FO371/170447/EQ1019/1.

45 Said Aburish, *A Brutal Friendship: The West and the Arab elite*, Indigo, London, 1997, p. 136; R. Allen to G. Hiller, 3 September 1962, FO371/164235/EQ1015/83.

46 Aburish, p. 98.
47 Kenneth Roth, 'War in Iraq: Not a humanitarian intervention', 27 January 2004, www.hrw.org.
48 See *Web of Deceit*, Chapter 15.
49 See *Web of Deceit*, Chapters 15 and 16.
50 House of Commons, *Hansard*, 15 June 2004, Cols. 34–5.

2 *The irrelevance of international law*

1   PM interview with the World Service, 9 October 2002, www.pm.gov.uk.
2   Clare Short evidence to FAC, Q64, 83, 124, 129.
3   'Prime minister's question time: the six crucial problems that Blair must solve', *Guardian*, 12 March 2003.
4   'Iraqi people facing humanitarian crisis: An interview with Dennis Halliday', *Between the Lines*, 7 April 2003.
5   Oliver Burkeman and Julian Borger, 'War critics astonished as US hawk admits invasion was illegal', *Guardian*, 20 November 2003.
6   Richard Norton-Taylor, 'Law unto themselves', *Guardian*, 13 March 2003, and other *Guardian* articles citing the 'near-unanimous view' among international lawyers; Mark Littman, 'A supreme international crime', *Guardian*, 10 March 2003; 'Was the war justified?: Leading international lawyers give their verdicts', *Guardian*, 2 March 2004; Richard Norton-Taylor, 'Whitehall united in doubt on war', *Guardian*, 27 February 2004; Norton-Taylor, 'Disputed advice helped quash opposition to war', *Guardian*, 28 February 2004.
7   Richard Norton-Taylor, 'A chance to name the guilty men', *Guardian*, 9 July 2004.
8   'PM statement following UN Security Council Resolution', 8 November 2002, www.pm.gov.uk.
9   Glen Rangwala, 'Changing stories on Iraq', 23 January 2004, www.middleeastreference.org.uk.
10 Jack Straw, evidence to the Foreign Affairs Committee, 4 March 2003, www.publications.parliament.uk/pa/cm/200203, paras 151, 178.
11 Jack Straw, evidence to the Foreign Affairs Committee, 29 April 2003, www.publications.parliament.uk/pa/cm/200203, para 290.
12 'Prime minister's question time: the six crucial problems that Blair must solve', *Guardian*, 12 March 2003.
13 House of Commons, *Hansard*, 17 March 2003, Col. 2; Paul Waugh, 'Attorney General conceded doubts over legality of war', *Independent*, 4 March 2004.

14 Keir Starmer, 'Sorry, Mr Blair, but 1441 does not authorise force', *Guardian*, 17 March 2003; Anne Penketh and Andrew Grice, 'Blix: Iraq war was illegal', *Independent*, 5 March 2004.

15 Butler report, paras 266–7.

16 'Prime Minister's address to the nation', 20 March 2003, www.pm.gov.uk; 'PM: Saddam and his regime will be removed', 25 March 2003, www.pm.gov.uk.

17 Mark Littman, 'A supreme international crime', *Guardian*, 10 March 2003.

18 Helena Smith, 'Greeks accuse Blair of war crimes in Iraq', *Guardian*, 29 July 2003; Ewen Macaskill, 'UK should face court for crimes in Iraq, say jurists', *Guardian*, 12 January 2004.

19 *A new chapter to the strategic defence review: Government response to the Committee's sixth report of session 2002–2003*, 21 July 2003, p. 11.

20 'PM warns of continuing global terror threat', 5 March 2004, www.pm.gov.uk.

21 P. Dean to Foreign Secretary, 25 September 1963, PREM11/4564.

22 Cabinet Office, Steering Committee, 'British overseas obligations', 14 April 1958, T234/768; see *The Great Deception: Anglo-American power and world order*, Pluto, London, 1998, p. 178.

23 Foreign Office, 'Regional Studies', September 1964, FCO49/302.

24 A. Douglas-Home, 'British policy towards the United Nations in the 1970s', 11 September 1970, FCO49/288.

25 See *Web of Deceit*, p. 404.

26 See *The Great Deception*, p. 179.

27 Minutes of a ministerial meeting, 2 December 1963, CAB 130/189; Memorandum of conversation, *Foreign Relations of the United States (FRUS)*, Vol. XXI, Document 68, www.state.gov.

28 D. Carden, Consul general, Muscat, 'Annual report on Muscat and Oman for 1965', 2 January 1966, FO1016/765.

29 *The Great Deception*, pp. 188–9.

30 Commonwealth Secretary to Lagos, 1 October 1968, PREM13/2260.

31 D. Brighty to E. Youde, 25 April 1969, PREM13/2820.

32 *The Great Deception*, p. 196.

3 Deceiving the public: The Iraq propaganda campaign

1 Clare Short, evidence to the House of Commons Foreign Affairs Committee, 17 June 2003, www.publications.parliament.uk/pa/cm200203, Q63; Glen Rangwala and Raymond Whitaker, '20 lies about the war', *Independent*, 15 July 2003; Rangwala, 'Changing stories on Iraq', 23 January 2004, www.middleeastreference.org.uk.

2   The quotation is from David Kelly in an email to a US journalist after giving evidence to a parliamentary inquiry. Cited in Simon Rogers (ed.), *The Hutton Inquiry and its Impact*, Guardian Books, 2004, p. 224.

3   Neil Mackay, 'Revealed: The secret cabal which spun for Blair', *Sunday Herald*, 8 June 2003.

4   Scott Ritter, letters, *Guardian*, 29 November 2003; Michael Meacher, 'The very secret service', *Guardian*, 21 November 2003.

5   Meacher, 'The very secret service'; House of Commons, *Hansard*, 12 January 2004, Col. 538.

6   Nicholas Rufford, 'Revealed: How MI6 sold the Iraq war', *Sunday Times*, 28 December 2003; 'MI6 ran "dubious" Iraq campaign', BBC News, 21 November 2003.

7   Seymour Hersh, 'Who lied to whom?', *The New Yorker*, 31 March 2003.

8   See David Miller, 'The propaganda machine', in Miller (ed.), *Tell Me Lies: Propaganda and media distortion in the attack on Iraq*, Pluto, London, 2004.

9   Defence Committee, *Lessons of Iraq*, Third report, Session 2003/04, 16 March 2004, paras 469–83, www.publications.parliament.uk.

10 David Leigh, 'False witness', *Guardian*, 4 April 2003; Stephen Dorril, 'Spies and lies', in Miller (ed.), *Tell Me Lies*, p. 112; Peter Beaumont, 'Allies fear Iraq plotting "scorched earth" war', *Observer*, 25 February 2003.

11 David Hencke and Andy Rowell, 'Battle the MoD lost: papers reveal failed bid to sway opinion on Iraq', *Guardian*, 19 November 2003.

12 'Sincere deceivers', *Economist*, 17 July 2004; 'He got it wrong', *New Statesman*, 19 July 2004.

13 *Butler report*, paras 433, 434, 435, 222, 240, 226, 261, 272, 295, 292.

14 *Government response to the intelligence and security committee report on Iraqi weapons of mass destruction – Intelligence and assessments 11 September 2003*, Cm.6118, February 2004.

15 Richard Norton-Taylor, 'Tell us the truth about the dossier', *Guardian*, 15 July 2003.

16 Robin Cook, 'Blair and Scarlett told me Iraq had no usable weapons', *Guardian*, 12 July 2004.

17 Cited in Rangwala, 'Iraq's weapons of mass destruction', www.middleeastreference.org.uk

18 *Butler report*, para 334.

19 Jack Straw evidence to the House of Commons Foreign Affairs Committee, 24 June 2003, Q735, www.publications.parliament.uk/ pa/cm200203

20 Jonathan Powell to John Scarlett, 17 September 2002, www.the-hutton-inquiry.org.uk

21 Jonathan Powell to Alastair Campbell and David Manning, 17 September 2002, www.the-hutton-inquiry.org.uk; emphasis in original.

22 'I was shocked by poor weapons intelligence – Blix', *Guardian*, 7 June 2003.

23 Robin Cook, 'We must not let one "dodgy dossier" distract us from more crucial questions', *Independent*, 26 June 2003.

24 Robin Cook, evidence to the House of Commons Foreign Affairs Committee, 17 June 2003, www.publications.parliament.uk/pa/cm200203, Q9; 'Iraq hits back with CIA offer', *Guardian*, 23 December 2003; 'Secret of Saddam's hidden arsenal', *Guardian*, 5 September 2002.

25 'Responsibility for the terrorist atrocities in the United States, 11 September 2001 – an updated account', www.pm.gov.uk.

26 Jason Burke, *Al Qaeda: Casting a shadow of terror*, I. B. Tauris, 2003, p. 19.

27 Peter Beaumont and Ed Vulliamy, 'Story of find in Afghan cave "was made up" to justify sending marines', *Observer*, 24 March 2002.

28 'Blair: I have secret proof of weapons', *Observer*, 1 June 2003; Clare Short evidence, Q89, 94.

29 Ewen Macaskill, 'Emails show how No. 10 constructed case for war', *Guardian*, 23 August 2003.

30 Daniel Pruce to Mark Matthews, 10 September 2002, www.the-hutton-inquiry.org.uk.

31 Daniel Pruce to Alastair Campbell, 11 September 2002, www.the-hutton-inquiry.org.uk; Tom Kelly to Alastair Campbell, 11 September 2002, www.the-hutton-inquiry.org.uk; Richard Norton-Taylor, 'Dossier was too static for No. 10', *Guardian*, 21 August 2003.

32 Richard Norton-Taylor, Nicholas Watt and Ewen Macaskill, 'The remaining questions', *Guardian*, 12 September 2003; Richard Norton-Taylor, 'Hoon has no defence for the dossier', *Guardian*, 1 October 2003.

33 '"There was a lack of substantive evidence"', *Independent*, 4 February 2004; Rogers (ed.), *The Hutton Inquiry*, pp. 219–21.

34 Richard Norton-Taylor, 'Hoon has no defence for the dossier', *Guardian*, 1 October 2003; Robin Cook, 'A sound judgment but it sidesteps the central issues', *Independent*, 29 January 2004.

35 Alastair Campbell to John Scarlett, 17 September 2002, www.the-hutton-inquiry.org.uk; Sarah Hall, 'Campbell misled us, says MP', *Guardian*, 22 August 2003.

UNPEOPLE

36 Ewen Macaskill and Richard Norton-Taylor, '10 ways to sex up a dossier', *Guardian*, 27 September 2003.
37 Evidence from journalist Tom Mangold to the Hutton inquiry, cited in Rogers (ed.), *The Hutton Inquiry*, p. 227.
38 Vikram Dodd, 'Hoon knew WMD press reports were wrong', *Guardian*, 23 September 2003; House of Commons, *Hansard*, 10 February 2004, Col. 1305; Clare Short evidence, Q103–4.
39 Sarah Hall, Patrick Wintour and Richard Norton-Taylor, 'Blair caught in Iraq arms row', *Guardian*, 5 February 2004.
40 House of Commons, *Hansard*, 12 February 2004, Col. 1677; Geoff Hoon, evidence to Defence Committee, 5 February 2004, www.publications.parliament.uk/pa/cm200304.
41 *Butler report*, para 497.
42 Richard Norton-Taylor, 'What David Kelly knew', *Guardian*, 24 July 2003; Ewen Macaskill, Richard Norton-Taylor and Vikram Dodd, 'The desperate search for the dossier evidence', *Guardian*, 27 August 2003.
43 Raymond Whitaker and Kim Sengupta, 'Is this the face of the man who gave Blair the cue for 45-minute WMD claim?', *Independent*, 22 February 2004.
44 '"A statement popped up and was seized on"', *Guardian*, 14 August 2003.
45 Cited in Justice Not Vengeance briefing, 'Gilligan 6:07: Dr Kelly was not the only source for the story', 5 February 2004, www.j-n-v.org.
46 Foreword, 'Iraq's weapons of mass destruction: The assessment of the British government', September 2002, www.fco.gov.uk.
47 House of Commons, *Hansard*, 23 January 2002, Col. 887 and 15 April 2002, Col. 721; 2 December 2002, Col. 522; 5 February 2003, Col. 266.
48 Richard Norton-Taylor, 'Iraq gave al Qaeda a base, says Blair', *Guardian*, 18 June 2004; *Butler report*, para 484.
49 Richard Norton-Taylor, 'UK spies reject al Qaeda link', *Guardian*, 10 October 2002.
50 'Iraq dossier fiasco rolls on', 12 June 2003, Jane's, www.janes.com.
51 Glen Rangwala, 'Paper written for the Foreign Affairs Committee', www.middleeastreference.org.uk.
52 Suzanne Goldenberg, 'Britain "knew uranium claims were false"', *Guardian*, 7 July 2003; Julian Borger, 'Democrats step up pressure on uranium claims', *Guardian*, 14 July 2003.
53 Seymour Hersh, 'Who lied to whom?'; Memorandum from the Foreign Office to the Foreign Affairs Committee, 28 July 2003, www.publications.parliament.uk.

54 Letters, *Guardian*, 15 July 2003.

55 *Butler report*, para 497.

56 'Prime Minister's interview with Arabic television', 4 April 2003, www.pm.gov.uk.

57 Nicholas Watt, 'Straw retreats on finding banned weapons', *Guardian*, 15 May 2003.

58 Jack Straw, evidence to the Foreign Affairs Committee, 24 June 2003, www.publications.parliament.uk.pa/cm200203, Q737, 845–6.

59 House of Commons, *Hansard*, 15 October 2003, Col. 234; Richard Norton-Taylor and Michael White, 'Report reveals Blair overruled by terror warning', *Guardian*, 12 September 2003.

60 'They won't go away', *Guardian*, 13 September 2003.

61 Memorandum from the Foreign Office to the Foreign Affairs Committee report on the foreign policy aspects of the war against terrorism, December 2003, www.publications.parliament.uk; Foreign Affairs Committee, Second report, Session 2003/04, Foreign policy aspects of the war against terrorism, 2 February 2004, para 23, www.publications.parliament.uk/pa/cm200304.

4 *The new Ministry of Offence*

1 DTI, *Our energy future – Creating a low carbon economy*, Cm 5761, February 2003, foreword, para 6.6, 6.13, 6.16, 6.17, 6.23, 6.25.

2 'US to move troops to Africa to protect oil interests', IPS, 9 July 2003, www.corpwatch.org; Ken Silverstein, 'US oil politics in the "Kuwait of Africa"', *The Nation*, 22 April 2002; Suraya Dadoo, 'When uncle Sam comes calling in Africa', *Media Review*, 30 April 2003, www.zmag.org.

3 Jean-Christophe Servant, 'The new Gulf oil states', *Le Monde Diplomatique*, January 2003.

4 Rob Evans and David Hencke, 'UK and US in joint effort to secure African oil', *Guardian*, 14 November 2003.

5 R. Butler to PM, 20 April 1964, DEFE 13/569.

6 Treasury, 'Overseas investment policy', 25 July 1956, T230/306.

7 Cabinet Office, 'Future policy study, 1960–1970', January 1960, CAB21/3847; Cabinet Office, 'Study of future policy, 1960–1970', Working Group, 14 October 1959, CAB21/3844.

8 Treasury, 'Overseas investment policy', 25 July 1956, T230/306; Foreign Office, 'Regional studies', September 1964, FCO49/302.

9 FCO, 'The British interest in oil', March 1967, FCO54/77.

10 Memorandum by Cabinet Secretary, 'Future defence policy', 7 June 1963, CAB21/5901.

11 MoD, *Strategic defence review*, 1998, Introduction para. 6, Chap. 4
    para. 61, chap. 5 para. 87, www.mod.uk.
12 *The strategic defence review: A new chapter*, July 2002, Cm 5566,
    Introduction, chap. 6 para. 89, 92; also 'Supporting analysis and
    information', section 4, para. 5, www.mod.uk.
13 MoD, *Operations in Iraq – Lessons for the future*, December 2003,
    Chapter 3 www.mod.uk.
14 MoD, *Delivering security in a changing world*, Defence white paper,
    December 2003, Introduction, para. 1.2, 2.14, 2.7, 3.1, 3.2, 3.5, 4.4, 4.9,
    4.10, 4.19, www.mod.uk.
15 FCO, *UK international priorities: A strategy for the FCO*, Cm 6052,
    December 2003, www.fco.gov.uk; Patrick Wintour, 'Ministers look
    for the lessons in Iraq failures', *Guardian*, 3 December 2003.
16 Geoff Hoon, speeches to RUSI, 9 December 2003, 26 June 2003;
    speech to the City forum, 27 November 2003, www.mod.uk.
17 Hoon, speech, 18 July 2002, www.mod.uk.
18 Robert Cooper, 'The new liberal imperialism', *Observer*, 7 April
    2002.

5 Massacres in Iraq: The secret history

1   British embassy, Baghdad, 'Annual report, 1958 – Iraq', 29 January
    1959, FO371/140896/VQ1011/1.
2   FO, 'The immediate outlook in Iraq', 24 July 1958, FO371/134201/
    VQ1015/162.
3   M. Wright to S. Lloyd, 22 April 1958, FO371/134198/VQ1015/36.
4   British embassy, Ankara to FO, 17 July 1958, FO371/134199/
    VQ1015/95.
5   Memorandum by IPC staff member, 'The political situation in Iraq',
    25 November 1962, FO371/170428/EQ1015/13.
6   See *Web of Deceit*, Chapter 12.
7   Aburish, *A Brutal Friendship*, pp. 139–40.
8   Ibid, pp. 137, 139.
9   F. Maynard, Note, 27 September 1962, FO371/164235/EQ1015/83; C.
    Cope, Note, 1 October 1962, ibid; R. Allen to S. Crawford, 31
    December 1962, FO371/170428/EQ1015/05.
10 R. Allen to S. Crawford, 28 January 1963, FO371/170428/EQ1015/26;
    R. Allen to FO, 9 February 1963, ibid, EQ1015/36.
11 D. Haskell to D. Goodchild, 15 February 1963, FO371/170432/
    EQ1015/104; R. Allen to FO, 11 February 1963, FO371/170431/
    EQ1015/68.

12 Report by military attaché, 'The revolution in Iraq', 19 February 1963, FO371/170434/EQ1015/126; Embassy, Baghdad to FO, 10 February 1963, FO371/170428/EQ1015/39; FO to Embassy, Tehran, 10 February 1963, ibid, EQ1015/33.

13 Embassy, Baghdad to FO, 11 February 1963, FO371/170431/EQ1015/64.

14 R. Munro to D. Goodchild, 26 February 1963, FO371/170434/EQ1015/129.

15 R. Lawson to G. Hiller, 2 March 1963, FO371/170434/EQ1015/131; D. Goodchild to R.Munro, 21 March 1963, FO371/170446/EQ1018/3.

16 R. Allen to Earl Home, 17 May 1963, FO371/170437/EQ1015/186; P. Cradock, Minute, 10 July 1963, FO371/170439/EQ1015/236.

17 FO to Embassy, Amman, 9 February 1963, FO371/170428/EQ1015/37.

18 R. Allen to FO, 15 February 1963, FO371/170502/EQ1532/23 and EQ1532/26.

19 FO to various embassies, 12 February 1963, FO371/170432/EQ1015/99.

20 FO, 'The outlook in Iraq', 15 February 1963, FO371/170433/EQ1015/111.

21 FO to Embassy, Ankara, 10 February 1963, FO371/170428/EQ1015/40.

22 A. Elwell to R. Munro, 14 March 1963, FO371/170446//EQ1018/3; written note by IRD official, ibid; FO, 'The outlook in Iraq'.

23 R. Munro to D. Goodchild, 6 March 1963, FO371/164235/EQ1018/3.

24 Embassy, Baghdad to FO, 10 February 1963, FO371/170428/EQ1015/53; D. Goodchild to R. Munro, 21 March 1963, FO371/170446/EQ1018/3; Embassy, Washington to FO, 10 February 1963, FO371/170430/EQ1015/46.

25 FO brief, 19 February 1963, FO371/170502/EQ1532/28.

26 R. Allen to FO, 13 February 1963, FO371/170432/EQ1015/82; R. Allen to FO, 15 February 1963, FO371/170433/EQ1015/120; R. Allen to Earl Home, 22 February 1963, FO371/170434/EQ1015/125; R. Allen to G. Hiller, 25 April 1963, FO371/170461/EQ1051/2.

27 D. Goodchild to H. Maynard, 17 May 1963, FO371/170446/EQ1018/10.

28 Aburish, *A Brutal Friendship*, p. 141.

29 Embassy, Washington to FO, 12 June 1963, FO371/170438/EQ1015/206; Embassy, Baghdad to FO, 21 June 1963, ibid, EQ1015/205; FO to various embassies, 14 June 1963, ibid, EQ1015/217; FO brief, 'Resumption of the Kurdish war in Iraq', 19 June 1963, FO371/170481/EQ1192/67.

30 E. Maynard to D. Goodchild, 22 June 1963, FO371/170447/EQ1019/4.

31 FO to various embassies, 14 June 1963, FO371/170438/EQ1015/217.

32 G. Hiller, 'Arms for Iraq', 7 June 1963, FO371/170489/EQ1224/8; FO to Amman, 10 April 1963, FO371/170479/EQ1192/21; Ministerial Committee on Strategic Exports, Brief for 8 April 1963 meeting, ibid, EQ1192/25.
33 G. Hiller, 'Arms for Iraq', 29 May 1963, FO371/170480/EQ1192/52.
34 Brief for Cabinet, 11 June 1963, FO371/170438/EQ1015/212.
35 FO brief, 25 June 1963, FO371/170480/EQ1192/57; P. Cradock to A. Campbell, 12 July 1963, FO371/170481/EQ1192/63; R. Allen to FO, 18 June 1963, FO371/170489/EQ1224/16; R. Allen to FO, 3 July 1963, FO371/170490/EQ1224/21.
36 FO to various embassies, 14 June 1963, FO371/170438/EQ1015/217.
37 D. Goodchild to H. Moreland, 27 August 1963, FO371/170490/EQ1224/24; J. Robey to FO, 9 July 1963, ibid.
38 D. Goodchild to R. Hutton, 20 September 1963, FO371/170485/EQ1194/6.
39 W. Morris, Minute, 8 October 1963, FO371/170482/EQ1192/91.
40 FO, Minute, 'Arms for Iraq', 13 September 1963, FO371/170492/EQ1224/70; E. Maynard to D. Goodchild, 6 July 1963, FO371/170448/EQ1019/21.
41 Draft FO brief, 12 September 1963, FO371/170449/EQ1019/45.
42 W. Morris, Minute, 26 September 1963, FO371/170449/EQ1019/54; W. Morris, 'Genocide in Kurdistan', 16 September 1963, ibid, EQ1019/45.
43 R. Allen to FO, 4 December 1963, FO371/170485/EQ1194/11; FO to Embassy, Tehran, 22 April 1963, FO371/170489/EQ1224/4.
44 E. Maynard to C. Brant, 30 July 1965, FO371/180813/EQ1019/75; Draft FO brief, June 1965, FO371/180830/EQ1192/29; S. Egerton to C. Brant, 15 January 1966, FO371/186747/EQ1019/2.
45 FO to Embassy, Baghdad, 8 July 1965, FO371/180830/EQ1192/41.
46 Draft FO brief, June 1965, FO371/180830/EQ1192/29.
47 Said Aburish, Saddam Hussein: The politics of revenge, Bloomsbury, London, 2000, p. 68; David McDowall, A Modern History of the Kurds, I. B. Tauris, London, 2000, p. 318.
48 M. Barzani to PM, undated in FO371/180814/EQ1019/87; P. Cradock, Note, 17 September 1965, FO371/180814/EQ1019/102.
49 E. Maynard to C. Brant, 2 January 1965, FO371/180812/EQ1019/1; E. Maynard to M. Burton, 13 March 1965, ibid, EQ1019/24.
50 E. Maynard to C. Brant, 2 September 1965, FO371/180814/EQ1019/95.
51 R. Allen to R. Butler, 20 December 1963, FO371/170445/EQ1017/19.
52 T. Evans to M. Stewart, 25 July 1968, FCO17/417/EQ 1/17; T. Evans to FO, 12 August 1968, FCO17/441/EQ3/24.

6 Psychological warfare beyond Iraq

1   David Miller, 'Information dominance: The philosophy of total propaganda control', *Coldtype*, January 2004.
2   Miller, 'Information dominance'.
3   Mark Leonard, *Public diplomacy*, Foreign Policy Centre, London, 2002, pp. 2–3; *Web of Deceit*, pp. 22–3.
4   Miller, 'The propaganda machine', p. 95.
5   See, for example, Robert Verkaik, 'Inquiries will test special relationship', *Independent*, 4 February 2004.
6   Dorril, 'Spies and lies', pp. 109–10.
7   Brian Jones, 'Were terrorists really planning a dirty bomb?', *Independent*, 9 April 2004.
8   David Leigh, 'Britain's security services and journalists: The secret story', *British Journalism Review*, Vol. 11, No. 2, 2000.
9   MoD, 'Operations in Iraq: Lessons for the future', 19 December 2003, www.mod.uk.
10   Defence Committee, Lessons of Iraq, Third report, Session 2003/2004, 16 March 2004, www.publications.parliament.uk.
11   Evidence to Defence Committee, 16 December 2000, Q1579, 1614, www.publications.parliament.uk/pa/cm200304.
12   See *Web of Deceit*, Chapter 20.
13   See Paul Lashmar and James Oliver, Chapter 1, pp. 17–18, 36, 175, 108.
14   'PM's talk with President Johnson', 22 December 1967, PREM 13/2459.
15   G. Etherington-Smith to E. Peck, 14 July 1965, FO371/180559/DV1051/216.
16   J. Cable to G. Etherington-Smith, 30 June 1965, FO371/180559/DV1015/189.
17   J. Cable, Minute, 29 June 1965, FO371/180559/DV1015/216.
18   C. Pestell, Minute, 3 January 1966, FO371/180559/DV1015/216.
19   UK embassy, Saigon, 'Information policy report annexes', undated [May 69], FCO 26/216, PBA 10/333.
20   Letter from Duncanson, British Advisory Mission, to Nguyen dinh Thuan, Le Secretaire d'Etat à la Presidence, 11 Jan 1962 DV1015/25, FO 371/166699.
21   Foreign Office note, 22 October 1961, FO371/160115/DV1015/151; H. Hohler to J. Russell, 29 April 1961, FO371/160119/DV1015/49; H. Hohler to E. Peck, 15 February 1962, FO371/166700/DV1015/49.

7 'Humanitarian intervention': The fraudulent pretext

1   See *Web of Deceit*, Chapter 12.
2   Jack Straw, 'A dynamic and ambitious approach to foreign policy', 11 June 2003, www.fco.gov.uk.
3   House of Commons, *Hansard*, 20 October 1999, Col. 599.
4   Human Rights Watch letter to Tony Blair, 5 February 2002; David Keen, 'Blair's good guys in Sierra Leone', *Guardian*, 7 November 2001.
5   Ewen Macaskill and Richard Norton-Taylor, 'Flawed evidence led to "mission creep"', *Guardian*, 16 May 2000.
6   House of Commons, *Hansard*, 6 April 2000, Col. 564; House of Commons, *Hansard*, 1 February 2000, Col. 525; Amnesty International, *Annual Report 1999*, Zimbabwe chapter.
7   House of Commons, *Hansard*, 3 May 2000, Cols. 149–57.
8   HRW, 'Fast track land reform in Zimbabwe', March 2002.
9   Ibid.
10 Chris McGreal, 'The trail from Lancaster House', *Guardian*, 16 January 2002.
11 HRW, 'Fast track land reform in Zimbabwe'.
12 Chris Talbot, 'Crisis in Zimbabwe: British military force poised to intervene', 1 May 2000, www.wsws.org.
13 House of Commons, *Hansard*, 3 May 2000, Col. 157.

8 From the horse's mouth: Whitehall's real goals

1   Foreign Secretary, 'Priorities in our foreign policy', July 1970, FCO49/303.
2   Permanent Under-Secretary's Steering Committee, 'British foreign policy: Brief by the Foreign Office', 26 January 1968, FCO49/13.
3   Cabinet Office, Steering Committee, 'British obligations overseas', 14 April 1958, T234/768; Interdepartmental Group on oil policy, Background paper on oil, 11 October 1968, FCO67/198.
4   FCO, 'The British interest in oil', March 1967, FCO54/77.
5   Guidance and Information Policy Department, Background paper No. 5, 'Expropriation of UK property in developing countries', 3 November 1970, FCO65/565.
6   Permanent Under-Secretary's Steering Committee, 'British foreign policy: Brief by the Foreign Office', 26 January 1968, FCO49/13.
7   Permanent Under-Secretary's Steering Committee, 'The basic assumptions', 20 October 1968, FCO49/23.

8   FO, 'Future policy: Review by the Foreign Office', January 1958, FO371/135623; Permanent Under-Secretary's Steering Committee, 'British foreign policy: Brief by the Foreign Office', 26 January 1968, FCO49/13.

9   *The Great Deception*, pp. 72–3.

10 FO, 'Future policy: Review by the Foreign Office', January 1958, FO371/135623.

11 FCO Planning Staff, 'Non-military means of influence in the Persian Gulf, SE Asia and Australasia', August 1968, FCO49/19.

12 *The Great Deception*, p. 18.

13 FCO, 'Future policy: Summary of memorandum by Colonial Office', February 1958, FO371/135624.

14 Cabinet Office, 'Future policy study 1960–1970', January 1960, CAB21/3847.

15 Ibid.

16 Introductory paper on the Middle East by the UK, 1947, *FRUS*, Vol. V, p. 569, 1947; O. Wright to PM, 8 April 1964, PREM 11/4679

17 Cabinet Office, Steering Committee, 'British overseas obligations', 14 April 1958, T234/768.

18 JIC, 'Outlook for Iran during the next twelve months', 31 August 1961, CAB 158/42.

19 See *Web of Deceit*, Chapter 16; FO, 'Regional studies', September 1964, FCO49/302; FO, 'Future policy: Review by the Foreign Office', January 1958, FO371/135623.

20 FO, 'Regional studies', September 1964, FCO49/302; Cabinet Office, 'Future policy study 1960–1970', Note by the Joint Secretaries, 14 October 1959, CAB21/3844.

21 Cabinet, Defence and Overseas Policy Committee, 'Future policy in Africa', October 1967, FCO46/90.

22 *The Great Deception*, p. 70.

23 FO, 'Future policy: Review by the Foreign Office', January 1958, FO371/135623.

24 FCO Draft paper, 'British foreign policy for the next three years', 9 January 1968, PREM13/2636.

25 A. Balfour to E. Bevin, 9 August 1945, Documents on British Foreign Policy, Series I, Vol. III, p. 17.

26 *The Great Deception*, p. 18.

27 Cabinet Office, 'Future policy study 1960–1970', January 1960, CAB21/3847; FO, 'Regional studies', September 1964, FCO49/302.

28 Cabinet Office, Steering Committee, 'British overseas obligations', 14 April 1958, T234/768.

29 *The Great Deception*, p. 119.

30 *The Great Deception*, p. 71.

31 Memoranda of conversation, 14 May 1965 and 27 January 1966, *FRUS*, Vol. XII, Documents 242 and 255, www.state.gov; Attachment to M. Bundy to L. Johnson, 10 September 1965, ibid, Document 250.

32 FO, 'Future policy: Review by the Foreign Office', FO371/135623.

33 FCO draft paper, 'Longer-term elements in Anglo/US relations', August 1968, FCO49/55; B. Trend to PM, 'Foreign policy', 26 February 1968; FCO Planning Staff, 'Non-military means of influence in the Persian Gulf, SE Asia and Australasia', August 1968, FCO49/19.

34 FCO, 'Relations between UK/US and Europe/US after enlargement', February 1972, FCO49/407.

35 G. Ball to L. Johnson, 22 July 1966, in *FRUS*, Vol. XII, document 264, www.state.gov.

36 Foreign Secretary to UK ambassadors, 2 April 1968, FCO49/23.

37 Cabinet Office, Steering Committee, 'British overseas obligations', 14 April 1958, T234/768.

38 National Intelligence Estimate, 24 June 1964, *FRUS*, Vol. XXI, Document 60, www.state.gov; State Department, 'US policy in the Middle East', 19 July 1968, *FRUS*, Vol. XXI, Document 30; JIC, 'Nasser's achievements, aims and future policies', 11 June 1959, CAB158/35.

39 FO, 'Future policy: Review by the Foreign Office', January 1958, FO371/135623.

40 Cabinet Office, 'Future policy study 1960–1970', January 1960, CAB21/3847.

41 JIC, 'Cuban developments and their impact on the Caribbean', 2 June 1961, CAB158/32.

42 JIC, 'The outlook for Latin America and the Caribbean', 18 July 1963, CAB158/49.

43 JIC, 'Cuba', 15 May 1970, CAB186/6.

44 *The Great Deception*, pp. 70, 128.

9 Friendly terrorists: New Labour's key allies

1 'Human costs of war mount', *Chechnya Weekly*, 1 May 2003; HRW, 'Human rights situation in Chechnya', 7 April 2003.

2 HRW, 'Russia: abuses spread beyond Chechnya', 16 July 2003.

3 *Web of Deceit*, pp. 163, 136, 171.

4 House of Commons, *Hansard*, 13 June 2003, Col. 1149, emphasis added; HRW, 'Inconsistent Blair urged to speak out on Chechnya',

20 June 2003; 'Press conference with the prime minister and President Putin', 26 June 2003, www.pm.gov.uk.

5   Nick Paton Walsh and Ewen Macaskill, 'Putin's brief encounter with Blair seen as snub', *Guardian*, 20 June 2003; House of Commons, *Hansard*, 10 September 2003, Col. 357; House of Commons, *Hansard*, 19 January 2004, Col. 966.

6   HRW, 'Inconsistent Blair urged to speak out on Chechnya', 20 June 2003; 'Diplomatic gains for Moscow', *Chechnya Weekly*, 5 June 2003.

7   Anna Neistat, HRW, 'What Mr Blair should say to the Russian president', *Independent*, 26 June 2003.

8   *Web of Deceit*, p. 174; 'Secret police caught red-handed', *Chechnya Weekly*, 27 March 2003.

9   HRW, 'Russian Federation/Chechnya: Briefing to the 60th session of the UN Commission on Human Rights', January 2004.

10 House of Commons, *Hansard*, 12 January 2004, Col. 525.

11 'Looking to the other way', *Guardian*, 2 October 2003.

12 Martin Hodgson, 'Innocent catch flak in dirty war', *Guardian*, 19 April 2000.

13 Doug Stokes, 'Colombia primer', Znet, 16 April 2002.

14 House of Lords, *Hansard*, 15 October 1997, Col. 540; House of Commons, *Hansard*, 24 November 1999, Col. 115 and 18 January 2000, Col. 675.

15 Robin, Kirk, 'Colombia and the "war" on terror: Rhetoric and reality', *The World Today*, March 2004, www.hrw.org

16 House of Commons, *Hansard*, 23 March 2004, Col. 239.

17 Isabel Hilton, 'Terror as usual', *Guardian*, 23 September 2003.

18 Bill Rammell, 'International community confirms support for Colombia at London meeting', 10 July 2003, www.fco.gov.uk.

19 Andy Higginbottom, 'Blair hands blank cheque to Uribe', undated, www.colombiasolidarity.org.uk; Bill Rammell, 'Building peace, security and prosperity in Colombia', 30 July 2003, www.fco.gov.uk.

20 David Pallister, Sibylla Brodzinsky and Owen Bowcott, 'Secret aid poured into Colombian drug war', *Guardian*, 9 July 2003.

21 Owen Bowcott and Rob Evans, 'MoD reveals aid to Colombian army', *Guardian*, 2 September 2003.

22 David Rhys-Jones, 'What's going on with Mo Mowlam', undated, www.colombiasolidarity.org.

23 House of Lords, *Hansard*, 15 October 1997, Col. 538; Bill Rammell, 'Building peace . . .'

24 Andy Higginbottom, 'BP – Blair's partner – and imperial power', undated, and 'BP and the US-Colombia business partnership', undated, www.colombiasolidarity.org.uk.

25 Michael Gillard, 'BP sacks security chief' and 'BP hands "tarred in pipeline dirty war"', *Guardian*, 17 October 1998.

26 Peter Hansen, 'Hungry in Gaza', *Guardian*, 5 March 2003; International Development Committee, Second report, Session 2003/2004, 15 January 2004, para. 6.

27 Memorandum from the Foreign Office to the Foreign Affairs Committee report into the foreign policy aspects of the war against terrorism, 28 January 2003, www.publications.parliament.uk.

28 House of Commons, *Hansard*, 3 June 2003, Col. 35.

29 House of Commons, *Hansard*, 10 February 2003, Col. 582; Rob Evans and David Hencke, 'Defence sales "hit by curbs on Israel"', *Guardian*, 29 July 2003; Richard Norton-Taylor, 'Arms sales to Israel breach guidelines', *Guardian*, 5 November 2003.

30 See, e.g., Jocelyn Hurndall, 'Rafah in miniature', *Guardian*, 20 October 2003.

31 Chris McGreal, 'Sharon's ally safe from arrest in Britain'. *Guardian*, 11 February 2002.

32 House of Commons, *Hansard*, 19 November 2003.

33 House of Lords, *Hansard*, 5 January 2004, Col. 4; Ewen Macaskill, 'Britain opposes international court review of security fence', *Guardian*, 30 January 2004.

34 Julian Borger, 'US in muted call for restraint while France and Germany condemn raid', *Guardian*, 6 October 2003.

35 Stephen Zunes, 'Undermining peace and law', Znet, 17 April 2004, www.znet.org; Press conference, 16 April 2004, www.pm.gov.uk; Nicholas Watt and Suzanne Goldenberg, 'Spurned Blair in plea to Bush', *Guardian*, 16 April 2004.

36 House of Commons, *Hansard*, 6 February 2003, Col. 392.

37 House of Commons, *Hansard*, 2 February 2004, Col. 678; Ian Black, 'UK leads push for EU crackdown on Hamas', *Guardian*, 27 August 2003.

38 Chris McGreal, '"We're air force pilots, not mafia. We don't take revenge"', *Guardian*, 3 December 2003.

39 FCO report, 'Future British policy toward the Arab/Israel Dispute', 14 September 1970, FCO 49/295.

40 JIC, 'British economic interests in Israel and the Arab world', 28 November 1969, CAB 188/5.

41 HRW, 'Nepal: Briefing to the 60th session of the UN Commission on Human Rights', January 2004.

42 'Nepal's war against terror', *CAAT* magazine, November 2002, www.caat.org.uk; David Hencke, 'Peace fund used to buy military planes', *Guardian*, 23 January 2003.

43 'Britain welcomes progress in Nepal ceasefire talks', 13 June 2003, www.ukindia.org; House of Commons, *Hansard*, 3 June 2003, Col. 35.

44 Helena Smith, 'Suicide bombers are buried in Turkey's breeding ground of extremism', *Guardian*, 27 November 2003.

45 Nick Hopkins and Rosie Cowan, 'Scandal of Ulster's secret war', *Guardian*, 17 April 2003; Angelique Chrisafis, 'Loyalist bombers "helped by British"', *Guardian*, 10 December 2003.

10 Nigerians: War for oil

1 Oronto Douglas, Von Kemedi, Ike Okonta and Michael Watts, 'Alienation and militancy in the Niger Delta', *Foreign Policy in Focus*, July 2003, www.fpif.org.

2 HRW, *The Warri crisis: Fuelling violence*, December 2003.

3 HRW, Letter to President Obasanjo, 3 July 2003.

4 Douglas et al., 'Alienation and militancy'; HRW, Letter to Obasanjo.

5 House of Commons, *Hansard*, 3 June 2003, Col. 35; HRW letter to Tony Blair, 5 February 2002.

6 Tony Blair, 'Nigeria needs to succeed if Africa is to succeed', speech, 7 February 2002, www.britainusa.com.

7 HRW, 'UK turns a blind eye to electoral violence in Nigeria', 2 May 2003; HRW, Letter to Jack Straw, 2 May 2003.

8 Robert Verkaik, 'Ministers attempt to halt US human rights cases against British firms', *Independent*, 11 February 2004.

9 Commonwealth Office to High Commission, Lagos, 5 November 1966, PREM13/1661.

10 F. Cumming-Bruce to Commonwealth Office, 30 January 1967, PREM13/1661.

11 FO and Commonwealth Office to Certain missions, Guidance no. 118, 25 May 1967, PREM13/1661.

12 G. Thomas to PM, 18 August 1967, PREM13/1661.

13 G. Thomas to PM, 8 August 1967, PREM13/1661.

14 Record of conversation between George Thomas and Nigerian High Commissioner, 28 April 1967, PREM13/1661; High Commission, Lagos to Commonwealth Office, 29 May 1967, PREM13/1661.

15 D. Hunt to Commonwealth Office, 12 June 1967, PREM13/1661.

16 O. Forster to M. Palliser, 7 July 1967, PREM13/1661.

17 Parker to Commonwealth Office, 22 July 1967, PREM13/1661; Commonwealth Office to Lagos, 24 July 1967, ibid; Lagos to Commonwealth Office, 21 July 1967, ibid.

18 Commonwealth Office to Lagos, 16 July 1967, PREM13/1661; Gowon to H. Wilson, 29 July 1967, ibid.

19 G. Thomas to PM, 18 August 1967, PREM13/1661; G. Thomas, 'Nigeria', August 1967, ibid.

20 Frederick Forsyth, *The Biafra Story: The making of an African legend*, Leo Cooper, London, 2001, p. 166.

21 FO and Commonwealth Office to Certain missions, 1 November 1967, PREM13/1661; G. Thomas to PM, 8 November 1967, ibid.

22 G. Thomson to D. Healey, 4 December 1967, PREM13/1661.

23 Commonwealth Office to Lagos, 12 December 1967, PREM13/1661; D. Healey to G. Thomson, 13 December 1967, ibid; Papers for Commonwealth Secretary, 12 June 1968, PREM13/2258.

24 Papers for Commonwealth Secretary, 12 June 1968, PREM13/2258; H. Wilson to Gowon in Commonwealth Office to Lagos, 5 April 1968, PREM13/1661.

25 Forsyth, *The Biafra Story*, p. 258.

26 Commonwealth Office to Lagos, 30 May 1968, PREM13/2258.

27 House of Commons, *Hansard*, 16 May 1968, Cols. 1397–8.

28 Papers for Commonwealth Secretary, 12 June 1968, PREM13/2258; FO and Commonwealth Office to Certain missions, 21 June 1968, ibid.

29 For example, Commonwealth Office to Lagos, 20 May 1968, PREM13/2258.

30 Commonwealth Office, 'Nigeria', 21 May 1968; G. Thomson to PM, 16 June 1968, PREM13/2258.

31 D. Hunt to Commonwealth Office, 6 June 1968, PREM13/2258; C. Godden to M. Palliser, 10 June 1968, ibid; Record of a meeting between Prime Minister and the Nigerian Commissioner for Information and Labour, 12 June 1968, ibid.

32 Record of a meeting between Prime Minister and the Nigerian Commissioner for Information and Labour, 12 June 1968, PREM13/2258.

33 Lord Shepherd to PM, 6 August 1968, PREM13/2259.

34 Record of meeting with Lord Hunt and Dr Lindt, 14 August 1968, PREM13/2260.

35 H. Wilson to Gowon, 24 September 1968, PREM13/2260.

36 FO, 'Nigeria', 7 December 1968, PREM13/2261.

37 Note of a meeting between the Prime Minister and the Committee for Peace, 6 November 1968, PREM13/2260.

38 Record of a meeting at Downing Street, 8 November 1968, PREM13/2260; Record of a meeting between Lord Shepherd and Chief Enahoro, 8 November 1968, ibid.

39 M. Stewart to Lagos, 23 October 1968, PREM13/2260.

40 Record of conversation between Lord Shepherd and Chief Enahoro, 13 November 1968, PREM13/2260; Mr Morris to Lord Shepherd, 13 November 1968, ibid; Record of meeting between Lord Shepherd and General Gowon, 11 December 1968, PREM13/2261.

41 FCO to Certain missions, 22 November 1968, PREM13/2260.

42 JIC, 'Nigeria', 26 March 1969, PREM13/2818.

43 FCO to Lagos, 10 December 1968, PREM13/2261; M. Stewart to Lagos, 12 December 1968, ibid.

44 Forsyth, *The Biafra Story*, p. 185.

45 See, e.g., M. Palliser to PM, 23 January 1969, PREM13/2263 and FCO, 'Relief for the Biafran enclave', 30 December 1969, PREM13/3374.

46 Text of interview by Prime Minister, 27 March 1969, PREM13/2819; FCO to Lagos, 27 March 1969, ibid.

47 J. Wilson to L. Monson, 26 March 1969, PREM13/2819.

48 Gowon to H. Wilson, 19 April 1969, PREM13/2820.

49 J. Gibbon to H. Wilson, 14 August 1969, DEFE24/589; D. Evans, Report on visit to Nigeria by RAF officers, 25 August 1969, ibid; A. Heskett to MoD, 24 July 1969, ibid.

50 M. Stewart to D. Healey, 8 December 1969, PREM13/2823.

51 Wilson to Gowon in FCO to Lagos, 12 January 1970, PREM13/3375.

52 I. Lucas, 'Random Reflections on the Northern states of Nigeria', 30 January 1970, DEFE31/27.

53 Lagos to FCO, 31 January 1970, FCO65/801.

11 Indonesians: Tools of covert action

1 Tapol, 'Backgrounder on Aceh', Indonesia, January 2002, www.tapol.gn.apc.org.

2 HRW, 'Aceh under martial law', 5 June 2002.

3 John Aglionby and Richard Norton-Taylor, 'British tanks used in Aceh', *Guardian*, 26 June 2003; John Aglionby, 'Battered people of Aceh take time out to party as Jakarta's crackdown drags on', *Guardian*, 20 August 2003; Tapol, 'High Court to hear arms to Indonesia case against UK government', 26 March 2004.

4   Tapol, 'Dismay as British armoured vehicles join war in Aceh', 28
     November 2003; HRW, 'Indonesia: refugees reveal widespread
     abuses in Aceh', 18 December 2003.

5   Sam Zafiri, 'A valid election in Aceh: Test-case for Indonesia's
     democracy', *Jakarta Post*, 3 July 2004, www.hrw.org

6   John Aglionby, 'Indonesia uses UK Hawks in Aceh offensive',
     Guardian, 20 May 2003; Tapol, 'The use of British military
     equipment in Aceh', 2 July 2003.

7   John Aglionby, 'Military chief defends use of British jets', *Guardian*,
     22 May 2003.

8   David Hencke and Rob Evans, 'UK warning to Indonesia over export
     licences for jets', *Guardian*, 21 June 2003.

9   Matthew Moore, 'Army defends use of British tanks in Aceh', *Sydney
     Morning Herald*, 24 June 2003; Tapol, 'Dismay as British armoured
     vehicles join war in Aceh', 28 November 2003.

10   John Aglionby, 'Indonesia ends use of British tanks', *Guardian*, 20
     January 2004.

11   Richard Norton-Taylor, 'Protests after UK drops Indonesia arms
     demand', *Guardian*, 11 February 2004.

12   FCO, 'UK and Australia joint statement on Aceh, Indonesia', 20 May
     2003, www.britainusa.com.

13   British embassy, Jakarta, Trade and Investment summary, October
     2003, www.Britain-in-indonesia.org.id.

14   Tapol, 'Military operations will never solve the Aceh conflict', 10 May
     2003.

15   Tapol letter to Mike O'Brien, 10 July 2003; Tapol, 'High Court to hear
     arms to Indonesia case against UK government', 26 March 2004.

16   Pranjal Tiwari, 'All in the timing', 26 May 2003, Znet; 'Aceh offensive
     intensifies', BBC news, 21 May 2003.

17   Kathy Marks, 'Summary executions become routine in Aceh',
     Independent, 27 May 2003.

18   Pranjal Tiwari, 'All in the timing', 26 May 2003, Znet; HRW, 'Aceh
     under martial law', 5 June 2002.

19   Pranjal Tiwari, 'All in the timing', 26 May 2003, Znet; Lesley
     McCulloch, 'Aceh, the more things change', *Asia Times*, 13 May
     2003.

20   F. Tomlinson, 'Indonesia', 11 March 1958, FO371/135849.

21   Ibid.

22   D. MacDermot, 'Annual report for the year 1958', 12 January 1959,
     FO371/144065.

23   H. Caccia to FO, 14 May 1958, PREM11/2730.

NOTES

24 Audrey Kahin and George Kahin, *Subversion as Foreign Policy: The secret Eisenhower and Dulles debacle in Indonesia*, New Press, New York, 1995.

25 R. Scott to FO, 12 December 1957, FO371/129531.

26 O. Morland, Minute, 13 December 1957, FO371/129531.

27 FO, 'Notes for discussion of Indonesia in Cabinet', 5 February 1958, FO371/135847.

28 Kahin and Kahin, *Subversion as Foreign Policy*, p. 156.

29 John Prados, *President's Secret Wars*, Elephant, Chicago, 1996, p. 140; Kahin and Kahin, *Subversion as Foreign Policy*, p. 120; D. MacDermot to FO, 2 May 1958, FO371/135851.

30 Kahin and Kahin, *Subversion as Foreign Policy*, pp. 120, 169, 121; Colonial Secretary to Various Governors, 28 February 1958, FO371/135848.

31 Kahin and Kahin, *Subversion as Foreign Policy*, p. 126.

32 Kahin and Kahin, *Subversion as Foreign Policy*, pp. 134, 148; Prados, *President's Secret Wars*, p. 144.

33 D. MacDermot to FO, 24 February 1958, FO371/135848.

34 FO to Washington, 27 June 1958, PREM11/2730.

35 Embassy, Washington to FO, 15 May 1958, PREM11/2730; FO to Washington, 14 May 1958, ibid.

36 Kahin and Kahin, *Subversion as Foreign Policy*, p. 205.

37 D. MacDermot to FO, 30 May 1958, FO371/135852.

38 Kahin and Kahin, *Subversion as Foreign Policy*, p. 211.

39 Commonwealth Relations Office to Various High Commissions, 22 April 1958; D. MacDermot to S. Lloyd, 4 July 1958, FO371/135853.

40 David Easter, 'British and Malaysian covert support for rebel movements in Indonesia during the Confrontation, 1963–1966', in Richard Aldrich (ed.), *The Clandestine Cold War in Asia, 1945–65*, London, Frank Cass, 2000.

12 *Vietnamese: Secret support for US aggression*

1 The Pentagon's final estimate of killed and wounded civilians from 1965 to 1972 ran from 700,000 to 1,225,000 while Senate numbers for the same period were 1,350,000. Deaths in these two assessments ranged from 195,000 to 415,000; 'enemy' killed were 850,000 minimum, a substantial proportion of which were civilians. This was in a country of 18 million people. Gabriel Kolko, *Anatomy of a War: Vietnam, the United States and the modern historical experience*, Phoenix, London, 1994, p. 200.

2   See, for example, Noam Chomsky and Edward Herman, *The Washington Connection and Third World Fascism*, South End Press, Boston, 1979; Chomsky, *Rethinking Camelot: JFK, the Vietnam war and US political culture*, South End Press, Boston, 1993; Kolko, *Anatomy of a War*.

3   Kolko, *Anatomy of a War*, p. 107.

4   Ibid, pp. 92–3, 65.

5   Ibid, pp. 93, 130, 75–6.

6   FO, 'The possibility of a negotiated solution of the conflict in Viet-Nam', 26 August 1965, FO371/180544/DV103145/218.

7   J. Cable to N. Trench, 4 June 1965, FO371/180541/ DV103145/117; FO, 'The possibility of a negotiated solution of the conflict in Viet-Nam', 26 August 1965, FO371/180544/ DV103145/218.

8   H. Hohler to Earl Home, 29 August 1962, FO371/166707/ DV1015/181; E. Peck, Minute, October 1962, ibid.

9   Military Attaché, 'Summary for January 1963', 26 February 1963, FO371/170132/ DV1201/36.

10 British embassy, Saigon to FO, 30 May 1961, FO371/160111/ DV1015/70; H. Hohler to Earl Home, 28 February 1962, FO371/166701/ DV1015/64; H. Hohler to Earl Home, 16 May 1962; FO371/166704/ DV1015/129.

11 E. Peck, Note, 14 June 1961, FO371/160112/ DV1015/83; J. Cable, Note, 19 June 1961, ibid.

12 E. Peck, Note, 10 November 1961, FO371/160118/ DV1015/203.

13 FO draft, 'Vietnam background', 13 June 1962, FO371/166705/ DV1015/141.

14 FO, minute, 31 July 1961, FO371/160114/ DV1015/129; F. Warner, Note, 26 July 1962, FO371/166706/ DV1015/173; FO brief, 4 November 1961, FO371/160117/ DV1015/192; H. Hohler to Earl Home, 5 June 1962, FO371/166704/ DV1015/140; C. Stewart to Earl Home, 2 June 1961, FO371/160112/ DV1015/87.

15 H. Hohler to Earl Home, 30 January 1963, FO371/170100/ DV1017/3; FO brief, 'Vietnam: The current situation', September 1963, PREM11/4759.

16 H. Hohler to FO, 12 April 1961, FO371/160109/ DV1015/29; Military Attaché, 'Summary for December 1962', 22 January 1963, FO371/170132/ DV1201/23; C. Stewart to G. Etherington-Smith, 26 May 1961, FO371/160111/ DV1015/73.

17 See Chomsky, *Rethinking Camelot*, p. 49.

18 C. Stewart to F. Warner, 3 July 1961, FO371/160113/ DV1015/116.

NOTES

19 H. Hohler to Earl Home, 20 December 1961, FO371/160121/ DV1015/295; R. Seconde, Note, 3 January 1962, ibid; J. McGhie, Note, 29 December 1961, ibid.
20 H. Hohler to Earl Home, 3 January 1962, FO371/1666698/ DV1015/6.
21 Foreign Secretary to Washington, 16 November 1961, PREM11/3736; D. Ormsby-Gore to FO, 13 November 1961, ibid.
22 FO, 'Vietnam', 16 January 1962, FO371/1666698/ DV1015/20; Earl Home to D. Rusk, 2 November 1961, PREM11/3736; E. Peck to H. Hohler, 22 February 1962, FO371/166700/ DV1015/49.
23 H. Hohler to FO, 14 July 1961, FO371/160114/ DV1015/133.
24 H. Hohler to Earl Home, 28 February 1962, FO371/166701/ DV1015/64; H. Hohler to E. Peck, 15 February 1962, FO371/166700/ DV1015/49.
25 R. Burrows to F. Warner, 4 July 1962, FO371/166705/ DV1015/148; FO, 'Vietnam', 16 January 1962, FO371/1666698/ DV1015/20.
26 Earl Home to Washington, 16 November 1961, PREM11/3736.
27 FO to Various embassies, 28 December 1961, FO371/1666698/ DV1015/9.
28 H. Macmillan to President Diem, 7 May 1962, PREM11/3736.
29 See FO371/166702, file DV1015/83.
30 H. Hohler to FO, 24 November 1961, FO371/160118/ DV1015/237; F. Warner to H. Hohler, 1 December 1961, ibid.
31 H. Hohler to Earl Home, 2 January 1963, FO371/1700088/ DV1011/1; FO, 'Vietnam', 4 April 1963, FO371/170090/ DV1015/23.
32 H. Hohler to Earl Home, 18 February 1963, FO371/170089/ DV1015/16.
33 H. Hohler to F. Warner, 12 December 1962, FO371/166708/ DV1015/215.
34 Cited in Chomsky, *Rethinking Camelot*, p. 51.
35 R. Burrows to R. Seconde, 25 January 1962, FO371/166699/ DV1015/31; F. Warner, Minute, 25 March 1963, FO371/170129/ DV1192/5.
36 Kolko, *Anatomy of a War*, p. 145.
37 H. Hohler to E. Peck, 6 March 1963, FO371/170129/ DV1192/1.
38 FCO Research Department, 'The British Advisory Administrative Mission to Vietnam (BRIAM), 1961–1971', 30 December 1971, FCO51/197; Peter Busch, *All the Way with JFK?: Britain, the US and the Vietnam war*, OUP, Oxford, 2003, p. 201.
39 FO, 'UK assistance to South Vietnam: Proposals by the Foreign Office', 21 July 1961, PREM11/3736; H. Hohler to Earl Home, 5 June 1962, FO371/166704/ DV1015/140; FCO Research Department; R. Thompson to A. Williams, 22 August 1963, FO371/170101/ DV1017/38.

40 Col. Lee to C. Jones, 17 September 1962, FO371/166751/ DV1201/71; H. Hohler to FO, 14 November 1962, ibid, DV1201/82; Chiefs of Staff meeting, COS(62) 72nd meeting, November 1962, ibid, DV1201/83; C. Howells, Minute, 14 November 1962, ibid, DV1201/89.

41 J. Denson to J. Petersen, 20 February 1961, FO371/160108/ DV1015/10G.

42 H. Hohler to FO, 6 November 1961, PREM11/3716; FO, 'Vietnam', 16 January 1962, FO371/1666698/ DV1015/20.

43 FCO Research Department.

44 J. Denson to R. Seconde, 9 February 1962, FO371/166700/ DV1015/43; State Department, Research Memorandum, 'Strategic Hamlets', 1 July 1963, FO371/170101/ DV1017/33.

45 H. Hohler to Earl Home, 18 February 1963, FO371/170089/ DV1015/16; Parliamentary answer provided on 29 April 1963, FO371/170090/ DV1015/23.

46 Kolko, *Anatomy of a War*, p. 133.

47 R. Thompson, 'Memorandum on strategic hamlets', 10 December 1963, FO371/170102/ DV1017/55.

48 FO brief, January 1964, FO371/175482/ DV1017/3; G. Etherington-Smith to E. Peck, 14 January 1964, ibid.

49 Col. Lee to C. Jones, 28 August 1962, FO371/166749/ DV1201/52.

50 R. Thompson to F. Warner, 29 January 1963, FO371/170100/ DV1017/5; FCO Research Department; F. Warner to G. Etherington-Smith, 25 September 1963, FO371/170093/ DV1015/84; R. Thompson to E. Peck, 19 December 1963, FO371/170096/ DV1015/144; Barry Petersen, *Tiger Men*, pp. 128–9.

51 Bloch and Fitzgerald, pp. 44, 64; Dorril, *MI6*, pp. 718–19.

52 FO to Various embassies, 21 August 1963, FO371/170092/ DV1015/62; G. Etherington-Smith to Earl Home, 25 September 1963, FO371/170093/ DV1015/86.

53 G. Etherington-Smith to E. Peck, 23 October 1963, FO371/170094/ DV1015/86G; G. Etherington-Smith to R. Butler, 4 December 1963, FO371/170095/ DV1015/134.

54 K. Blackwell to F. Warner, 23 May 1963, FO371/170090/ DV1015/35.

55 G. Etherington-Smith to P. Gordon Walker, 1 January 1965, FO371/180511/ DV1011/1.

56 G. Etherington-Smith to M. Stewart, 14 June 1965, FO371/180542/ DV103145/139.

57 Kolko, *Anatomy of a War*, p. 201.

58 P. Wilkinson to G. Brown, 16 January 1967, FCO15/487/ DV1/5.

59 House of Commons, *Hansard*, 3 March 1964, in PREM11/3736.

NOTES

60 Brief, 'Viet-Nam: Anglo-United States relations', May 1965, PREM13/695; Speech by Michael Stewart, 28 June 1965, FO371/180542/ DV1013145/156; FO brief for PM, 13 July 1965, FO371/180559/ DV1051/211.

61 FO brief, 'Visit to Washington by Prime Minister and Foreign Secretary', December 1964, PREM13/692.

62 R. Thompson to E. Peck, 19 December 1963, FO371/170096/ DV1015/144.

63 J. Wright to PM, 1 March 1965, PREM13/693.

64 PM's office to J. Henderson, 11 March 1965, FO371/180539/ DV103145/47; FO to Washington, 9 February 1965, PREM13/692; M. Stewart to PM, February 1965, ibid.

65 J. Wright, Note, 11 February 1965, PREM13/692.

66 'Record of discussions with Mr Bundy', 29 May 1964, PREM11/4759.

67 'Record of a telephone conversation between the Prime Minister and President Johnson', 11 February 1965, PREM13/692.

68 'Record of a conversation between the Prime Minister and the US ambassador, Mr David Bruce', 17 February 1965, PREM13/692; M. Stewart to PM, 17 March 1965, FO371/180539/ DV102145/69.

69 FO brief, 'US air attacks against North Viet-Nam', 15 March 1965, FO371/180539/ DV103145/47.

70 House of Commons, *Hansard*, 25 March 1965, Col. 736; P. Dean to FO, 9 April 1965, PREM13/694.

71 Lord Harlech to FO, 9 March 1965, FO371/180557/ DV1051/51; 'Record of a meeting between the Prime Minister and President of the United States', 15 April 1965, PREM13/694; P. Dean to J. Wright, 13 April 1965, FO371/180541/ DV103145/98.

72 G. Etherington-Smith to M. Stewart, 22 March 1965, FO371/180515/ DV1015/81; G. Etherington-Smith to M. Stewart, 3 March 1965, FO371/180594/ DV1094/42.

73 G. Etherington-Smith to E. Peck, 10 March 1965, FO371/180514/ DV1015/76; G. Etherington-Smith to FO, 18 March 1965, ibid.

74 G. Etherington-Smith to E. Peck, 13 March 1965, DV1093/55; G. Etherington-Smith to M. Stewart, 14 June 1965, FO371/180542/ DV103145/139.

75 G. Etherington-Smith to J. Cable, 25 May 1965, FO371/180596/ DV1093/90; Kolko, *Anatomy of a War*, p. 190.

76 G. Etherington-Smith to M. Stewart, 24 March 1965, FO371/180515/ DV1015/82; FO brief, 10 March 1965, FO371/180557/ DV1051/57; G. Etherington-Smith to J. Cable, 10 March 1965, FO371/180609/ DV1192/30.

77 D. Murray, Minute, 11 June 1965, FO371/180541/ DV103145/141.

78 PM to President Johnson, 2 August 1965, PREM13/697.

79 G. Etherington-Smith, 'Assessment of the situation in Viet-Nam', 31 August 1965, FO371/180517/ DV1015/165.

80 FO, 'Secretary of State's visit to Washington', 30 September 1965, FO371/180560/ DV1051/269.

81 PM adviser [unclear which] to PM, 16 June 1966, PREM13/1274.

82 PM to President Johnson, 10 June 1966, PREM13/1274.

83 PM to President Johnson, 23 June 1966, PREM13/1275.

84 House of Commons, *Hansard*, 29 June 1966, Col. 1796.

85 P. Dean to FO, 29 June 1966, PREM13/1275.

86 PM to President Johnson, 1 July 1966, PREM13/1275.

87 House of Commons, *Hansard*, 21 June 1966, Col. 287.

88 N. Trench to J. Cable, undated [June 1965], FO371/180596/ DV1093/97.

89 J. Cable, Minute, 1 January 1965, FO371/180539/ DV1013145/32; FO brief, 'Visit to Washington by Prime Minister and Foreign Secretary', December 1964, PREM13/692.

90 FO brief, 'Secretary of State's visit to Washington and New York', 19 March 1965, DV103145/120.

91 E. Peck to G. Etherington-Smith, 14 July 1965, FO371/180542/ DV103145/139.

92 FO, 'The possibility of a negotiated solution of the conflict in Viet-Nam', 26 August 1965, FO371/180544/ DV103145/218; FO, 'Background brief on Viet-Nam', 13 July 1965, FO371/180559/ DV1051/211; J. Cable to G. Etherington-Smith, 4 August 1965, FO371/180559/ DV1051/231.

93 FO brief, 'The situation in South Viet-Nam', 4 February 1965, FO371/180514/ DV1015/49; G. Etherington-Smith to FO, 1 February 1965, FO371/180539/ DV103145/15.

94 Lord Walston to M. Stewart, 17 November 1964, FO371/180557/ DV1051/55.

95 Parliamentary answers in FO371/180596/ DV1093/93.

96 M. Palliser, Minute, 28 July 1965, FO371/180543/ DV103145/188.

97 FO brief, 'Aid to South Viet-Nam', 13 April 1965, FO371/180541/ DV103145/105; FCO Research Department.

98 FO to Saigon, 12 December 1963, FO371/170095/ DV1015/139.

99 J. Cable to O. Forster, 28 October 1964, FO371/175483/ DV1017/37; MoD report, 'Information on operations in Vietnam', 11 October 1965; FO371/180610/ DV1192/71.

100 Chiefs of Staff Committee, 'Information on operations in Vietnam', 18 January 1968, DEFE11/696; FO, Minute, 16 December 1965, FO371/180610/ DV1192/78.

101 D. Murray, Minute, 12 November 1964, and written note on this minute by FO official, FO371/175483/ DV1017/39.

102 J. Cable to G. Etherington-Smith, 11 March 1965, FO371/180608/ DV11192; D. Murray, Minute, 30 September 1965, FO371/180610/ DV1192/58; J. Cable to G. Etherington-Smith, 6 August 1965, ibid, DV1192/68.

103 FO to Washington, 21 June 1965, FO371/180610/DV1192/58.

104 House of Commons, *Hansard*, 27 June 1967, Col. 254.

105 PM to President of Board of Trade, undated [May 1967], FCO46/203/ ZDS41; Political Adviser, Singapore to FO, 20 June 1967, FCO24/133/ HAA3/2; D. Gordon, Minute, 17 September 1970, FCO15/510/ FAV10/2.

106 C. MacLehose, 'South Viet-Nam: Annual review for 1967', 6 February 1968, FCO15/487/ DV1/5; Defence Attaché, 'Prisoners of war and detainees', 22 March 1967, FCO15/482/ DV1/2; D. Gordon to J. Moreton, 21 January 1970, FCO15/1325/ FAV1/3; J. Moreton, 'South Viet-Nam: Annual review for 1969', 23 January 1970, FCO15/1325/ FAV1/3.

107 Chomsky and Herman, *Washington Connection*, pp. 313, 324.

108 'Record of a conversation between the Prime Minister and the Vice President', 2 April 1967, PREM13/1919; E. Youde to J. Graham, 25 November 1969, PREM13/3552.

109 J. Moreton to D. Gordon, 21 June 1971, FCO26/652/ PBA10/333.

110 D. Murray to J. Colvin, 1 February 1967, FCO15/585/ DV10/4.

111 J. Colvin to FO, 22 May 1967, FCO15/587/ DV10/4; P. Wilkinson to D. Murray, 27 March 1967, FCO15/586/ DV10/4.

112 Air Attaché, Saigon, 'The air war over Viet-Nam', 18 September 1968, FCO15/1083/ FAN10/1/2.

113 Brief for PM, 26 October 1967, FCO15/588/ DV10/4; MoD, 'The air war in the North', August 1967, ibid.

114 FO to Washington, 27 November 1967, FCO15/588/ DV10/4; FO to Washington, 11 January 1968, FCO15/589/ DV10/4.

115 A. Burgess, Minute, 23 December 1971, FCO15/1493/ FAV10/9; K. Wilford, Note, 29 December 1971, ibid.

116 FO Planning Committee, 'United States policy and British interests in South-East Asia after Viet-Nam', 28 June 1968, FCO49/32/ ZP4/14.

117 Ibid; FO Planning Committee, Minutes of meeting of 9 July 1968, 12 July 1968, ibid.

118 D. Murray, 'Vietnam negotiations: British interests', 16 May 1968, ibid.

119 FO brief, 'Vietnam: An assessment of the present position and, in particular, of the probable consequences of any precipitate American withdrawal', January 1970, FCO15/1354/ FAV3/548.

120 J. Moreton to D. Gordon, 11 May 1970, FCO15/1218/ FAC10/6; H. Brown to M. Stewart, 8 June 1970, FCO15/1218, FAC10/6.

121 E. Heath to President Nixon, 21 July 1970, PREM15/673.

122 Contained in J. Freeman to FCO, December 1970, PREM15/1281.

123 Embassy, Washington to FCO, 18 April 1972, ibid; P. McCormick to Lord Bridges, 6 April 1972, ibid; J. Graham, Minute, 18 April 1972, FCO15/1692/ FAV3/304.

124 PM to President Nixon, 9 May 1972, PREM15/1281.

13 Ugandans: The rise of Idi Amin

1   'Amin's son runs for mayor', BBC News, 3 January 2002; 'Amin has escaped justice', BBC News, 16 August 2003.

2   John Fairhall, 'Afterword: Idi Amin', *Guardian*, 19 August 2003; Richard Norton-Taylor, 'Amin hailed as splendid, but not very bright', *Guardian*, 23 June 2000.

3   R. Slater, 'Uganda: Annual review for 1970', 14 January 1971, FCO31/1022.

4   High Commission, Kampala to FCO, 22 October 1970, FCO45/687; R. Slater to H. Smedley, 20 July 1970, ibid.

5   East African Department, FCO, 'Incoming government: Uganda – Nationalisation', 1 June 1970, FCO31/722.

6   East African and Mauritius Association, Aide memoire to HMG, 30 July 1970, FCO31/727.

7   A. Douglas-Home to Kampala, 8 September 1970, FCO31/727.

8   R. Slater, 'Uganda: Annual review for 1970', 14 January 1971, FCO31/1022.

9   E. le Tocq to D. Miler, 27 November 1970, FCO31/710; High Commission, Kampala, 'Survey of events in 1970', 10 April 1970, FCO31/710.

10 FCO, 'Uganda', 27 January 1971, FCO31/1023; FCO brief, 'Uganda: Note for the Secretary of State', 3 February 1971, FCO31/1024.

11 H. Smedley, Note, 27 January 1971, FCO31/1028; R. Slater to FCO, 3 February 1971, ibid; R. Slater to A. Douglas-Home, 'Military coup in Uganda', 15 February 1971, FCO31/1024.

12 E. Counsell to S. Crawford, 26 January 1971, 21 January 1971.

NOTES

13 H. Smedley, Note, 27 January 1971, FCO31/1028; R. Purcell, Note, 1 February 1971, FCO31/1024; R. Slater to FCO, 27 January 1971, ibid.

14 'Idi Amin's untold story', *Monitor* (Kampala), 11 April 1999.

15 E. le Tocq to H. Smedley, 4 March 1971, FCO31/1024.

16 E. le Tocq, 27 April 1971, ibid; FCO, 'Visit of Mr Wakhweya', 7 April 1971, ibid.

17 P. Redshaw to R. Purcell, 5 February 1971, FCO31/1024; R. Purcell to R. Slater, 22 February 1971, ibid.

18 R. Byatt to R. Purcell, 2 March 1971, FCO31/1019; R. Purcell to P. Redshaw, 30 March 1971, FCO31/1017.

19 E. le Tocq to H. Smedley, 18 February 1971, FCO31/1056.

20 B. Bradbrook to MoD, 26 April 1971, FCO31/1056; J. Willson [sic] to D. Hawkins, 5 April 1971, ibid; E. le Tocq to H. Smedley, 1 April 1971, ibid.

21 P. Redshaw to E. Counsell, 14 May 1971, FCO31/1019; R. Byatt to E. Counsell, 18 May 1971, FCO31/1017.

22 P. Moon to N. Barrington, 6 July 1971, FCO31/1072; J. Graham to P. Moon, 2 July 1971, ibid.

23 FCO brief, 'General Amin's visit', July 1971, FCO31/1073; C. Booth to D. Brinson, 6 July 1971, FCO26/747.

24 Record of conversation between Foreign Secretary and President of Uganda, 13 July 1971, FCO31/1073; 'Commonsense Uganda', *Daily Telegraph*, 15 July 1971.

25 E. le Tocq to Renwick, 13 August 1971, FCO31/1017.

26 G. Duggan to E. le Tocq, 16 August 1971, FCO31/1017.

27 R. Slater to A. Douglas-Home, 'The first six months of General Amin's government', 6 August 1971, FCO31/1017.

28 G. Duggan to E. le Tocq, 16 August 1971, FCO31/1017.

29 FCO, 'General Amin's prospects', November 1971, FCO31/1018.

30 G. Duggan to E. Counsell, 10 November 1971, FCO31/1018.

31 P. Grattan to Lord Bridges, 6 March 1972, PREM15/1257; R. Anderson to S. Dawbarn, 1 February 1972, ibid.

32 R. Slater to S. Dawbarn, 8 February 1972, FCO31/1324.

33 E. Heath to Idi Amin, 23 March 1972, PREM15/1257; Enclosure to Lord Aldington's letter of 5 April 1972, ibid.

34 S. Dawbarn to Mr Le Quesne, 20 March 1972, FCO31/1327.

35 G. Duggan to FCO, 6 March 1972, FCO31/1327; G. Duggan to E. Counsell, 14 February 1972, ibid.

36 A. Douglas-Home to Kampala, 16 May 1972, FCO31/1328.

37 R. Slater to S. Dawbarn, 30 May 1972, FCO31/1328.

38 S. Dawbarn to H. Smedley, 21 June 1972, FCO31/1328.

39 P. Grattan to Lord Bridges, 2 June 1972, PREM15/1257.
40 E. Heath to Idi Amin, 8 August 1972, PREM15/1258.
41 FCO to Kampala, 9 September 1972, FCO46/936.
42 H. Phillips to FCO, 8 February 1971, FCO31/1032.
43 Campbell to FCO, 8 June 1972, FCO31/1328; R. Slater to S. Dawbarn, 13 June 1972, ibid.
44 House of Commons, *Hansard*, 8 December 1998, Col. 169.

14 Chileans: Protecting a dictator

1   Jamie Wilson, 'How the General escaped trial', *Guardian*, 12 January 2000.
2   House of Commons, *Hansard*, 22 October 1998, Col. 1206; Amelia Gentleman, 'Thatcher takes elevenses with old ally', *Guardian*, 27 March 1999.
3   Giles Tremlett, 'Pinochet's torture ship heads into storm', *Guardian*, 6 June 2003.
4   The *Guardian* devoted two pages to the release of government documents on 1 January 2004, mainly covering ministers forced to quit in sex scandals and the 1973 fuel shortages owing to the Arab-Israeli war. The story of British support for the overthrow of democracy was one that was ignored, even though a picture of Allende was printed along with mention of the coup.
5   Quoted in Hugh O'Shaughnessy, *Pinochet: Politics of torture*, LAB, 2000, p. 38.
6   CIA document, 'CIA activities in Chile', released September 2000, see National Security Archive, 'CIA acknowledges ties to Pinochet's repression', 19 September 2000, www.gwu.edu/~nsarchiv.
7   Quoted in Chomsky, *Year 501*, p. 36.
8   CIA, 'CIA activities in Chile'.
9   JIC, 'Chile: Economic prospects', 3 September 1971, CAB188/17; JIC, 'The Chilean economy: Allende takes charge', 10 February 1971, CAB188/15.
10 R. Seconde, Record of conversation with US ambassador, 30 May 1973, FCO7/2427.
11 Conservative Research Department, Foreign Affairs background brief, 'Chile – A reason why', 19 November 1973, FCO7/2416.
12 R. Seconde to FCO, 'Chile: First impressions', 3 September 1973, FCO7/2412.
13 JIC, 'The Chilean economy: Allende takes charge', 10 February 1971, CAB188/15.

NOTES

14 R. Seconde to FCO, 'Chile: First impressions', 3 September 1973, FCO7/2412.

15 R. Seconde to FCO, 14 September 1973, FCO7/2411; R. Seconde to A. Douglas-Home, 1 October 1973, FCO7/2414.

16 Conservative Research Department.

17 R. Seconde to FCO, 14 September 1973, FCO7/2411; R. Seconde to H. Hankey, 14 September 1973, FCO7/2413.

18 A. Douglas-Home to Various embassies, 13 September 1973, FCO7/2411.

19 R. Seconde to FCO, 18 September 1973, FCO7/2412; R. Seconde to H. Carless, 23 November 1973, FCO7/2416.

20 R. Seconde to H. Hankey, 19 September 1973, FCO7/2412.

21 FCO to Certain missions, 21 September 1973, FCO7/2412.

22 R. Seconde to FCO, 21 September 1973, FCO7/2412.

23 R. Seconde to FCO, 22 September 1973, FCO7/2414.

24 Ibid.

25 A. Douglas-Home to R. Seconde, 4 October 1973, FCO7/2414.

26 FCO brief to Secretary of State, 19 September 1973, FCO7/2412.

27 Cabinet meeting, 13 September 1973, CM(73) 40th, CAB128/53.

28 R. Seconde to A.Douglas-Home, 1 October 1973, FCO7/2414.

29 C. Crabbie to A. Walter, 14 December 1973, FCO7/2416; H. Hankey to R. Seconde, 28 September 1973, FCO7/2413.

30 J. Hunter to H. Hankey, 12 October 1973, FCO7/2415.

31 R. Seconde to H. Hankey, 14 September 1973, FCO7/2413.

32 P. Fullerton to R. Seconde, 2 November 1973, FCO7/2415.

33 H. Carless to R. Seconde, 28 December 1973, FCO7/2416.

34 R. Seconde to A. Douglas-Home, 1 October 1973, FCO7/2414; A. Douglas-Home to Certain missions, 21 September 1973, FCO7/2412.

35 Beckett, Pinochet in Piccadilly, pp. 139–40.

36 Mark Phythian, *The Politics of British Arms Sales Since 1964*, Manchester University Press, 2000, p. 110.

37 Caroline Moorehead, 'Amnesty and unions deplore lifting of Chile arms embargo', *The Times*, 25 July 1980; Phythian, p. 116 [Ridly quote].

38 Phythian, p. 116.

39 Phythian, p. 118.

40 Phythian, p. 117.

41 Barnes, 'Birds of a feather', in LAB, *The Thatcher Years: Britain and Latin America*, LAB, London, 1988, p. 57.

42 Alejandro Foxley, 'The neo-conservative economic experiment in Chile', in Samuel Valenzuela and Arturo Valenzuela, *Military Rule in Chile: Dictatorship and opposition*, Johns Hopkins University Press, London, 1986, p. 44.

43 Cited in Barnes, 'Birds of a feather'.

15 Guyanans: A constitutional coup

1   *Web of Deceit*, Chapter 17.
2   D. Sandys to PM, 11 January 1962, PREM11/366; B. Trend to PM, 26 March 1963, CAB21/5523.
3   US Special National Intelligence Estimate, 'The situation and prospects in British Guiana', 11 April 1962, *FRUS*, 1961–1963, Vol. XII, USGPO, Washington, 1996, Document 274.
4   JIC, 'The outlook for British Guiana', 3 September 1964.
5   Special National Intelligence Estimate, 'Prospects for British Guiana', 21 March 1961, *FRUS*, ibid, Document 242.
6   Hilsman to Deputy Under Secretary of State for Political Affairs (Johnson), 17 October 1961, *FRUS*, ibid, Document 258; Special National Intelligence Estimate, 'The situation and Prospects for British Guiana', 11 April 1962, *FRUS*, ibid, Document 274.
7   A. Schlesinger to D. Bruce, 27 February 1962, *FRUS*, ibid, Document 267; 'Brief for the Prime Minister's talks with President Kennedy: British Guiana', June 1963, CO1031/4402.
8   State Department, 'Possible course of action in British Guiana', 15 March 1962, *FRUS* ibid, Document 272.
9   Special National Intelligence Estimate, 'Prospects for British Guiana', 21 March 1961, *FRUS*, ibid, Document 242.
10 Record of a meeting, 6 April 1961, PREM11/366; A. Douglas-Home to D. Rusk, 18 August 1962, *FRUS*, ibid, Document 246.
11 A. Schlesinger to President Kennedy, 30 August 1961, *FRUS*, ibid, Document 249; R. Hilsman to Johnson, 17 October 1961, *FRUS*, ibid, Document 258.
12 US State Department to Embassy in UK, 19 February 1962, *FRUS*, ibid, Document 264.
13 PM to A. Douglas-Home, 21 February 1962, PREM11/366; A. Douglas-Home to D. Rusk, 26 February 1962, ibid.
14 Hugh Fraser to Secretary of State, 20 March 1962, ibid; Special National Intelligence Estimate, 'The situation and prospects for British Guiana', 11 April 1962, *FRUS*, ibid, Document 274.
15 PM to N. Brook, 3 May 1962, PREM11/366.
16 M. Bundy to President Kennedy, 13 July 1962, *FRUS*, ibid, Document 281; A. Schlesinger to President Kennedy, 5 September 1962, *FRUS*, ibid, Document 288.
17 William Blum, *The CIA: A forgotten history*, Zed, London, 1986, p. 120.
18 E. Melby to State Department, 14 March 1963, *FRUS*, ibid, Document 290.

19 'Brief for the Prime Minister's talks with President Kennedy: British Guiana'.
20 Memorandum of conversation, 30 June 1963, *FRUS*, ibid, Document 295.
21 President Kennedy to PM, 10 September 1963, CAB21/5523.
22 PM to President Kennedy, 27 September 1963, CO1031/4402.
23 FO to Various embassies, 1 November 1963, FO371/167689; C. Jagan to PM, 7 November 1963, ibid; 'Record of a conversation at HM embassy, Washington', 26 November 1963, FO371/167690.
24 Blum, *CIA*, p. 122.
25 A. Schlesinger to D. Bruce, 27 February 1962, *FRUS*, ibid, Document 267.
26 'Brief for the Prime Minister's talks with President Kennedy: British Guiana'.

16 Arabians: Dirty wars

1 Clive Jones, *Britain and the Yemen Civil War, 1962–1965*, Sussex, Academic Press, 2004.
2 C. Gandy to FO, 6 October 1962, PREM11/3877; A. Douglas-Home to PM, 22 January 1963, paraphrasing Gandy's views, 22 January 1963, PREM11/4357.
3 C. Gandy to FO, 6 October 1962, PREM11/3877; C. Gandy to FO, 31 October 1962, PREM11/3878.
4 O. Wright to PM, 18 July 1964, PREM11/4929; Minutes of a meeting, 5 February 1963, CAB130/189; A. Douglas-Home to PM, 25 October 1962, PREM11/3877.
5 A. Douglas-Home to Embassy, Washington, 14 October 1962, PREM11/3877; Brief for PM, January 1963, DEFE13/398; Minutes of a meeting, 31 October 1962, CAB130/189.
6 K. Trevaskis to D. Sandys, 14 October 1963, PREM11/4928; Minutes of a meeting, 2 December 1963, CAB130/189.
7 K. Trevaskis to D. Sandys, 14 October 1963, PREM11/4928.
8 Minutes of a meeting, 5 February 1963, CAB130/189; 'Record of a conversation between President Kennedy and the PM', 15 November 1962, PREM11/3878; Note to PM, 22 November 1963, PREM11/4928; P. de Zulueta to PM, 26 October 1962, PREM11/3877.
9 Stephen Dorril, *MI6: Fifty years of special operations*, Fourth Estate, London, 2000, pp. 679–80.
10 R. Crawford to A. Douglas-Home, 12 October 1962, PREM11/3877; PM, Minute, 6 October 1962, PREM11/3877; R. Butler to PM, 20 April 1964, DEFE13/569.

11 C. Johnston to Colonial Secretary, 26 October 1962, PREM11/3878; Dorril, *MI6*, pp. 680–1; FO, 'The Yemen', 19 November 1963, CO1055/2.

12 Dorril, *MI6*, p. 682; C. Johnstone to Colonial Secretary, 17 December 1962, DEFE13/398.

13 H. Beeley to FO, 6 January 1963, PREM11/3878; Dorril, *MI6*, p. 683.

14 Dorril, *MI6*, pp. 383–4.

15 C. Johnstone to Colonial Secretary, 6 March 1963, PREM11/4928; Dorril, *MI6*, p. 684.

16 Dorril, *MI6*, pp. 684–6.

17 Ibid, pp. 688, 690; Note to PM, 18 December 1963, PREM11/4928.

18 R. Butler to PM, 20 March 1964, PREM11/4678.

19 P. Thorneycroft to PM, 22 April 1964, DEFE13/569; Enclosure to R. Butler to PM, 21 April 1964, 'Yemen: Range of possible courses of action open to us', DEFE13/569; N. Fisher to D. Sandys, 14 July 1964, DEFE13/570; 'Yemen: Memorandum for consideration by Ministers', July 1964, ibid; MoD, 'Aid to the Royalists', 19 July 1964, ibid.

20 Enclosure to R. Butler to PM, 21 April 1964, 'Yemen: Range of possible courses of action open to us', DEFE13/569.

21 R. Butler to PM, 21 April 1964, DEFE13/569; House of Commons, *Hansard*, 14 May 1964, Col. 605.

22 P. Thorneycroft, 'Maintaining our position in South Arabia', 13 July 1964, DEFE13/570; N. Fisher to D. Sandys, 14 July 1964; MoD, 'Aid to the Royalists'; C. Crow to FO, 29 July 1964, DEFE13/570.

23 Dorril, *MI6*, pp. 689, 691.

24 M. Webb to J. Amery, 20 August 1964, DEFE13/570; R. Butler to PM, 11 September 1964, ibid; Dorril, *MI6*, p. 693.

25 Dorril, *MI6*, p. 694; FO to M. Palliser, 12 May 1967, PREM13/1923.

26 Dorril, *MI6*, p. 697; D. Greenhill to B. Trend, 31 March 1967, DEFE13/571; M. Palliser to B. Trend, 23 March 1967, ibid; 'South Arabia: Paper by Lord Shackleton', June 1967, DEFE13/572.

27 Dorril, *MI6*, pp. 698–9.

28 K. Trevaskis to Colonial Secretary, 15 March 1964, PREM11/4678; C. Harington to Earl Mountbatten, 11 June 1964, DEFE13/570.

29 D. Sandys to PM, 21 April 1964, DEFE13/569; K. Trevaskis to Colonial Secretary, 11 May 1964, ibid.

30 MoD to CINC Mideast, 15 May 1964, DEFE13/569; MoD to CINC Mideast, 20 May 1964, ibid; Defence Secretary to Acting Chief of the Defence Staff, 21 May 1964, ibid.

31 Report by the Commander in Chief, Radfan, April–July 1964, 27 November 1964, DEFE13/710; D. Sandys to PM, 21 April 1964,

DEFE13/569; K. Trevaskis to Colonial Secretary, 15 March 1964, PREM11/4678; Colonial Secretary to High Commissioner, Aden, 24 July 1964, DEFE13/570.

32 FO to Embassy, Washington, 22 July 1957, PREM11/1944.

33 B. Burrows to S. Lloyd, 29 January 1957, ibid; B. Burrows to FO, 23 March 1958, PREM11/2402; B. Burrows to FO, 21 July 1958, ibid.

34 G. Middleton to D. Riches, 29 December 1958, PREM11/4360; J. Amery, Minute, 19 January 1959, ibid.

35 FO to Various embassies, 19 July 1957, PREM11/1944; FO to Washington, 21 July 1957, ibid; C. Gault to FO, 21 July 1957, ibid.

36 C. Gault to FO, 21 July 1957, PREM11/1944.

37 B. Burrows to FO, 23 March 1958, PREM11/2402; B. Burrows to FO, 11 April 1958, PREM11/2402.

38 Note to PM, 28 April 1958, and PM's approval, PREM11/2402; FO to Bahrain, 4 August 1957, PREM11/1944; Unsigned brief, 'Oman', 4 August 1957, ibid.

39 FO, Minute, 29 October 1957, FO 371/126890/ EA1015/440; British Forces Arabian Peninsula, Commander's report on operations in Oman, October 1957–February 1959, DEFE11/402.

40 G. Middleton to FO, 18 November 1958, PREM11/4360.

41 British Forces Arabian Peninsula, Commander's report.

42 FO, Oman Working Party, 'Future of Muscat and Oman', 31 July 1959, DEFE11/401.

43 FO brief, June 1971, PREM15/1761.

44 D. Carden to S. Crawford, 8 October 1966, FO1016/766.

45 S. Crawford to M. Stewart, 7 July 1969, FO1016/790; J. Godber to P. Jenkin, 17 August 1972, PREM15/1761.

Table: Britain and global deaths

1 See Chapter 1.

2 Figures vary widely. The *Guardian* estimated 10,000–20,000 civilian deaths as an indirect result of the bombing. Estimates of the military deaths are usually in the 3,000–6,000 range. *Web of Deceit*, p. 49.

3 Human Rights Watch estimates 500 civilian deaths ('Civilian deaths in the NATO air campaign', February 2000, www.hrw.org). Some estimates, which include military deaths, are often over 1,000. *20th Century Atlas: Alphabetical list of war, massacre, tyranny and genocide*, www.users.erols.com.

4 *20th Century Atlas.*

5   Figures vary very widely; see *20th Century Atlas*. Immediately after the war the US government estimated 100,000 deaths. Other independent estimates are much lower, others much higher.

6   Figures vary very widely, from hundreds of thousands to 4 million. Most deaths were those of Vietnamese, with figures usually ranging from 1–3 million. Hundreds of thousands were also killed in Cambodia and Laos.

7   Some estimates are as low as 300,000 but most credible figures are much higher and some estimate over a million.

8   See *Web of Deceit*, Chapter 20.

9   Estimated number of deaths due principally to the brutal 'resettlement' operations. Estimates of number of Mau Mau killed in actual fighting vary from 10,000–13,000.

10 See *Web of Deceit*, Chapter 15.

11 See *Web of Deceit*, Chapter 16.

12 Figures unknown.

13 *20th Century Atlas*.

14 Prados, p. 43.

15 See Dorril, *MI6*, chapter 16.

16 See *Web of Deceit*, Chapter 14.

17 Figures vary very widely. This is approximate figure for North Korean and Chinese deaths.

18 This is approximate figure for deaths on the rebels (i.e. EAM/ELAS) side.

19 Figures vary extremely widely. See *20th Century Atlas*.

20 Figure from September 2000 (beginning of second intifada) to March 2004; Palestinian Red Crescent Society, www.palestinercs.org.

21 Nigerian police and army are complicit in many of these killings; see Chapter 10.

22 Russia provided an official number of 15,000 Chechen deaths by August 2003 (AFP, 'Russia underplays Chechnya deaths', 8 August 2003). This is likely to be a severe underestimate, especially in light of the ferocious attack on Grozny in 1999/2000.

23 Number of deaths by government forces from 1996–2002; *Web of Deceit*, p. 81.

24 Figures vary. 35,000–40,000 is a commonly cited figure since 1990; some current estimates, however, state 15,000 in the past 10 years.

25 The UN estimated half a million deaths of children under five as a result of the 1991 war and sanctions. Former UN Coordinator for Iraq, Denis Halliday, has given a figure, including adults, of over a million. *Web of Deceit*, p. 29.

26 See *Web of Deceit*, Chapter 21.
27 The Turkish government in 2001 gave a figure of 23,000 Kurds killed; www.harpers.org/warcrime.html; independent estimates are usually higher.
28 See *Web of Deceit*, Chapter 1.
29 See *Web of Deceit*, p. 111; Chomsky, *Hegemony or Survival*, p. 206.
30 See *Ambiguities of Power*, pp. 119–29.
31 The Central American Human Rights Commission estimates 2,000–3,000; Physicians for Human Rights estimates 300 civilian deaths and 50 military deaths ('Panama: Operation Just Cause', December 1990).
32 See *Web of Deceit*, Chapter 1.
33 See *Web of Deceit*, Chapter 4.
34 See *Web of Deceit*, Chapter 14.
35 See *Web of Deceit*, Chapter 21.
36 Figures vary widely; *20th Century Atlas*.
37 See especially Brendan Sims, *Unfinest Hour: Britain and the destruction of Bosnia*, Allen Lane, London, 2001.
38 See *Web of Deceit*, Chapter 18.

Conclusion

1   George Orwell, *Homage to Catalonia*, Penguin, 1989, p. 187.

INDEX